Further praise for
Winning at Active Management

"The chances of success in fund management, as in professional sports coaching, are inversely proportional to time. The longer you are in the game, the greater your chance of having a poor run over a measurable window (say, three years), and involuntarily exiting the field. So the thoughts of a manager with 50 years' experience are worth reading. This book, unlike many written by active managers, does not claim to have found El Dorado and a path to untold riches; indeed, it acknowledges that passive investment may be appropriate for some applications.

The reason Bill has succeeded for so long comes across well in his and his co-authors' approach to culture, and in their dismissal of the Price-Earnings Ratio – a figure that whilst discredited, and never used in private markets, remains a mainstay of most active managers' processes. Economies and markets do not stand still, and yet many active and quant managers believe that what worked before will work again without the need to change and evolve their processes. It is in this area, more than any other, that 50 years of experience is invaluable."

**Robert Waugh
Chief Investment Officer
The Royal Bank of Scotland Group**

"One of the most difficult aspects of consulting to institutional investors is finding active investment managers who will produce consistent results over a long period. While an investment process that is both sound and repeatable across different market environments is critical, it is insufficient unless implemented in a thoughtful way by an investment team that possesses the skills and values, and is offered the right incentives, to make optimal investment decisions. To my mind, a firm's leadership must inculcate and manage this sort of culture within the entire team in order to remain successful over a long period, and the first part of this book highlights that cultural challenge.

Technology has become a game changer in the investment industry, and the organizations that apply it most effectively will be the long term winners. Given the incredible amount of information that is now available, winnowing the critical insights to a manageable amount and sharing them among the investment team has become essential to an investor's success. In addition, using technology to better understand the factors behind market behavior can help an investment firm to evaluate its own performance. Again, the book speaks effectively of the need to make better use of technology within all parts of the investment industry."

David Service
Director, Investment Consulting
Willis Towers Watson
(Retired)

"Bill Priest, a leading practitioner of free cash flow-based investing, explains why that philosophy has been so successful. And much more: he and his co-authors tackle the most difficult issue in the investment management business – culture – and demonstrate how to maintain it in challenging periods. The book also addresses the industry's latest challenge, the proliferation of quantitative algorithms in every corner of the investment world, and describes how the value of judgment has increased as machines have come to exploit the short-term relationships that can be tested. Recommended reading for this generation of investors, and the next one."

Michael Goldstein
Managing Partner
Empirical Research Partners

WINNING AT ACTIVE MANAGEMENT

WINNING AT ACTIVE MANAGEMENT

The Essential Roles of Culture, Philosophy, and Technology

William W. Priest
Steven D. Bleiberg
Michael A. Welhoelter
with John Keefe

WILEY

Published by John Wiley & Sons, Inc., Hoboken, New Jersey.
Published simultaneously in Canada.

For general information on our other products and services or for technical support, please contact our Customer Care Department within the United States at (800) 762-2974, outside the United States at (317) 572-3993 or fax (317) 572-4002.

Wiley publishes in a variety of print and electronic formats and by print-on-demand. Some material included with standard print versions of this book may not be included in e-books or in print-on-demand. If this book refers to media such as a CD or DVD that is not included in the version you purchased, you may download this material at http://booksupport.wiley .com. For more information about Wiley products, visit www.wiley.com.

Library of Congress Cataloging-in-Publication Data:
ISBN 9781119051824 (Hardcover)
ISBN 9781119051770 (ePDF)
ISBN 9781119051909 (ePub)

Printed in the United States of America

10 9 8 7 6 5 4 3 2 1

To Jack L. Treynor – the Albert Einstein of Finance, a man of great principle, a co-author, and a friend, from whom I learned more finance and economics than any other person.

And to my family – wife Katherine, Jeff, Karen, Amanda, Jack, Jacob, Hayley, Spencer, Joan, and Steve, who provide support, questions, and the occasional "what in the world were you thinking!" – William W. Priest

To Terri, Ben, Katie, and Ellie, and to my father, Lawrence Bleiberg, in whose footsteps I have followed – Steven D. Bleiberg

To my wife, Leslie, and my children, Christopher, Megan, and Lindsay – Michael A. Welhoelter

CONTENTS

PART II

Philosophy and Methodology

Active Management is Not Dead Yet

During a writing project like this one, once the key ideas are established, a question nags at the authors: What should we call it? Early on we came up with a working title "Not Dead Yet."[1] It was meant as a tongue-in-cheek response to the stream of reports over the past few years on the decline of active management of equity portfolios flowing from financial journalists and market observers—as well as the marketers of index funds, exchange-traded funds and other products that compete with actively managed strategies. To an extent, they make a valid point: the performance of active managers as a group has been less than desired. But there are several reasons to explain managers' underperformance: some are cyclical, as markets of recent years have been affected by new sorts of macro influences, while others are secular, and related to how managers carry out their investment processes (Chapter 6).

However, the markets have not changed inalterably, at least not in our view. The essence of active management is a well-designed investment process that measures the relative value of individual stocks, and takes advantage of the many mispricings that result from less-than-optimal actions of investors, both individuals and professionals (Chapter 5). Granted, the stock market may have become harder for many managers to beat for several years. But inefficiencies in the pricing of stocks are timeless, and we believe that active equity management still works, and that the best managers can deliver excellent performance over the long term (Chapter 7). *Active management is not dead.*

This book is a second installment to a volume that I authored in late 2006 with Lindsay McLelland, *Free Cash Flow and Shareholder Yield: New Priorities for the Global Investor*, published by John Wiley & Sons in early 2007. A few years after the founding of Epoch Investment Partners in 2004, I wanted to share views on what we saw as crucial investment issues of the day, and relate insights from the perspective of the firm's investment process. The factors that would lead to the global financial crisis had just started to surface, and while we weren't prescient on every topic in the book, we got many of them right as evidenced in white papers Epoch published at the time. (For example, see "The Canary in the Coal Mine: Subprime Mortgages, Mortgage-Backed Securities and the U.S. Housing Bust" from April 2007, reprinted in Appendix A.) More important, Epoch's strategies fared well in the markets that followed, so the firm and its clients came through the global financial crisis in good stead.

A couple of years ago, I decided to write a second book. People that I talked with assumed it would take the form of a memoir about my 50 years in the investment industry. That idea had some appeal, as the markets of those years were varied and dynamic, and I have been "in the room" at critical junctures of market volatility with important and colorful people, and have plenty of stories and lessons to share.

But I am not a historian—I am an investor, and as such I am much more oriented to the future than the past. Of course, history is often the best guide to the future, but the "present" that today's investors are facing—which includes the recent unusual period of the global financial crisis, and how governments, corporations, and markets have contended with the world since— make the further past of my career seem less and less relevant going forward.

Still, my experience has been pretty interesting, so I will share a bit. I joined the industry cavalcade in July 1965 at a mutual fund management firm, working as a research analyst initially and eventually a portfolio manager. I joined BEA Associates in New York, as a portfolio manager and partner of the firm, in July 1972. That November the Dow Jones Industrial Average closed above 1,000 for the first time. (The 1,000 mark on the Dow presented a challenging summit for equity investors: the average broke through 1,000 in intraday trading three times in early 1966, but did not end the day there.[2]) The firm's staff numbered 11, and BEA managed less than $300 million in client assets—pretty small even in 44-year-old dollars. Not only was BEA a minor force in the market; the firm also had a weak balance sheet and at the beginning operated hand-to-mouth.

Shortly after I joined the firm, there was a significant collapse in stock prices—from its peak in December 1972 through December 1974, the Dow dropped 44 percent.[3] My timing in leaving a large firm for the entrepreneurial excitement of a startup could not have been worse: the resulting decrease in assets and management fees led to a few BEA staff (of whom I was one) having to forego cash compensation for several weeks. However, BEA was fortunate to have a strong culture—one based on personal integrity, the motivation for the work that lay ahead of us, and the drive to provide superior performance for our clients.

There's a saying in the stock market, which applies to life in general: *Timing Is Everything*. For BEA Associates, it was everything, and more. In 1974 Congress passed the Employee Retirement Income Security Act—ERISA—for the protection of employee pension funds, requiring employers to adequately fund them, and segregate the assets in formal pension plans. (The expanded requirements for recordkeeping, regulatory compliance and investment mandated by ERISA were so sweeping that those in the business jokingly called it the "Accountants,

Lawyers and Money Managers Relief Act.") The resulting flow of contributions from corporations to the pension funds they sponsored launched a new era for institutional asset management. The passage of ERISA was prompted by "the most glorious failure in the [automobile] business." In 1963, after stumbling financially for many years—a strong postwar market for U.S. car sales notwithstanding—the Studebaker-Packard Company closed its plant in South Bend, Indiana. Workers aged 60 and over received their expected pensions, but younger workers received a fraction of what was promised or nothing at all. The shutdown helped advance a growing debate on pension reform into the national legislative arena, leading to the passage of ERISA in 1974.[4]

The new regulations forced the financial analysis underlying pension funding to a higher level, and to meet some of that need, I was fortunate to co-author, with financial scholar Jack L. Treynor and fellow BEA partner Patrick J. Regan, *The Financial Reality of Pension Funding Under ERISA*, published by Dow Jones-Irwin in 1976. Our conclusions grabbed the attention of legislators, and I testified before a congressional committee that influenced later regulations on the viability of insuring pension plans via the Pension Benefit Guaranty Corporation (PBGC). My co-authors and I were concerned that under certain circumstances, the PBGC could go broke, and Congress did indeed repeal and amend the section known as CELI—Contingent Employment Liability Insurance.

BEA expanded rapidly in the new era: by 1980 our managed assets had climbed to $2 billion, and the firm was recognized as a leader in U.S. institutional money management. In 1989, I became the CEO of BEA Associates, but continued to manage institutional portfolios. A year later the firm entered into a formal partnership with global bank Credit Suisse, although BEA Associates maintained its name until early 1999, when it became Credit Suisse Asset Management-

Americas and I continued as the CEO. We then acquired Warburg Pincus Asset Management in spring 1999, at which point the fully built-out CSAM-Americas managed assets of nearly $60 billion. In 2000, Credit Suisse purchased the brokerage firm Donaldson, Lufkin & Jenrette, and its asset management arm also joined CSAM-Americas, bringing total assets to about $100 billion.

Over the course of those 30 years, as BEA Associates grew from a startup to the cornerstone of a large global institutional firm with offices in New York, Tokyo, London, Zurich, and Sydney, I witnessed the full life cycle of an asset manager—from the diseases of infancy that infect and threaten all new companies, to the limitless potential of vibrant middle age, to the comfortable but sclerotic bureaucracy that constrains complex global firms that grow too large.

Then in 2001, Credit Suisse's corporate policies caused me to "retire": the bank had a policy of "60 and out" for executives at my level. I was always aware that such a policy existed—I just didn't think it would apply to me! Having no desire to retire, in March 2001 I joined Michael Steinberg, an excellent investor I had known for some time, and we formed Steinberg Priest Capital Management. The firm's managed assets grew from $800 million to over $2 billion in three years, but the partners had differing ambitions and we disbanded the structure in 2004.

But I still had a desire to build a firm of substance, and in 2004 three partners—Tim Taussig, David Pearl, and Phil Clark—and I started once again, creating Epoch Investment Partners with 11 employees and initial managed assets of $640 million. As of the end of 2015, less than 12 years after its founding, Epoch oversaw nearly $50 billion in long-only equity strategies, and employed over 100 people.

So much for the memoir. In this book I have assembled a discussion that I hope will prove interesting and valuable to people in investment management—what's happening today, and what the industry might look like in 5 or 10 years, both in the "investing business" (that is, the selection of securities and the managing of portfolios), as well as "the business of the investing business" (managing the many non-investment functions—product management and client services, and a firm's information technology, operations, and compliance functions).

To be successful, an investment firm must clear three hurdles—its clients must reap superior investment performance; its employees must find desirable long-term employment; and its owners must earn fair financial returns. In this book, I have tried to share what I believe to be the required and essential elements to achieve these goals. Two of these are timeless, while the third reflects the growing dominance of information technology in every aspect of today's personal and business life.

The first is firm culture, which is the bedrock of success for any firm, regardless of its industry. (Management theory pioneer Peter Drucker is supposed to have said, "Culture eats strategy for breakfast.") In investment management—a people business based on shared efforts and rewards—culture is the *sine qua non*. The first section of this book is devoted to culture and includes a number of rough-and-ready observations on its importance in investment management.

As of early 2016, investment managers as a group are faring well but face challenges—like any other incumbent industry in a world moving at a rapid pace. After several slow years following the financial crisis, growth in new business has resumed in the industry, such that the total pool of assets available to managers in the United States is well above its 2007 precrisis highs. Since then, however, the center of gravity of the industry has shifted: whereas traditional defined benefit pension plans were once the largest source of new business, today's inflows of assets are dominated by defined contribution retirement plans, as well as insurance companies, sovereign wealth funds, and high-net-worth investors resident in emerging markets. In the market for individual investors in the United States, market share is slipping away from large old-line wirehouse brokerage firms, in favor of independent investment advisers. (And lately, a wave of low-cost "robo-advisory" firms has been challenging them both.) These changes in the landscape are forcing traditional investment managers to reorient their marketing efforts, and contend with a new layer of costs.[5]

The focus of this book, however, is more the business of investing—managing client assets. While the business of the investing business has experienced an evolution, traditional active portfolio management has been under full-out assault. Many investors have favored passive investment products, such as conventional index funds and exchange-traded funds (ETFs) tracking market indexes, over active strategies trying to outperform the general market. A more recent marketing idea known as "smart beta" represents another group of semi-active products; like index funds and ETFs, they are able to deliver concise portfolios at fee rates below those of active managers.

This displacement, amounting to many billions of investment dollars owned by both institutional and individual investors, has occurred in part as the result of a shortfall by active managers in delivering market-beating performance. As the book discusses, it's partly a cyclical phenomenon, but a great proportion of active managers have underperformed common benchmarks, and many of today's investors seem willing to trade off the potential upside that active managers may provide in exchange for market performance and the certainty of lower fees.

Therefore, the second section of this book offers background on the debate over the merits of active management versus passive alternatives and points out that active investment managers have been challenged by an array of difficult market conditions. Among active managers, however, the industry also has become increasingly competitive: people are highly trained and talented, and armed with more relevant and timely data than I might have dreamed of in the 1980s, or even 10 years ago. (The competition is only growing, and becoming smarter: the CFA Institute, which confers professional certification on people in the investment business, counted about 135,000 members in 2015; during that year, an additional 80,000 new candidates sat for the qualifying exams.)

The second section also discusses Epoch's view of the investment world, and what the firm sees as the most effective investment process for outperforming the general equity market. In brief, Epoch believes that the source of value in a company is its free cash flow, and that superior returns to stocks come from identifying those companies that generate substantial cash flow, and then allocate it wisely—reinvesting in the business when it is sufficiently profitable, and distributing the remainder to the owners. The philosophy can be expressed simply, but executing it effectively requires intensive fundamental research and insightful forecasting from analysts that know their companies well.

The human effort required for the analytical process is increasingly being supplemented by information technology, which is the focus of this book's third section. For years, investors have applied scientific rigor to investing, whether from using mathematical frameworks for valuation, to borrowing models from the physical sciences for insights into the functioning of markets. As a result of their increasing power and decreasing cost, computers have taken over much of the burden of raw data analysis, and the widespread digitization of information of all kinds—economic reports, corporate financials, market prices, and the growing analysis of real-time consumer and business data, as well as the traffic on social media—has broadened and deepened the research process. At the same time portfolio management has become a global undertaking, and it demands from practitioners a grasp of many more markets, companies, and economic forces.

The changes in the investment business over 50 years have been monumental: the increased speed and complexity of the markets; how managers react to them; and managers' understanding of the factors behind investment returns. The industry has more sophisticated tools for analysis and forecasting, but these have been matched by the volume and variety of information to be dealt with. The book concludes with our thoughts on how an optimal investment management process should be dominated neither by human judgment nor computer algorithms, but by an informed combination of the two—*racing with the machine*. Indeed, the last section previews an investment strategy that Epoch has developed over several years—one that likely would not have been possible without today's rich resources for gathering and processing information.

Thank you for this opportunity to share my views.

William Priest

Notes

1. With a nod to the movie *Monty Python and the Holy Grail* (Michael White Productions: 1975).
2. Jason Zweig, "The 11-Year Itch: Still Stuck at Dow 10000," *The Wall Street Journal*, June 12, 2010.
3. S&P Dow Jones Indices. McGraw-Hill Financial. Accessed at: www.djaverages.com/?go=industrial-index-data.
4. Wooten, James A., "The Most Glorious Story of Failure in the Business": The Studebaker-Packard Corporation and the Origins of ERISA. *Buffalo Law Review,* Vol. 49, p. 683, 2001. Available at SSRN: http://ssrn.com/abstract=290812 or http://dx.doi.org/ 10.2139/ssrn.290812.
5. These observations have been measured and documented by consultants McKinsey & Company in their 2015 industry review, "Navigating the Shifting Terrain of North American Asset Management." Accessed at: http://www.mckinsey.com/client_ service/financial_services/latest_thinking/wealth_and_asset_ management.

WINNING AT ACTIVE MANAGEMENT

PART I

Culture

CHAPTER 1

Culture at the Core

Every organization—whether a business, a not-for-profit entity, or government—reflects and operates from a unique culture. It's an inherent and essential element that brings order to the internal and external environments[1] and reduces uncertainty[2] among members of the group. The quality and strength of cultures explain many of the differences in organizational performance. But culture often operates below the surface of an organization, so that studying the abstraction of culture is elusive.

Organizational culture is especially important to the workings of a knowledge transfer business, such as investment management, because much of the work produced is intangible, and the environment changes so rapidly. Accordingly, culture is a critical component of any professional service firm, and we have made culture the introductory topic for this book.

Culture is a subject that has occupied management consultants and academics since the 1950s. One definition that we have found useful was put forward by Edgar Schein, an early scholar on culture and leadership, and today professor emeritus of MIT's Sloan School of Management. He writes:

"The culture of a group can ... be defined as a pattern of shared basic assumptions learned by a group as it solved its problems of external adaptation and internal integration, which has worked well enough to be considered valid and, therefore, be taught to new members as the correct way to perceive, think and feel.[3] ... Culture is to a group what a personality or character is to an individual."[4]

Schein adds that culture often is those principles and beliefs a founder or leadership set has imposed on a group—and which have worked out well: "[The] dynamic processes of culture creation and management are the essence of leadership, and make you realize that leadership and culture are two sides of the same coin."[5]

The owners or managers of an organization might consciously work at developing a culture, or a culture may evolve on its own as the result of years of decision making, but a culture is present in any setting where people are working toward common goals. In a new organization, culture can be very strong, as it is one of its few assets, and crucial to its early efforts.

Employees have a hand in corporate culture as well. "Not all of corporate culture is created from the top down," wrote Andrew Lo, a professor of finance at Massachusetts Institute of Technology, in a paper on corporate culture in finance. "A culture is also composed of the behavior of the people within it, from the bottom up. Corporate culture is subject to compositional effects, based on the values and the behaviors of the people it hires, even as corporate authority attempts to inculcate its preferred values and behaviors into its employees."[6] Indeed, an organization benefits from a diversity of opinions to prevent "groupthink."

"Most companies' culture just happens; no one plans it. That can work, but it means leaving a critical component of your success to chance," wrote Eric Schmidt and Jonathan Rosenberg, executive chairman and adviser to the CEO, respectively, at global technology giant Google Inc.[7] They observe that the right time to plan a culture is early on, because after it takes shape—consciously or not—the founding principles are likely to reinforce themselves, as like-minded people will be attracted by them to join an organization, and those with other viewpoints may not.

The values and principles of a culture permeate every aspect of a business: operating strategy; products, services, and relationships with customers; firm structure and business model; "people processes"; and governance. Culture determines relationships among authority and peers, an organization's common language, granting rewards and status, and the measures of success.[8]

Thus, culture is a shared view of how to carry out day-to-day tasks, as well as dealing with unusual conditions—how the firm's long-term principles inform short-run actions. Culture also determines how a firm treats its customers and employees, and how the employees treat each other. Accordingly, organizations fortunate enough to arrive at the right culture gain a competitive advantage that carries the firm toward its long-term goals. In this section, we will consider the different approaches firms take to building and expressing culture and, in particular, its importance to success in the investment management industry.

The Original Organizational Culture: Command-and-Control

Cultures vary according to the sizes and activities of individual groups, and are intertwined with an organization's structure. One combination of structure and culture, however, has prevailed during most of the evolution of corporate America, and probably for most of human history: "command-and-control." (It's often illustrated in management textbooks by a pyramid, but anyone reading this book has seen that image a thousand times, so we don't repeat it here.)

The command-and-control structure assumes that one person, or a few people, at the top of an organization can determine the best direction, and that subordinates should carry out leaders' decisions without inserting any ideas of their own—a principle called the *great person theory.*[9] It's the operative, and necessary, culture in any sort of military operation, or police and firefighting unit, where lots of people have to be trained to do the same thing, in exactly the same way quickly and without doubt or question, often in dangerous settings.

"In corporate cultures that lack the capacity to incorporate an outside opinion, the primary check on behavior is the authority," wrote Andrew Lo: "From within a corporate culture, an authority may see his or her role as similar to the conductor of an orchestra, managing a group of highly trained professionals in pursuit of a lofty goal." Others looking from the outside in might see a particular organization's authority as blatantly forceful.[10]

Command-and-control became the favored form of culture in American business starting in the late nineteenth century, when standardized processes and behaviors were essential to the rapid growth of the manufacturing economy. The idea was advanced by Frederick W. Taylor, who was very successful as an engineer but also invented the profession of management consulting. For a growing manufacturing sector that had lots of workers, who possessed varying levels of skill and were accustomed to carrying out their work by hand in their own different ways, he developed a structure that imposed defined tasks—rewarding successful workers with high pay and terminating those who failed.[11]

Command-and-control cultures still prevail in most industries[12] because, in many settings, a rigid hierarchy is useful and desirable. For instance, manufacturing organizations often need central control over the use of resources and quality control over processes, and to be able to respond swiftly to emerging problems. It also can work well in single-line businesses operating in stable markets, where little flexibility is called for. The short leash of command-and-control also is essential in situations where the organization's goal is cutting costs.

It's also suitable where creative thinking and initiative can create risks.[13] For instance, a pharmaceutical maker has to follow strict controls over the manufacture of its products, and how they are sold: a drug firm's Western region sales head could hardly decide to come up with his own custom version of the company's big cholesterol drug. Organizations such as electric and gas utilities or hospitals must adhere to well-defined practices to ensure reliable service and the safety of their customers and employees. Similarly, bank credit officers have to follow standardized processes for lending, with decisions and approvals at several levels, to allow for systematic credit rating and proper allocation of the firm's capital. Accordingly, command-and-control structures and cultures are often present in highly regulated industries.

Drawbacks of Command-and-Control

Although command-and-control allowed the industry of a young America to flourish, in the past couple of decades the structure has been discredited. Command-and-control is not an agile form, and in industries that are rapidly changing, a few senior managers don't have enough time to micromanage an entire company. Moreover, the structure is not equipped to allow individuals further down in an organization to contribute their ideas upstream: a one-way information flow from the top of the pyramid to the bottom can result in significant missteps or missed opportunities. In many cases, people in the field may have better information about product and competitor dynamics, while those at the top may possess the least relevant information and therefore lack the insights needed for optimal decisions.[14] The gap between the leadership team and the customer or client—that is, an organization's layers of management—is often too wide in command-and-control cultures. Some firms have layers of reporting structure numbering into the teens. Many management consultants recommend a maximum of six to eight.

In human terms, employees in command-and-control structures have well-defined boundaries, duties, and career paths. Such a work environment may be desirable for many people, but current thinking in management science and practice recognizes that employees want to contribute ideas to their organizations, and argues in favor of fostering collaboration and creativity. For instance, IBM Corporation published a study in 2012 that surveyed corporate CEOs around the globe, who said they were aiming to change the nature of work "by adding a powerful dose of openness, transparency and employee empowerment to the command-and-control ethos that has characterized the modern corporation for more than a century."[15] As a practical matter, corporations, large and small, may have little choice: through the Internet and various social media, employees are probably sharing and collaborating whether management wants it or not.

An Alternative Culture for Knowledge Businesses

In contrast to the rigidity of the command-and-control model, professional service businesses such as legal and management consulting firms—as well as investment managers—often develop structures and cultures that better suit the nature of their work and the economics of their businesses.

Unlike manufacturers, which can carefully specify their standardized products, professional firms offer no tangible goods to sample or road test, and there are no set manufacturing processes: each lawsuit, audit, or financial market environment is unique, and a firm's reputation and brand is built from past successes in contending with the varying circumstances. Accordingly, predicting product and service outcomes is much less certain for most investment managers, as well as other services businesses such as law firms, management consultants and medical practices. Prospective customers can look to firms' prior work to understand their areas of expertise and skill, and even the reliability of their services in the past, but a firm's success depends greatly on the context—for a law firm, the facts of a court case, or for a consultant, the state of a client's affairs before a business is redesigned. Compared to a physical, manufactured product, the design of which can be reworked over many years, the environments in which professional service businesses work are often too complex, varied and rapidly changing to provide reasonably objective evaluations ahead of time.

The identity of professional service firms is closely tied to the people in possession of skills—individual lawyers, consultants or asset manager teams. (An investment industry bromide says that a firm's most valuable assets leave by the elevator every night.) Accordingly, successful employees in these firms are highly compensated and often hold equity stakes, in order to tie their day-to-day efforts and resulting personal wealth to their firms' long-term success.

Of course, professional partnerships have senior management teams: a completely flat organization, where everyone is enabled to decide and act on anything, would be chaotic. Senior management's role, however, is more about leadership—guiding firm strategy, high-level business development and problem solving—as their detailed involvement in every client situation would be impractical and unnecessary. Professional partnerships operate by a set of rules, but don't have a single absolute ruler, as do command-and-control organizations.

Senior management also typically sets compensation and controls the addition of new partners. Importantly, in less tangible matters, senior managers provide practical examples of the firm's culture and what constitutes good behavior. Meanwhile, in handling client engagements, client teams apply their own experience and judgment to handling challenges as they arise rather than follow specific directives made at the top.

The differing characteristics of command-and-control versus professional partnerships will attract different sorts of people to each type of culture. Professional partnership careers tend to require more extensive training just to enter, and typically call for greater commitments of time to the job. Taking intelligent risks and raising individual initiative also are central to professional work. People with risk-seeking natures are more likely than not to be attracted to the more complex and challenging careers of professional partnerships, while risk-averse people may prefer a different environment.

The Partnership Culture Model

With less involvement of senior management in day-to-day decisions, the economic success of a professional firm is dependent on "multiple leadership," that is, key decisions being made at many points in the firm. Figure 1.1 illustrates the relationships among the financial and working elements of a partnership: interdependence in carrying out their work, and support that individuals offer and rely on from one another. Both are built on a foundation of economic interests shared among the partners.[16]

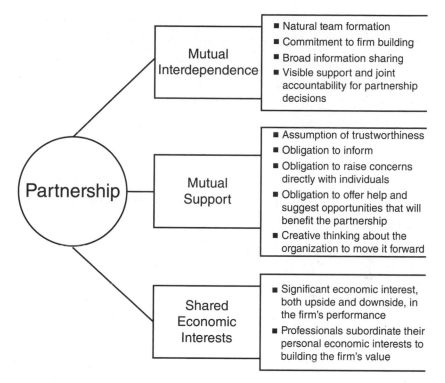

FIGURE 1.1   Tenets of Professional Partnership

Source: Epoch Investment Partners

Interdependence

In serving the complexities of a given assignment, client-serving teams at professional partnerships often are likely to draw on the expertise in several areas of the firm. Attorneys, consultants, and investment analysts should be eager to share their knowledge, both within and among teams, in the interest of providing the best service to clients and moving the firm forward. Implicit in those goals, of course, is that the hard work and judgment has to be reciprocated among all members of the group when called for.

An illustration: in an investment management setting, it's typical for analysts and portfolio managers in a firm's equity group to share insights on the prospects for individual companies or industries with those running fixed-income portfolios. Each approaches the analysis a bit differently, providing complementary (and sometimes opposing) views.

Narrow views and overspecialization often get in the way of idea sharing, typically to organizations' detriment. Gillian Tett, the U.S. managing editor of the *Financial Times*, has written on corporate culture and idea sharing from the perspective of an anthropologist, noting: "We need specialist, expert teams to function in a complex world. But we also need to have a joined-up flexible vision of life."[17] She cites companies hobbled by the "silos" within their structures, for example, Sony Corporation beginning in the 1980s, and the turnaround potential of removing them, such as at IBM Corporation in the mid-1990s.

Ms. Tett lauds Facebook, Inc. for its resistance to building silos, instead promoting an open organization where employees rotate through various teams, and come to know people in all parts of the company. It's not the most efficient structure, she concedes, but citing a senior executive, "[It's] a small price to pay to meet the goal of keeping the organization fluid and connected; it was crucial to have a bit of slack, or inefficiency, to breed creativity and give people time to stay connected."[18]

Rotating people through the firm's various departments isn't feasible for us at Epoch (or for many asset managers). The knowledge needed to work on the investment teams, for instance, is quite specialized, and assigning people without in-depth training to our portfolio teams would fall short of our fiduciary obligations to clients.

In the case of Epoch Investment Partners, we manage several complementary strategies—all in equities, but investing in various markets and company sizes, and we encourage analysts and portfolio managers to share whatever they know about their companies with anyone else who might be able to use it. We don't obligate people to rely on others' decisions, but what counts is that the information—in the forms of both data and opinions—is freely available for everyone's use. (Epoch maintains a research database that is open to all analysts and portfolio managers.) It is not uncommon in some firms to find people who feel protective of their hard work and want to keep it for their sole benefit, but in our case not sharing insights with another analyst or portfolio manager will lead to a collective loss—or at least a forgone opportunity to enhance the returns of another strategy. And since we reward employees on the firm's overall results, the effect on returns from not sharing affects everyone's rewards.

Fostering that sort of sharing is not easy, however. Some people that are drawn to the specialized, expert nature of investment management are introverts, and would be more comfortable in their offices than handing away their insights (or fitting the insights of others into their own work). We try to create a natural environment for sharing and collegiality with a set of regular meetings, on companies' earnings reports, portfolio performance reviews, and the like, to give people a chance to hear what others are saying, and to offer their own ideas. By so doing we hope to avoid the NIH ("Not Invented Here") syndrome—"If I did not invent it, the idea has little or no value."

Epoch's ultimate success in winning for our clients depends in large part on our ability to transfer knowledge from one person to another. Firm meetings are a platform for people to then form their own groups, where they discuss in greater depth the good and bad points of different ideas or decisions. In turn, we hope the individuals in those groups will reach out to other portfolio managers, or the senior management team, and share their thoughts, even if their points include disagreement or opposition. What counts is that all the ideas are given air time: for the interdependence principle to work, people at all levels in a professional partnership need to know that their opposing views, and their reasoning behind them, are welcome.

"Everything we do should be about transferring knowledge with one another."

—Bill Priest

At Google, Eric Schmidt and Jonathan Rosenberg caution against the encroachment of HiPPOs, (or Highly Paid Persons' Opinions): "When it comes to the quality of decision making, pay level is intrinsically irrelevant and experience is valuable only if it is used to frame a winning argument. Unfortunately, in most companies experience *is* the winning argument."[19] The best decisions are reached from considering the best ideas, rather than one person's opinion, and the ability to participate in decision making will encourage all team members to make a contribution.

Schmidt and Rosenberg also believe that team members have an obligation to speak up when inferior ideas make their way to the table, and that they later share the responsibility for decisions that don't work out: "If they don't [raise their concerns], and the subpar idea wins the day, then they are culpable. ... [D]issent must be an obligation, not an option."[20]

"An organization is like a tree full of monkeys, all on different limbs at different levels. The monkeys on top look down and see a tree full of smiling faces. The monkeys at the bottom look up and see an entirely different perspective."

—Anonymous

Support

A companion to interdependence is support among team members, although it operates more at a personal level. Support includes encouraging people to advance their ideas, as well as formal and informal coaching and mentoring.

An equally important aspect of such support is offering candid feedback on the decisions of team members—simply stated, discussing their mistakes as well as their successes. Hospitals hold regular reviews of mortality and morbidity, which look into the how and why of patients' outcomes, with an eye toward safety and quality improvement. Professional firms can conduct similar postmortem reviews and make them a regular part of the management process, in a forum that is not critical or threatening, but intended instead to gain understanding of how mistakes have come about, and how to minimize and avoid repeating them.

Support also calls for raising concerns, both at an individual level and for the benefit of the organization as a whole, when an individual believes a mistake or incorrect judgment is "in process." For this facet of support to have value, however, individuals and managers have to be receptive to such ideas and seek them out, even when they face challenges or criticisms.

Ray Dalio, the founder of Bridgewater Associates, a highly successful investment organization, has codified over 100 pages of cultural and management principles published on the firm's web site.[21] On the topic of support (of both sorts—coaching and candid feedback), he states that he expects people in his organization to:

- Stress-test their opinions by having the smartest people they can find to challenge them;
- [Be] wary about overconfidence, and [be] good at not knowing; and
- Wrestle with reality, experiencing the results of their decisions, and reflecting on what they did to produce them so that they can improve.

It's a part of human nature to avoid these sorts of conflicts, but in an open and thoughtful professional partnership, people need to feel free to take the other side—even if it means questioning a decision by the boss—and point out something that might have been missed. By the same token, it's up to senior people in the firm to both advocate—and accept—that sort of candor.

> *"If you don't know what you don't know, you can get the organization into a lot of trouble, but if you do know what you don't know, you can seek help from others, and everyone just gets better."*
> —Bill Priest

Shared Interest

Because so many people in professional organizations have direct input and influence to the success and quality of client engagements, everyone in the firm owns the responsibility to move the firm forward. In turn, for individuals to be motivated to engage and commit deeply with clients and colleagues, they need to have a significant financial interest in the firm's performance. This calls not just for an expectation of bonuses every year to reward good work, but a participation in both the potential upside and downside, and a long-term tie to the firm that comes from equity ownership (or often in the case of an investment management firm, a stake in the strategies it offers to clients).

A shared financial interest requires a great commitment from a firm's partners. Aside from the long and hard working hours and commitment of personal life, there can be significant financial commitments—contributing to the firm in times of financial difficulty, of course, but often during good times as well, when a firm is growing and requires reinvestment of profits that might otherwise be paid out to the owners. Accordingly, balancing short-term rewards with the best interests of the firm through compensation policies is a crucial role for senior management.

Partnerships' policies vary on what they emphasize in professional compensation—events of individual merit, or collaboration that contributes to firm continuity. A "lockstep" model is formulaic, with compensation based on seniority and contributions to the firm over time, while a discretionary "eat what you kill" model, paying out bonuses tied to specific revenue events, recognizes particular successes in a given year.[22] Most firms, including Epoch, opt for the flexibility of combining the two in some fashion, to allow both *fairness* and *justice* in compensation.

"Tell me how a person is paid, and I'll tell you how he'll behave."
—Bill Priest

Justice and Fairness

"Fairness seems to have three main features: equality, agreement, and transparency," wrote Paul Woodruff, professor of philosophy at the University of Texas at Austin.[23] With respect to compensation, he adds, "transparency allows anyone to predict accurately what results to expect." Woodruff goes on to caution leaders, however, that "fairness is a trap, because once you commit yourself to it, you must submit to it. You are no longer in control because you have waived the right to exercise good judgment," and any deviations from established rules would appear unfair.

Justice in a corporate culture is a subtly different concept, Woodruff says, calling for judgment and leadership rather than formulas. Having a discretionary component in compensation combines fairness and justice, giving a firm's leaders leeway, and the ability to reward both individual achievement and teamwork, and thus reinforce the culture.

Justice has the greater challenge. It goes to the heart of preserving "the community," and the attributes valued by the community—frequently at times when the application of rules based in fairness might have the opposite and negative effect.

For a professional firm to be viable for the long term, however, the shared interest of the partners has to transcend the financial rewards, and include the intangible achievement of helping to build a quality organization. This calls for assembling a group of partners with complementary values and temperaments who will be able to work together, to understand each other, and to put up with each other during hard times over many years.

Notes

1. Edgar H. Schein, *Organizational Culture and Leadership*, 4th ed. (San Francisco: Jossey-Bass, 2010), 16.
2. Roger Urwin, "The Impact of Culture on Institutional Investors," Towers Watson/Thinking Ahead Institute, 2015.
3. Schein, *Organizational Culture and Leadership*, 18.
4. Ibid., 14.
5. Ibid., 3.
6. Andrew W. Lo, "The Gordon Gekko Effect," NBER Working Paper Series, Working Paper 21267, National Bureau of Economic Research, 2015, p 6. Accessed at: http://www.nber.org/papers/w21267
7. Ric Schmidt and Jonathan Rosenberg, with Alan Eagle, *How Google Works* (New York: Grand Central Publishing, 2014), 29.
8. Edgar H. Schein, *The Corporate Culture Survival Guide*, New and revised ed. (San Francisco: Jossey-Bass, 2009), 52–58.
9. Booz Allen Hamilton, "Beyond Command-and-Control: Managing the Diverse Corporation in Today's Turbulent Times," 5. 2000. Accessed at: http://www.boozallen.com/content/dam/boozallen/media/file/80674.pdf
10. Lo, "The Gordon Gekko Effect."
11. "Frederick Winslow Taylor, *The Principles of Scientific Management* (New York: Harper & Row, 1911). Accessed at: marxists.org/reference/subject/economics/taylor/.

12. Booz Allen Hamilton, "Beyond Command-and-Control," 4.

13. Ibid., 4.

14. Joel Spolsky," The Command and Control Management Method," Joel on Software (joelonsoftware.com), 2006.

15. IBM Corporation, "Leading through Connections: Case Studies from the Global Chief Executive Officer Study," IBM Institute for Business Value, 2012. Accessed at: http://www-01.ibm.com/common/ssi/cgi-bin/ssialias?subtype=XB&infotype=PM&appname=GBSE_GB_TI_USEN&htmlfid=GBE03535USEN&attachment=GBE03535USEN.PDF

16. This framework for describing investment management culture arose from an offsite meeting many years ago, between the management of Credit Suisse Asset Management-Americas (at the time, led by William Priest) and consultants McKinsey & Company. We have found it to be a durable and reliable guide.

17. Gillian Tett, *The Silo Effect: The Peril of Expertise and the Promise of Breaking Down Barriers* (New York: Simon & Schuster, 2015), 19.

18. Ibid., 179.

19. Schmidt and Rosenberg, with Alan Eagle, 29.

20. Ibid.

21. Ray Dalio, *Principles* (2011), 40. Accessed at: http://www.bwater.com/Uploads/FileManager/Principles/Bridgewater-Associates-Ray-Dalio-Principles.pdf

22. Maxine Boersma, "My Job Is to Protect the Firm's Culture," *Financial Times*, May 9, 2012.

23. Paul Woodruff, *The Ajax Dilemma: Justice Fairness and Rewards* (Oxford, England: Oxford University Press, 2011), 120.

CHAPTER 2

Culture in Investment Management

Investment managers present a puzzle to understanding the prospective value of their work, even when compared to other services business. The measurement of portfolio performance has evolved considerably in the past 30 years: evaluated against a particular benchmark, the wisdom of a manager's past decisions can be analyzed in great detail, with a galaxy of custom-designed statistics.

That said, portfolio mathematics still have trouble in definitively distinguishing luck from skill in historical results (particularly over short periods). Even the most skillful active managers sometimes underperform their benchmarks, and less skilled managers can be blessed with lucky streaks. A great active manager might outperform 60 percent of the time, but still underperform during the other 40 percent (and in truly challenging market environments, such as the one following the global financial crisis, it's likely that many active managers will fall short).

Even more challenging is the prediction of future performance from the results of the past: some of the earliest research from financial academics went in search of predicting performance, although its success has been fleeting. One early example is the Sharpe ratio, proposed 50 years ago by Stanford professor William Sharpe, initially as a tool for forecasting the returns of mutual funds.[1] More recently, the financial economists Martijn Cremers and Antti Petajisto hit on a new statistic that they hoped would have predictive value, named *active share.*[2] Subsequent research has shown both the Sharpe ratio and active share to be informative in measuring past performance, but the industry is still in search of an effective predictor. (Investment manager skill is a topic covered in detail in Chapter 6.)[3]

Accordingly, prospective clients, and the consultants that assist them, supplement return histories with additional characteristics of investment managers. A firm's culture is a distinguishing feature and part of its value proposition to clients, alongside its investment process and the pedigrees of its team. It's our view that even in the largest firms that manage hundreds of billions of dollars in client assets—and accordingly may need greater structure—there exists a desire and effort to create a partnership-like environment within teams.

Values

Underlying an investment firm's culture is a set of values—beliefs and principles that guide its employees in their work, and its leaders in their strategic decisions for the organization. Some firms articulate their values in a written statement that becomes part of the processes of hiring and orientation, and is useful to both the firm and employees in identifying the kind of people who should be hired, as well as providing practical guidelines on how to succeed.

At Epoch we don't maintain a detailed list of values; instead, we express them through an aspiration statement, which we developed at the founding of the firm in 2004:

To provide superior risk-adjusted results using a transparent approach based on our free cash flow philosophy;

To serve investors who seek and value Epoch's investment approach;

To continue as a thought leader and innovator in global investment management.

The first aspiration, setting out the goal of superior performance, calls for a strong work ethic, a solid base of knowledge that people refresh through curiosity, and consistency and good judgment in security selection and portfolio construction, among other things.

The second requires candor and sincerity in dealing with clients, and taking responsibility for our results. This point is especially important, as it addresses Epoch's investment style: it's essential that clients understand what sort of risk-adjusted results our approach is trying to achieve, and when it is most likely to succeed (or to underperform).

Meeting the last goal also calls for hard work, but in the sense of a separate effort—thinking creatively outside one's silo of experience and knowledge, to anticipate developments in the global economy and financial markets, shape the results into new investment strategies, and articulate them to clients in our resource of white papers and other investment insights.

Epoch's second aspiration deserves amplification. We think of ourselves as owners of businesses, not as traders of stocks. We don't buy companies because we think their stock prices are temporarily depressed after having disappointed the markets, and might stand to benefit from a short-term pickup in their outlook. Rather, we look for firms that have the ability to grow the value of their businesses over the long term, through a combination of superior returns on their invested capital, and management teams who understand that value is created by successful capital allocation decisions.

Deb Clarke, the global head of investment research at consultants Mercer LLC, has written on the distinction between the two investment viewpoints, and advocates that a long-term orientation is likely to better match the liabilities and objectives of the institutions that own the managed assets. She identifies two groups of such investors: one invests in established businesses expected to earn superior long-term returns on their high-quality operations and finances. The second type of long-term investor finds companies that may already be recognized as high-growth, but believes that the market lacks the imagination or time horizon to appreciate just how far they can go.

She points out that conventional performance measures, such as quarterly or annual returns, are not sufficient to evaluate such broad-based, long-term investing, and that additional measures of risk—geopolitical, environmental and technological—should be part of the dialogue. Ms. Clarke explains that "it is possible to succeed with this approach if investors genuinely understand ... the manager's strategy, and agree at the outset on the measures that will be used to monitor the progress of the portfolio on a regular (but not too frequent) basis. This is likely to align investors and managers more closely and make for a much better-informed discussion ... ultimately leading to ... better long-term performance."[4]

Clients that hire Epoch simply from a few years' superior returns in a performance record would probably dismiss us when returns fall short, so we look for clients who subscribe to the economic logic behind our strategies, and appreciate the benefits of investing with Epoch for the long term. Importantly, we want to be seen as providing thoughtful insights on the investment issues of the day.

> *"Clients that hire you by the numbers will fire you by the numbers, too, so we look for clients that understand and value the methodology behind our strategies."*
>
> —Bill Priest

A complementary set of values is proposed by Mike Krzyzewski, coach of Duke University's basketball team. His Duke teams have won five national championships, and "Coach K" has led all his teams to over 1,000 wins—the most in NCAA history.[5]

Coach K has developed a framework for team building, promoting five key values expressed in the analogy of a fist. "[M]y goal as a leader is to create a dominant team where all five fingers fit together into a powerful fist," he wrote in his 2001 book *Leading with the Heart*. "So in order to make it happen, the team has to learn how to think as one."[6]

His first value is communication: Duke's teams feature offensive and defensive systems, but also build in a system for communication. We add that as an investment firm grows, the permutations among the employees grow exponentially, and management needs to ensure that communication expands to where it's needed. That expansion can be accomplished with planned meetings, or informal get-togethers, or just establishing places in the office for people to gather, but management must do what it can to nudge team members to exchange ideas. (By the same token, leaders also should seek advice from their team members.)

Coach K's second value is trust, which he casts in terms of telling the truth—identifying team members' shortfalls, but in a constructive way. His third value is collective responsibility: teams win and lose together, and when a finger points blame, the group no longer has a fist. Caring is essential as well, toward individuals and the team, as well as caring about group goals of performance and excellence. The fifth value is pride—individuals trying hard enough, and putting a personal signature on everything they do. Overall, the goal of his value system—which has shown great results—is to convince team members that they are part of something bigger than themselves.

During year-end reviews at Epoch, we ask people two questions, in the spirit of Coach K's values of collective responsibility and caring. The first is directed at the individual: "What can we as management provide to allow you to do your job more effectively?" The second is directed back at management: "What can we do to make the organization more effective?" Everyone has to own the effort in his individual way, and asking these questions leads to valuable conversations—causing staff and management to think about how they can help one another, and bringing us together as a team.

> *"'Evolve We Must' is our mantra. Standing still usually means that at the end of the day you will not still be standing."*
>
> —Bill Priest

Integrity

Financial businesses have unique obligations to their clients. Companies in many lines of business follow a *caveat emptor,* or "buyer beware," business model, where customers are expected to be their own judges of product and service quality. Not so with investment management: asset managers are fiduciaries, and held to a higher standard of putting the interests of clients above their own. This places an emphasis on *trust*—both among the firm and its clients, and within the firm among its employees—and *integrity.* Werner Erhard and Michael Jensen, prominent scholars of human behavior and achievement and financial economics, respectively, have developed an extensive framework around integrity in finance,[7] motivated by their disappointment with the behavior of some financial institutions leading up to the 2008 financial crisis. Their work focuses on corporate financial management and compensation policies, as well the underwriting of securities, but Erhard and Jensen's ideas have broad application to a great many other businesses, and certainly are relevant to the cultural aspects of investment management. They line up with our thinking as well.

Erhard and Jensen construct a detailed model of integrity, which states, in summary, that people with integrity know what's expected of them; that they keep their word; and that they carry out what they've said they would. Importantly, when people fail to keep commitments—as will happen—they must acknowledge that they have and, as Erhard and Jensen put it, make provisions to clean up any messes they've created for colleagues or customers who were counting on them.

In Erhard and Jensen's model, integrity is not just a desirable, intangible virtue, but is a "positive phenomenon"—a definite cause, with observable effects. As they state: "[W]ith any positive phenomenon—for example, gravity—there are effects caused by actions related to that phenomenon. The action of stepping off a cliff will, as a result of gravity being a positive phenomenon, cause an effect (whether one likes the effect or not)."[8] The implication of their work is that integrity is a factor of production—"heretofore hidden, ... as important as knowledge, technology, entrepreneurship, human capital, and physical and social capital."[9] In their 2014 paper, the two scholars noted that empirical tests of integrity were under way at a large financial services firm.

We add another criterion that is implicit in the Erhard-Jensen integrity framework, but with little specific mention: accountability. In the wake of the 2008 financial crisis, regulators in the United States and elsewhere brought many actions against financial companies for marketing toxic investment products, but there were few consequences for the individuals involved.

Gretchen Morgenson, writing in the *New York Times* in August 2015, highlights the lack of accountability with an example of a 2015 settlement around a municipal bond strategy sold by Citibank from 2002 through 2008 to thousands of high-net-worth investors. It was marketed as a safe investment despite its considerable leverage, and triggered losses to customers estimated at $2 billion. The bank is said to have paid investors about $700 million to compensate for losses, as well as $180 million in a settlement with the U.S. Securities and Exchange Commission (SEC).

"Most disturbing . . . is the settlement's lack of accountability," Ms. Morgenson wrote: "As is all too common, Citigroup's shareholders are footing the $180 million bill associated with it. But they didn't devise the toxic bond strategy, sell it or hide its risks to investors." The SEC's action pointed out the role of the fund manager in failing to properly oversee the fund, but the accountability was apparently plea-bargained away, and the SEC settlement did not name the individual ultimately responsible (although Ms. Morgenson's story did so). She asks: "How can we expect Wall Street's me-first culture to change when regulators won't pursue or even identify the me-firsters who are directly involved?"[10]

As for Epoch, we are inclined to leave detecting and measuring integrity to the experts, but we have always emphasized its importance. In a firm with integrity nothing is hidden, and deception and untruth are not tolerated. Therefore, the compliance function—following regulations of legal authorities, as well as the rules of conduct a firm has developed on its own—is paramount. As a firm our compliance record has been excellent, as validated by the results of audits by various regulatory bodies.

Trust

Trust is an essential value within professional partnerships, where people need to know that they can depend on their colleagues to deliver quality results. Creative thinking and collaboration are essential, again highlighting the shortcomings of a command-and-control culture—in some settings.

"After all, bureaucracies are based on the assumption that people will abuse power if we entrust them with it," wrote management consultant Robert Bruce Shaw: in such situations, "Trust is replaced by formal regulations that force people to behave in ways deemed appropriate by those in positions of authority."[11] Shaw goes on to say that "new" competitive demands—he was writing in 1997—render such tight controls too restrictive and time consuming.

He sets out three "trust imperatives" for building trust in an organization: achieving results (possessing the right skills and getting the intended results); acting with integrity (behaving consistently and following through on commitments); and demonstrating concern (respecting the well-being of others). Unlike formal regulations, however, an environment of trust does not become effective immediately upon management's pronouncements; instead, it must be built up over time among colleagues, and at different levels of the organization, as they meet each other's expectations.[12] (However, it is constructive for management to keep trust in mind while making and keeping organizational and individual commitments.)

Trust has a special role in investment management, one that is pervasive and transcendent. Clients must intrinsically trust the firms working for them to be capable stewards of their assets, and deliver the best performance their strategies allow.

Investment management firms operate in two spheres. One concerns the "business of investing"—managing clients' money capably, and delivering the best returns possible, in the context of the firm's philosophy and investment process. The other focuses on the "business of the investing business," which revolves around gathering assets, providing career opportunities for the firm's employees, and making a profit for its owners. Individual firms tend to be either client-centric or self-centric,[13] emphasizing the two parts in different ways depending on their ownership structures, and what revenue and profit targets they are obligated to reach. Ideally, the business of investing takes priority; when that job is well done, the clients, employees, and owners all will be rewarded.

In the relationships among asset managers and asset owners, the elephant in the room is often a gap of trust between the two. Asset managers are generally for-profit shareholder entities, while asset owners tend to be profit-for-members entities, and a lack of congruence can cause a breakdown in trust, and a short-lived relationship.[14] The sub rosa question for both parties is "What kind of asset manager are you?" That is, are you investing-led, or commercial-led? Long-lived relationships require the former element to dominate, and it needs to reflect itself not only in performance metrics, but in thought leadership—allowing for partnering efforts of knowledge exchange, going well beyond just run-of-the-mill quarterly reviews.

"There's the business of investing, and the business of the investing business. Of course, when conflict arises, the business of investing should dominate."

—Bill Priest

At another level, a firm's employees have to trust their leaders to use the company's resources well, and make equitable decisions on compensation and advancement. (Because bonuses and other incentives typically make up a large and variable proportion of compensation, this trust is probably more important in investment management than in other knowledge businesses.) And leaders have to trust employees, to whom they have granted such important roles in the fortune and reputation of the firm. Finally, the employees have to trust each other in order to make mutual interdependence a workable proposition.

A firm's clients have an advantage in placing their trust with a manager: they can turn to investment management consultants, who in addition to vetting a firm's performance record also make a tacit, or even explicit, endorsement such as, "We've known these guys for a while, and you can trust them." It's not as easy for employees: even with plenty of research into how a firm operates, for a new employee entering a firm, coming to trust leaders and colleagues will likely require the successful completion of a few performance and compensation cycles.

At Epoch Investment Partners, we were able to expand the trust within the firm upon the arrival of the global financial crisis in September 2008—a very challenging time indeed. While the senior members of Epoch's investment team had decades of experience, the firm was only four years old, and assets under management were about $6 billion. How would the firm fare in such an uncertain time?

When the crisis hit, Epoch's leadership faced three difficult challenges at once: what to tell clients about the health of the firm; how to manage the work force in the face of what might be a great contraction in business; and how to protect the investment of the firm's owners. (Epoch was a public company at the time.)

We also wanted the actions to be consistent. We started to become wary of the state of the financial markets in 2007, as evidenced by several white papers Epoch published during that period. By August 2008 the markets and the global economy were already in serious trouble, and we couldn't rule out that they might get worse. (A few of our most relevant white papers are reprinted in Appendix A.)

Then on Sunday, September 15, 2008, Lehman Brothers Holdings filed for bankruptcy, and the global financial markets went into freefall. Lehman's failure also had an immediate impact on the global real economy, as Lehman had grown to become the principal counterparty to letters of credit, which are crucial to international trade.[15,16] That evening, we sent out a note to everyone in the firm, saying that we would hold an "all-hands" meeting Monday morning at 9 o'clock.

In that meeting, I said, "Look—we are about to go through something that none of us has ever seen before. It's an enormous threat to the world as we know it, and no one, not even me, has seen anything like it, and it's going to be absolutely terrifying."

"However, because we have a balance sheet that can withstand a prolonged period of market correction"—at that point, the cash on the balance sheet was greater than our annual revenues!—"there will be no layoffs, so long as all of us do our jobs." I went on to declare that there would be a bonus pool for the year, albeit a reduced one.

So as leaders, we took the long view, deciding that we would not lay off any employees despite the downturn sure to come, and would be better off keeping our staff at the ready for a recovery. Fortunately, the firm was in a strong financial condition. However, Epoch's leaders chose to cut their own compensation drastically and allocate those funds to salaries and bonuses of the staff, to ensure that client portfolio objectives were pursued with full focus and resources. We mention this not because we are looking for a pat on the back, but rather as an example of the importance of bringing justice, rather than formulaic fairness, to a difficult situation. Employees appreciated that action, and it certainly enhanced trust and loyalty throughout the firm: the choice showed employees that management valued them and their efforts, and strengthened the connection among Epoch's staff and leadership.

Culture and Clients

While the culture of an investment manager is developed and refined within the firm, culture is also important in distinguishing a firm to the outside world, and should be an important consideration to clients in manager hiring. A firm's track record is obviously important to the decision to engage and keep a manager, but in isolation investment performance, particularly over shorter periods, can be an unreliable indicator of investment skill and returns to be earned in the future. Thus, institutional investors, and the consultants that advise and assist them, take culture into account when choosing and monitoring investment managers.

"We don't make a specific assessment of a firm's culture, but we look at six areas of investment skill, and culture is included in each one," says James MacLachlan, Global Head of Equity Research in the New York office of global investment consultants Willis Towers Watson. "Skill without culture doesn't get you there, and neither does culture without skill."[17]

Much of Willis Towers Watson's analysis looks at the alignment of the firm with its clients—whether the manager is living up to the spirit of its obligations as a fiduciary, putting the interests of clients ahead of those of the firm, and resolving any conflicts in favor of the client.

An important culture-skill consideration is how the manager addresses the capacity of its investment strategies. For most asset classes, and for most investment styles, the size of a portfolio and the probability of outperformance work at cross purposes: once a strategy grows beyond a critical mass, the portfolio manager faces challenges in finding the right securities, acquiring them at the right prices, and then selling them in a timely fashion when necessary. Thus, the client's interest is best served by keeping the portfolio within its capacity limits. However, managers of successful strategies face the temptation of bringing in new clients and letting the portfolio grow further to increase fee revenues, and then possibly jeopardizing future investment returns. James MacLachlan observes: "We spend a lot of time looking at how managers handle capacity issues proactively, and how they trade off the interests of long-time clients against the additional revenues new clients will bring in, and not hurt their ability to generate alpha." He points out that few organizations truly constrain their capacity.

In a similar vein, Willis Towers Watson looks at how a firm's managers are compensated—whether on the basis of the returns on client portfolios (how well the clients do) or on the growth in assets under management (how well the firm does). Paying incentives to employees on asset growth can work against the principle of observing capacity limits on investment strategies, and MacLachlan asks: "Is a firm led by its investment managers, who are likely to be more attentive to performance, or by its business managers, who might seek to maximize assets beyond a limit that serves clients?"

At Epoch, we align the firm's interests with those of clients in several ways. One is fee rates: clients with similar-sized accounts are charged equal fees (a practice known in the industry as a "most favored nation" policy). Another is compensation: bonuses are paid on the performance of the portfolios, rather than the volume of new business in a given year. And as mentioned earlier, instead of receiving bonuses in cash, employees are required to hold a portion in Epoch's investment strategies—so employees are investing alongside the clients, and earn those same returns on a significant amount of their net worth. Such co-investment also aligns the time frame of the firm with that of the client: investment people shouldn't be focused just on the current year, but instead on the multi-year life span of a client relationship.

Firm Culture under Stress

A firm's culture is tested and evolves over time as the organization expands, and is subjected to sudden shocks. One instance highlighting the strength of Epoch's culture involved the seemingly innocent issue of our firm party for the winter holidays in 2008, a few weeks after the full arrival of the financial crisis. Some financial firms throw legendary holiday parties, but as a relatively small company with a fairly conservative group of employees, ours have tended to be more modest. Still, employees and management both were wondering whether to have one at all: given how terrible the markets were, and the economy seemed to be, might a party be disrespectful of the many people already enduring hard times? Should we give the money to a charity instead? Or put it into staff bonuses? People had worked hard, especially so, in 2008. Along with the many other issues to be addressed in the face of the crisis, our management team seriously debated the Christmas party, and the message that having one—or not—would send.

Thus, at the end of November, I penned a memo to the entire firm, which said in part:

> Having a holiday party perpetuates a culture of shared values, demonstrates a sense of collective appreciation for the year's efforts, and allows all of us a few moments of pleasure before returning to the more somber world around us. Everyone works hard to move the firm forward. Sometimes our best efforts are not good enough, and this year may be one of those years. Nevertheless, let us come together for an evening and celebrate a year of common effort. ... [A]fter all, is this not the season of promise and renewal? Please save December 12th for the Holiday Party and we look forward to seeing you there.

Culture in Recruiting

Shocks such as big market downdrafts are among the most trying events an investment firm's culture is called on to survive, but keeping culture on track can also be a challenge during periods of more normal organic growth. Determining which prospective employees will best fit and carry the culture forward is very difficult, because the intangible traits of culture are hard to observe in the course of a few interviews.

Some firms supplement their hiring practices with standardized personality tests, but in my long career I have never believed that such measures added much insight to the interview process. Standardized tests provide only an indirect view of each individual, and the means for evaluating the results of tests—grouping people into categories from very broad averages—are indirect as well. Moreover, investment firms are often hiring for specialized positions, where it's desirable that someone has gained a special knowledge as an analyst, or shown skill as a portfolio manager. Therefore, our starting point may be the resume and what an individual has already achieved.

The folks at Google take an alternative approach, focused on the individual rather than past accomplishments. Their prodigious growth has required adding many thousands of people every year, so that hiring is a continuous and substantial effort. In many cases, however, people don't stay in one position for a long time, and as Eric Schmidt and Jonathan Rosenberg write: "Hiring decisions are too important to be left in the hands of a manager who may or may not have a stake in the employee's success a year later."[18] Therefore, Google assigns its hiring decisions to small committees, based on a standard set of information on all candidates and four interviews of a half-hour each, without giving much weight to relationships a person might already have with people in the company, or the subjective opinions of the committee members. Still, they believe that hiring is an essential part of everyone's job, including senior management, and too important to be consigned to recruiters alone.

The staffing needs of Epoch, and many other investment managers, are quite different in the sense that we seek to form lasting teams and relationships, because in our business, long tenures and stable staff are a desirable trait. We don't hire that many people, so our process is not regimented, but instead driven by our qualitative assessments of candidates' skills and values. Thus, rather than look to tests of general potential, we ask candidates to meet with all the people they will be working with at our firm—which could entail 15 or more separate interviews—and we make decisions from our aggregate impressions.

My philosophy, admittedly simple, is to seek out candidates who are "decent."[19] Decency is not easy to define or measure, but if people don't like who they work with, they can't work with them for long periods of time, or at least not productively.

Moreover, decent people tend to be likeable—they share traits such as fairness, generosity, sincerity, and curiosity. They have a moral compass and don't want to disadvantage other people. Bringing in the wrong person, at whatever level, can be toxic to an organization, and reduce everyone's interest in their work and detract from the culture of the firm.

Thus, decency is an essential trait in the staff of an investment management firm, or any professional environment. I used to set out to recruit the smartest people we could find, hoping that they would turn out to be decent as well. But after a few particularly painful lessons in my career, where people brought in for their extreme smartness turned out to be destructive to the organization, I came to realize that decency takes higher priority. So I've flipped the criteria and now first look for people who I think are decent and hope that they turn out to be as smart as they appear to be.

As a generality, there are three reasons that people join, stay with, or leave a given firm. One is that they like their colleagues—if not, day-to-day life can become pretty miserable. Second is being offered a platform from which people can grow their human capital—to become more valuable in the future, whether at that firm or some future employer.

Third is whether they are rewarded appropriately. This comes in two parts, of which the first is money: are people paid appropriately? The other is whether each individual can make a contribution to the firm—to "move the needle." This element is crucial at a firm such as Epoch: we have just over 100 employees, so every person matters, and all help to move the firm forward.

Making an identifiable contribution is possible in a smaller firm such as Epoch, but what goes along with it is taking high-profile risks, and enjoying or suffering the consequences. There's no achievement without effort; unfortunately, however, there can be effort without commensurate achievement. Not everyone who wants to make a positive difference achieves that, and it's hard to know in advance exactly which people will, but the willingness to put in the time and hard work is a trait we value highly.

Acquisitions

Aside from market catastrophes, another class of stressful event for the culture of an investment manager is a merger or acquisition. And it happens frequently: by the numbers, asset management is an attractive part of the financial services sector. Revenues tend to be pretty steady, profit margins are typically higher than those in other financial business lines, and the capital requirements are comparatively low. Accordingly, during the decades of the 1990s and 2000s, many banks and insurance companies decided to acquire investment management firms.

Companies acquire asset managers for cultural reasons as well: investment management firms are full of people with entrepreneurial outlooks, and acquirers might believe that adding an asset management arm could infuse a new spirit and reinvigorate a staid organization.

But such acquisitions bring many challenges. One economic reality is that clients and consultants place managers under special scrutiny after they are acquired, expecting that the new owners might impose big changes to the investment style and marketing approach. That's a logical view because it's not uncommon that an investment firm's top portfolio managers depart after an acquisition, fearing that they will chafe under the new ownership.

But even assuming the acquired firm stays intact, in many cases there can arise a cultural conflict between the acquirer and the new subsidiary, particularly if the parent is given to a command-and-control view of the world and requires that from all business units. The two cultures, and often the personalities of people at the two firms, just don't match up. One conflict is dictating growth targets: big parents tend to set systematic asset and revenue objectives for acquired asset manager units that are unlikely to correlate with the natural cycles of the financial markets. Another, noted above, is setting the manageable size of strategies: for many types of strategies, asset management is often best performed on smaller scales, and forcing growth and building beyond their natural capacities can impair portfolio returns.

Buyers can also make the mistake of admiring firms for their component parts, and then inadvertently destroy the culture and success they coveted ("I can't wait to get hold of this firm. We'll send Mary to our London office, and Joe's a star—he'll be great in Tokyo"). Sellers are not without fault, however, as some can become mercenary ("We want you to buy us out, but we don't really want to be part of your organization." Or put more crudely, "We want your money but we don't want you").

"[S]urprisingly little attention is paid to culture before the new organization is created, and it is often a surprise to the parent that it now has to deal with powerful subcultures. . . ." commented culture scholar Edgar Schein, on the topic of acquisitions.[20] The parent may lay out a plan to take the best elements from both cultures, but that is seldom possible, because each subculture will want to stick to its own way of doing things.

Clayton Christensen, a prolific scholar on management and innovation, addressed the particular threat to the culture of acquired companies. Before undertaking a purchase, the acquiring firm needs to understand the strengths and limitations of its own culture, and study the culture of the target as well. On the challenge of combining the two, he wrote:

> At a minimum, there is a clash of cultures. Often, however, the result is that while many of the acquired company's resources are retained, its culture—those processes and the business model that made it attractive in the first place—[is] vaporized very quickly. In some cases this may have been the acquiring company's intent. But in many cases it was not.[21]

An exception has been our association with Toronto Dominion Bank. We entered into a business combination with TD, whereby it acquired Epoch, in March 2013. Recognizing the importance of the continuity of culture, TD wanted Epoch to operate as autonomously as possible. Aside from meeting certain requirements of regulatory authorities, that continues to be the case, and the culture that existed before the acquisition is very much intact today.

Evolution of Culture

Cultures can evolve in several different ways: organic evolution from reacting to changes in circumstances; guidance from cultural insights of leaders; or planned change through directed group efforts.[22] Or they may not: "If an organization's internal and external environments remain stable, strongly held assumptions can be an advantage," writes Edgar Schein. "However, if there is a change in the environment, some of those shared assumptions can become a liability, precisely because of their strength," and limit the group's ability to adapt, innovate and grow.[23]

From a standing start, more or less, in 2004, Epoch grew its business to nearly $50 billion of assets under management and advisement by the end of 2015. The mantra "Evolve We Must" has been a constant thread in the firm's DNA, and present in our attitude and energy from the start. Thus in charting the course for the firm's future, Epoch leadership considered several new directions in order to build on our specialty of equity management. We ruled out an expansion into fixed income strategies, believing we would not likely reach the scale necessary to compete with established firms. There was also an active debate about adding strategies in emerging market equities, but that, too, seemed unproductive, as that skill set was not present in our team at the time and the prospects for emerging markets equities did not appear to be attractive.

However, we saw important opportunities in two important trends reshaping the industry. First, equity investors were moving their focus from their home markets and regions to more diversified strategies with a global scope. We were confident that Epoch's investment philosophy would be well received outside the United States and that our global strategies would expand our client base.

Second, distribution in the industry was shifting its center of gravity from institutional investors, which made up most of

Epoch's clients, to retail investors. But our background was predominantly institutional, and we realized that Epoch would need to work through partners who could put our strategies in the hands of retail investors. Accordingly, we cultivated distribution relationships with key insurance companies.

The evolution of our strategy got off to a strong start, and between 2009 and 2012 assets under management rose to $24 billion. Epoch had correctly anticipated the expansion to global markets with the design of several strategies, including our successful Global Equity Shareholder Yield. Accordingly, as the client base and assets grew, their composition became increasingly global, and between 2009 and 2012 the share of Epoch's managed assets in global strategies rose from 40 percent to 60 percent.

Growth called for a response of expanding the staff, and some structural modification of the company, with the goal of broadening the transfer of knowledge among the larger team. Given the greater importance of global strategies, separate regional research meetings evolved into global sessions, and additional teams were created to support the greater range of strategies.

Evolution of Culture: A Parable

"[C]ulture is very much a product of the environment," wrote Andrew Lo, "and as environments change, so too does culture."[24]

On the isolated Chatham Islands, 500 miles southeast of New Zealand, the Moriori people migrated from the mainland to establish settlements, probably about the year 1500.[25] Over 24 generations their population grew to 2,000, and through time they followed the proscription of an ancestor, Nunuku, against violence, developing a culture based on a law of peace (unique in a part of the world known for its tribal wars and cannibalism). Then in 1835, 900 of the mainland Maori tribe reached the Moriori's shores, in search of new territory. The Moriori welcomed the Maori's arrival, and even nursed them back to health after a difficult journey.

But the Maori started a campaign of war, prompting a Moriori council on how to handle the situation. Younger Morioris wanted to stand their ground and fight back, but the tribe's elders insisted on keeping the pacific tradition of Nunuku's Law. The results were disastrous, as many Moriori were killed, and the rest enslaved; by 1862 only 101 of the 2,000 had survived. The conquering Maori eventually left the islands, but the New Zealand government added insult to the Moriori injuries and granted the Maori ownership of the islands anyway. A few Moriori went on to prosper nonetheless, and the twentieth century brought a modest revival of their people and culture.

Cultures are meant to be stable, and in a business such as investment management, where the financial markets are moving every day, employees need a set of principles to guide them in meeting the challenges the markets present. But as the example of the Moriori shows, if a culture is too rigid at the wrong time it will undermine a group's mission, so a culture may need to adapt to change—in the organization, as well as in the world at large.

At Epoch we have great faith in the principles that make up our culture—mutual interdependence, support, and shared interest—and our central values of integrity, trust, and alignment of our interests with those of our clients. Our culture is therefore much the same as what we set out at the founding of the firm in 2004, and those principles will likely be in place as long as there are "spear carriers" for the values we represent.

"Cultures don't necessarily deserve to survive. For our culture to endure, we have to evolve, and keep winning for our clients."

—Bill Priest

What will change, however, is how we apply those values to carry out portfolio management. The world's economy is shifting, in its sources and uses of the factors of production (land, labor, and capital, broadly stated), the need to preserve the environment, the role of governments and central banks, the balance of growth and power among developed and developing countries, and the reach of wireless communication and digitization into every corner of the world. The investing world itself is changing, too, as many investors redefine their needs and turn to new strategies and products. In the last section of this book, we offer a few hypotheses on the role of technology in investment management, and how Epoch and the industry might adapt its research methodology and investment processes.

Notes

1. William F. Sharpe, "Mutual Fund Performance." *The Journal of Business*, Vol. 39, No. 1, Part 2: Supplement on Securities Prices (January 1966): 119–138. Accessed at http://www.edge-fund .com/Shar66.pdf.

2. Martijn Cremers and Antti Pettajisto, "How Active Is Your Fund Manager? A New Measure That Predicts Performance," March 31, 2009. AFA 2007 Chicago Meetings Paper; EFA 2007 Ljubljana Meetings Paper; Yale ICF Working Paper No. 06-14. Available at SSRN: http://ssrn.com/abstract=891719 or http://dx.doi.org/ 10.2139/ssrn.891719.

3. A similar challenge of prediction plagues another service industry—Major League Baseball. In spite of a rich database of performance statistics, managers have a poor record of choosing future all-stars, even in the game's comparatively well-controlled conditions. "The draft has never been anything but a ... crapshoot," said Oakland A's manager Billy Beane, in Michael Lewis's book *Moneyball* (New York: W.W. Norton and Company, Inc., 2004), 17. "We take fifty guys and we celebrate if two of them

make it. In what other business is two for fifty a success? If you did that in the stock market, you'd go broke." After 2002, however, the intensive application of sabermetrics statistical analysis transformed baseball to a somewhat more disciplined business. (Sabermetrics is the empirical study of in-game baseball statistics, and takes its name from the Society for American Baseball Research.)

4. Deb Clarke, "A Broader View of Risk," Top1000funds.com, January 20, 2016. Accessed at: http://www.top1000funds.com/featured-homepage-posts/2016/01/20/transforming-decision-making-of-long-horizon-investors/.

5. Duke Athletics, goduke.com/ViewArticle.dbml?ATCLID=152844.

6. Mike Krzyzewski and Donald T. Phillips. *Leading with the Heart: Coach K's Successful Strategies for Basketball, Business and Life* (New York: Grand Central Publishing, 2001), 70.

7. Werner Erhard and Michael C. Jensen, "Putting Integrity into Finance: A Purely Positive Approach," Harvard NOM Unit Research Paper 12-074 (2014), 4. Accessed at: http://ssrn.com/abstract=1985594.

8. Ibid., 6.

9. Ibid., 3.

10. Gretchen Morgenson. "An S.E.C. Settlement with Citigroup That Fails to Name Names," *The New York Times,* August 28, 2015.

11. Robert Bruce Shaw, *Trust in the Balance: Building Successful Organizations on Results, Integrity and Concern* (San Francisco: Jossey-Bass, 1997), 6.

12. Ibid., 23.

13. Roger Urwin, "The Impact of Culture on Institutional Investors," Towers Watson/Thinking Ahead Institute, 2015.

14. Ibid.

15. A letter of credit is a letter from a bank guaranteeing that payment from a buyer to a seller will be made on time and in the correct amount. If the buyer cannot make payment, the bank would be required to make good on the full or remaining amount.

16. Roger B. Porter, Robert R. Glauber, and Thomas J. Healey, *New Directions in Financial Services Regulation* (Cambridge, MA: MIT Press, 2011), 40.

17. James MacLachlan, in discussion with authors, 2015. The comments of Mr. MacLachlan and the related processes of Willis Towers Watson should not be interpreted as an endorsement of any particular manager.

18. Eric Schmidt and Jonathan Rosenberg, with Alan Eagle, *How Google Works* (New York: Grand Central Publishing, 2014), 121.

19. Webster's *Third New International Dictionary* defines decent as "marked by a combination of goodwill, sincerity, tolerance, uprightness, generosity or fairness; not cruel, repressive, or vindictive.

20. Edgar H. Schein, *The Corporate Culture Survival Guide*, New and revised ed. (San Francisco: Jossey-Bass, 2009), 12.

21. Clayton M. Christensen, "What Is an Organization's Culture?" Harvard Business School case 9-399-104, August 2006.

22. Ibid., 221–222.

23. Ibid., 218.

24. Andrew W. Lo, "The Gordon Gekko Effect," NBER Working Paper Series, Working Paper 21267, National Bureau of Economic Research, 2015, p 21. Available at: http://www.nber.org/papers/w21267.

25. Denise Davis and Māui Solomon, "Moriori—The Impact of New Arrivals," *Te Ara: The Encyclopedia of New Zealand,* updated July 12, 2012. Available at: http://www.TeAra.govt.nz/en/moriori/page-4.

PART II

Philosophy and Methodology

Watching over the world's wealth is a big business: For North America alone, consultants McKinsey & Company put total assets managed at $31 trillion for the end of 2014, generating revenues for the year of $111 billion.[1] And there are plenty of managers at work: in the United States, more than half the industry's assets were managed by 128 large firms, but the Securities and Exchange Commission reports a total of over 11,000 registered investment advisers (RIAs). Managers can be grouped according to what types of assets they manage and what sorts of clients they serve, but each goes about the process of investing a little differently.

The next eight chapters of this book examine those differences and consider the details of the investment process, in particular for equities. To begin, Chapter 3 examines the relationship between the real economy and financial markets, as well as the makeup of returns to equities, and contributions to returns over time of earnings growth, dividends and changes in valuations. We then consider the philosophical debate among investment practitioners, financial economists, and investors on whether the best long-term results are achieved through portfolios actively managed by professionals, or by more passively "owning the markets" with low-cost index funds. Chapter 4 lays out a classic theoretical case in favor of passive management, while Chapter 5 counters with a more contemporary and practical view of real-world investor behavior. In Chapter 6 we review the performance record of active managers, and consider some of the challenges they have faced in recent markets. Epoch is firmly in the active investment camp, and in Chapter 7 we build our case in favor of active management. Chapters 8 through 10 review the process of researching and selecting securities for investment, emphasizing Epoch's focus on companies' ability to generate free cash flow and build their long-term value through wise allocation of capital.

Note

1. McKinsey & Company, "Navigating the Shifting Terrain of North American Asset Management," 2015.

CHAPTER 3

The Nature of Equity Returns

Linkages: The Real Economy and the Financial Economy

Observers of the U.S. economy often draw a distinction between Main Street and Wall Street, as though the business and financial worlds operate in their own spheres. However, the real economy of Main Street—the production and consumption of goods and services—and the financial economy of Wall Street—the financial markets where stocks and bonds are traded—can be viewed as two sides of the same coin. Two important factors link the two aspects of the overall economy.

The sum of all goods and services produced in the real economy in a given year is measured by gross domestic product (GDP). Real GDP, which measures output in constant prices, emphasizes the growth in quantities produced, while nominal GDP adds in inflation, to take into account changes in both quantities and prices. The share of businesses' profits in nominal GDP in the real economy, profit margins, corresponds to corporate earnings per share in the financial economy—the first important link (Figure 3.1).

The second key link between the real and financial economy is interest rates, which underlie the valuation of financial

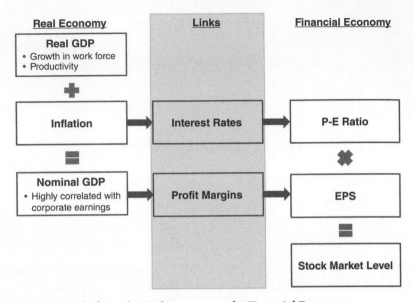

FIGURE 3.1   Links from the Real Economy to the Financial Economy
Sources: Crestmont Research; Epoch Investment Partners

assets. Interest rates include a component to provide lenders with a real return and contain a second component to account for inflation: in order to preserve the purchasing power of their capital, lenders factor inflation into the rates they charge borrowers.

In the case of equities, the rate of inflation is embedded in the price-earnings ratio: low inflation leads to lower interest rates and higher price-earnings ratios, while higher inflation raises interest rates, and compresses price-earnings ratios. (Appendix B reviews the mathematical relationship between interest rates and the valuation of financial assets.)

The linkages between the real and financial economies are not just conceptual: over time, the trends in U.S. GDP and corporate profits have tracked each other quite closely. Figure 3.2 plots the two series on log scales from 1947 through 2015.

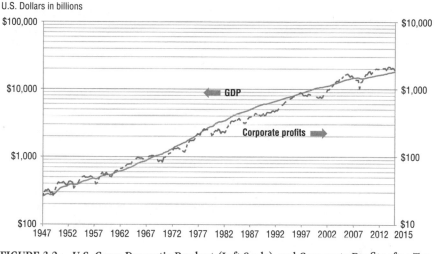

FIGURE 3.2   U.S. Gross Domestic Product (Left Scale) and Corporate Profits after Tax
(Right Scale), 1947–2015
Source: St. Louis Federal Reserve Bank

Components of Stock Returns

In simple terms, the return on an investment in equities can
be split into three components: dividends received (including
reinvestment of dividends), growth in earnings per share, and
changes in valuation (as measured by the price-earnings ratio).
(Multiplying growth in earnings per share by the change in the
price-earnings ratio produces the change in price.)

Sharing a trajectory with the U.S. and global economies,
earnings per share for companies in the S&P 500 (the top line
in Figure 3.3) rises during expansions (such as the growth years
of the mid-1990s, and 2002 through 2008) and loses ground
during periods of recession (as in the early 1990s, early 2000s,
and in the weakness following the global financial crisis). Dividends (the lower line) tend to be more steady, although many
companies choose to cut them back when decreased profits
don't justify maintaining a dividend, such as in 2008 and 2009.[1]

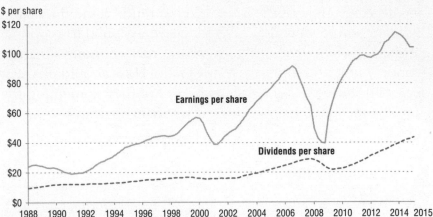

FIGURE 3.3   S&P 500 Operating Earning per Share and Cash Dividends Share, Latest 12 Months, December 1988–December 2015

Source: S&P Dow Jones Indices

Although annual earnings per share of the S&P 500 track U.S. GDP pretty closely, the linkage between the real economy and the value of stock prices has not been as systematic. Figure 3.4 illustrates the variation, plotting nominal U.S. GDP against earnings per share and the price index level of the S&P 500 from

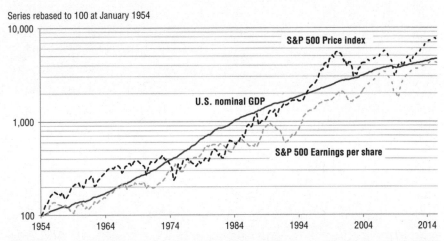

FIGURE 3.4   S&P 500 Price Level and Earnings per Share, versus U.S. Nominal GDP, 1954–2015

Source: Bloomberg LP

1954 to 2015. Most of the difference in trends is the fluctuation over time in the valuation investors have assigned to corporate earnings, through the volatility of the real economy/financial economy link of the price-earnings ratio. How should investors deal with these changes in valuation? Are they something that can be anticipated as part of an investment strategy?

Price-Earnings Ratios

To answer those questions, we need to better understand what a price-earnings ratio really is and what it is not. It's a simple measure, but the concept behind it is elusive. The price-earnings ratio equates a stock's current price with some measure of earnings per share—perhaps actual earnings over the latest 12 months, or an estimate of the coming year. Price-earnings (P/E) ratios can be measured for individual companies, or for an index of stocks in the aggregate.

It is important to recognize that the *P* and the *E* in a P/E ratio are somewhat mismatched. Looking at stock prices and earnings over the long term, the stock market seems to anticipate changes in earnings (or, at least, what investors expect the change in earnings to be) with about a nine-month lead. In other words, investors aren't usually focused on what earnings are doing at the moment—instead, they look forward to what they expect about nine months ahead. That's why, for example, in the worst of the global financial crisis, stocks started rising in March 2009 even though earnings didn't hit bottom until the fourth quarter of that year.

P and E are a bit of an odd couple: ultimately they reflect the same underlying fundamental reality, but from different perspectives in time. The *P* in a P/E ratio is a forward-looking number, valuing shares based on expectations of where earnings are likely to be in the future. Meanwhile, the *E* is a backward-looking number, measuring what earnings have been over the last twelve months. (Even when investors calculate a "forward P/E" based on earnings for the year ahead, the E is only looking out 12 months, while the P is based on expectations about earnings for many years beyond that.) To get a sense of the odd dance that makes up a P/E ratio, imagine two dancers trying to accomplish a waltz, under unusual conditions: one partner is hearing the music live as the band is playing it, while the other is listening to the music through headphones on a 15-second delay.

Looking at the P/E ratio in this light, it's evident that deriving meaning from short-term changes in the ratio itself—much less anticipating those changes—is not straightforward, because both the numerator and the denominator are always in motion. Moreover, multiple combinations of changes in prices and earnings can produce an equal change in the P/E ratio. For example, a 20 percent rise in price accompanied by a 10 percent rise in earnings will bring an increase in the P/E ratio of roughly 10 percent. But a 5 percent gain in price accompanied by a 5 percent fall in earnings would produce that same 10 percent increase in the P/E ratio, as would a 10 percent fall in price accompanied by a 20 percent drop in earnings. However, each of these three cases would probably arise from quite different scenarios in the economy and the market environment. In other words, focusing on changes in P/E in isolation doesn't reveal whether prices or earnings are rising or falling, or whether the economy is growing or shrinking.

Stock prices do not change because investors consciously decide to apply a different P/E ratio to a company's reported earnings. Rather, the P/E ratio changes, at least in part, because investors change their view about a company's future earnings prospects, and as a result change their view of what the company is worth today. In other words, P/E changes don't drive stock prices; changes in stock prices drive changes in P/E. (We say *in part* because the P/E can change even when prices don't change at all, as long as the trailing earnings are changing—which they almost always are.)

This is not to say that investors can't make assumptions about how P/E ratios will change: all other things being equal, changes in interest rates and inflation will affect P/E ratios. As discussed in Appendix B regarding the math of valuing financial assets, for a given stream of cash flows, lower interest rates result in higher asset prices (and vice versa). Similarly, lower inflation tends to result in lower interest rates, which in turn result in more favorable pricing of financial assets, theoretically leading to higher P/E ratios.

We say theoretically because, again, that assertion assumes all other conditions are equal. But all other conditions rarely stay equal in the stock market. Consider Figure 3.5, which plots the aggregate P/E ratio of the S&P 500 from 1988 to 2015, together with the yield of the 10-year U.S. Treasury bond (on an inverted scale).

During some periods, such as from 1989 to 1997, or from 2003 to 2007, interest rates and the S&P 500 P/E ratio moved

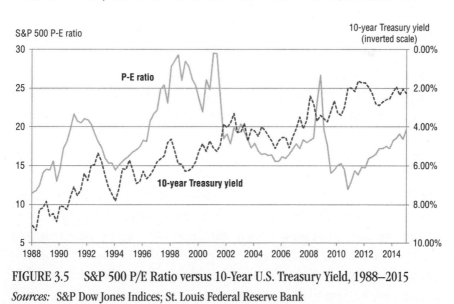

FIGURE 3.5   S&P 500 P/E Ratio versus 10-Year U.S. Treasury Yield, 1988–2015

Sources: S&P Dow Jones Indices; St. Louis Federal Reserve Bank

in opposite directions pretty reliably: changes in interest rates, and the impact that those changes had on present value calculations, appear to have been the main driver of changes in the market P/E.

At other times, the P/E ratio displays seemingly contrary behavior. From 1997 to 2002, for instance, the P/E ratio rose disproportionately versus the drop in interest rates. At work during this period was the other crucial factor in P/E ratios—investor sentiment.

Greater optimism over prospects for the economy leads investors to raise their expectations about the size of future profits, driving today's prices higher, and increasing the P/E ratio as a result. Investor enthusiasm is what propelled P/E ratios during the tech-telecom boom of the late 1990s, when investors valued the S&P 500 at between 25 and 30 times earnings for several years. In that case, investor sentiment took over as the dominant driver of the market P/E, as expectations called for future profits to soar. As a result, the market P/E ratio rose far faster than interest rates fell.

The global financial crisis brought on unusual behavior in P/E ratios from 2008 through 2011. In the second half of 2008 the market P/E rose modestly as interest rates fell—their typical interaction, at least at first glance. However, the real driver was not lower interest rates but, instead, the fact that while stock prices were falling, earnings were falling even faster. (Thus, the rising P/E ratio during that period was certainly not the product of investors' optimism.)

Then in mid-2009, the market's P/E ratio spiked sharply higher. In this instance, investor optimism *was* the driver: share prices started to discount the coming recovery in earnings, even as trailing earnings were still collapsing. The extreme extent of the rise in the P/E was due to the mismatch between forward-looking prices and backward-looking earnings: as reported earnings finally turned up in late 2009 and into 2010, the P/E ratio fell back. But neither the spike in the P/E ratio, nor its later drop, was the result of conscious decisions by investors— either to first pay more for earnings, or then less. Instead, the P/E ratio responded to inflection points in the earnings stream, and the wild gyrations arose from the mismatch between forward-looking prices and historical reported earnings.

What turned the P/E around and put it on an upward path in 2011 was the Federal Reserve's policy of quantitative easing. Quantitative easing—or at least the first stage of it— had begun just after the onset of the financial crisis in 2008, but it took time for investors to realize that the illiquidity that had triggered the crisis was not going to recur. As investor confidence in future profit growth returned—slowly, because the strength of the economic recovery was below average— the influence of lower interest rates on the market P/E began to dominate again. The influence on the financial markets of quantitative easing since 2008 cannot be overemphasized, and we direct readers to Epoch's May 2014 white paper, "The Power of Zero + the Power of the Word," presented in Appendix A.

These examples illustrate the challenge in anticipating changes in valuation: its two main factors—interest rates and opinions about future earnings—do not work independently of each other. A fall in interest rates might seem to imply higher P/E ratios (because a lower discount rate raises the present value of future cash flows), but if interest rates are falling because the economic outlook is deteriorating, as was the case in 2008 and 2009, then investors will also be lowering their expecta- tions for future earnings at the same time. Which effect will predominate—lower interest rates pushing P/E ratios higher, or increased pessimism about future earnings pushing P/E ratios lower? There is no way to say with certainty, and the relation- ship between interest rates and P/E is neither linear nor easily predictable.

Analysts at Pavilion Global Markets have studied this phenomenon, and derived what they see as a simple conclusion: "[W]hen the economy is in trouble, governments lower interest rates to bolster consumption. Equities are under pressure in those times and P/E multiples are depressed. When the economy picks up again, market interest rates start to move up as do P/Es. This multiple expansion continues until we get to an interest rate 'bliss point,' which we have calculated to be around 5.5 percent."[2]

Accordingly, when scatter plots of interest rates and P/E ratios are fitted with a polynomial trend line, rather than slope downward—the relationship that generally prevailed from 1988 to 2002 (as in the left panel of Figure 3.6)—the curve forms what Pavilion Global Markets calls a P/E ratio "dome" for the full period including quantitative easing (as in the right panel of Figure 3.6).

Further complicating matters for investors, for an individual stock, at a given point in time the P/E ratio will reflect not only the factors driving market valuation, but also factors specific to the company—tangible factors such as its recent earnings growth and outlook for the future, as well as intangibles such as intellectual property, management acumen, and other

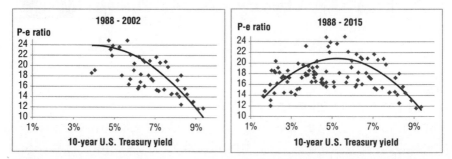

FIGURE 3.6   P/E versus 10-Year, 1988–2002 (Left Panel) and P/E versus 10-Year, 1988–2015 (Right Panel)

Sources: Pavilion Global Markets; Epoch Investment Partners

unique characteristics. Typically, the more (or less) favorably the market views a company, the higher (or lower) will be its P/E ratio relative to other stocks versus peers in its industry, or in the market in general.

The Historical Makeup of Stock Returns

Changes in P/E ratios are just one factor in the returns on stocks: dividends and changes in earnings per share make contributions as well. Figure 3.7 illustrates the three components of return for the S&P 500, over 10-year periods going back to 1927. Over the very long run—the 88 years from 1927 through 2015—the total return to the S&P 500 averaged 9.8 percent annually (see the summary column on the far right in Figure 3.7).

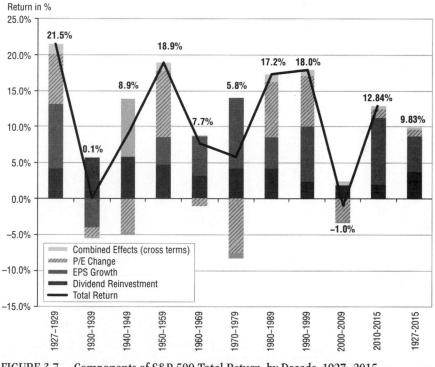

FIGURE 3.7   Components of S&P 500 Total Return, by Decade, 1927–2015

Source: Standard & Poor's; Epoch Investment Partners

Dividends always make a positive contribution to returns (illustrated by the black bars). Growth in earnings per share, depicted by the gray bars, usually is additive, too, depending on the length of the period being measured. In Figure 3.7, the 1930s was the only 10-year period where earnings per share growth was negative, and thus detracted from total return. Also note that from 2000 through 2009, the contribution to total return from earnings growth was positive but minimal, as a result of the collapse in earnings, especially for the banking sector, in the global financial crisis.

Figure 3.8 presents a more granular picture, showing a series of rolling 10-year periods from 1936 through 2015 that better demonstrates the cycles in the components of return. Dividends are represented by the medium gray portion of each column, while earnings per share growth is shaded in light gray, and P/E ratio changes are shown by the dark gray parts. The black line depicts total return.

Slicing the data this way, dividends still have always made a positive contribution to return. As for earnings, they detracted

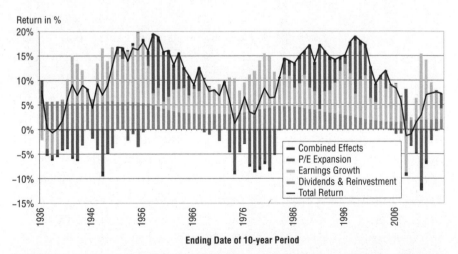

FIGURE 3.8   Components of S&P 500 Total Return, Rolling 10-Year Periods, 1927–2015
Source: Standard & Poor's; Epoch Investment Partners

from total stock returns during the Great Depression, but since then earnings have made a positive contribution, with one exception—the 10 years ending in 2008, which encompassed two recessions.

In contrast, contributions from changes in the P/E ratio tend to rise and fall significantly over short periods. For instance, changes in P/E ratios contributed 7.8 percentage points to the total annualized return of 17.2 percent in the 1980s, and 7.1 percentage points to the 18.0 percent total return of the 1990s. But in the 1970s, the change in the market P/E ratio deducted 7.6 percentage points from total return, which managed to significantly undermine the combined 14 percentage point contribution of dividends and earnings per share growth for those years. Changes in interest rates explained much of this pattern: rising rates in the 1970s pushed P/E ratios down, while falling interest rates in the 1980s and 1990s pulled valuations back up.

Clearly, over shorter periods, the impact of changes in the price-earnings ratio on returns is often quite large. In the fullness of time, however—over the 88 years covered in Figure 3.7—the net changes in P/E ratios have not been a significant factor in returns. Of the S&P 500's total annual return for the full period of 9.8 percent, 3.8 percentage points came from dividends and 4.9 percentage points from growth in earnings per share. Changes in valuation, through the P/E ratio, added just 0.9 percentage points on average. (In addition to the three primary components, the presentation of total return of the S&P 500 also includes an amount we call "combined effects," which is the result of converting the geometric returns of the index to an arithmetic computation. That component is positive in some periods and negative in others, but is consistently small.)

With this background on the links from the economy to the financial markets, and the importance of earnings growth, dividends and changing valuations to moves in share prices, we are prepared to discuss in depth the process of equity investing. As a first step, we look at decades of academic study by financial economists, developing hypotheses and models constructed by financial economists to explain the behavior of investors, and how their actions aggregate into the movements of the financial markets. Chapter 4 looks at earlier classic models that aimed to fit the markets into a sleek framework of rational decision making, and Chapter 5 considers more recent work that describes the markets—more accurately, in our view—from the perspective of a wide range of less well organized investor behavior, including misperceptions of risk and reward, and many investors' disproportionate reactions to economic and corporate financial events.

Notes

1. The S&P 500 is a widely used market index, published by S&P Dow Jones Indices since 1957. It includes 500 leading U.S. companies weighted in proportion to their market values, and captures approximately 80 percent of the value of the U.S. stock market.
2. Pavilion Global Markets, "A Fair Value Dome to Replace the Broken Fed Model," April 11, 2013.

CHAPTER 4

The Great Investment Debate: Active or Passive Management?

I nvesting in the world's financial markets is a varied, complex and important undertaking. Every investor should have a formal plan, in two parts: a philosophy or strategy for guiding the investment; and a methodology, or set of tactics, for carrying it out. A well-designed plan includes a viewpoint on how the financial markets should react to a range of developments in the real economy, what assets to invest in or avoid, and the likely range of returns a portfolio might earn, as well as yardsticks for measuring success or disappointment—a set of principles for monitoring the results, and signaling to the asset owners that they need to adjust the plan if something goes awry.[1]

For institutional investors, a reasoned investment policy statement is often a legal requirement, and certainly part of the overseers' fiduciary duty. For many other investors, however, an investment philosophy may develop over time through trial and error, even unconsciously—not unlike an organizational culture. But developing an informed investment plan presumes a knowledge of the financial markets that many people lack, and this shortage has created the need for an enormous industry of investment consultants, managers and advisers for institutions, businesses, and individuals.

Of the many options investors face, in this discussion we are most concerned with the final stages of this complex portfolio decision tree—the crucial, practical choice of how to manage the assets from day to day, with a focus on equities. Specifically, are investors better off in the long run by owning passive port-folios that aim to own every stock in the market, and therefore earn market-like results? Or should they invest in actively man-aged portfolios? That is, should they hire specialist firms pursu-ing more narrow portfolios intended to outperform the market?

The choice goes beyond philosophy. The investment out-comes can differ greatly, between "owning the market," per-haps through an index fund that tracks the S&P 500 or the MSCI World Index by effectively owning every stock, versus the return on an actively managed strategy, where a manager narrows the portfolio to, say, 50 or 100 securities he believes will outperform the broad market. (The MSCI World Index, published by MSCI Inc., includes roughly 1,600 stocks in 23 markets in developed economies around the globe, and cap-tures approximately 85 percent of the capitalization in each market. In much of the discussion that follows, we use the S&P 500 as a proxy for "the stock market." A global index like the MSCI World Index is a better proxy for today's investor, but we rely instead on the S&P 500 for its richer and more accessi-ble history.) Consider a hypothetical $1,000 invested in the U.S. stock market in January 1990. From then through December 2015, the annualized return from the S&P 500 was 9.3 percent. Note that this is a hypothetical return, rather than an actual one. Performance of an index does not reflect actual results, although the managers of funds tracking indexes can closely approximate the hypothetical returns. Had the portfolio owned an S&P 500 index fund charging an annual management fee of 0.10 percent, its value would have grown to $9,814 at the end of 2015 (assuming the reinvestment of dividends, and no additions or withdrawals from the account, and no taxes). An actively managed fund that earned an average of 1.50 percent above the benchmark each year, even while charging an annual management fee of 0.75 percent, would have grown to $12,207, or about 24 percent greater.

But that example is simple arithmetic, calculated in a vacuum. A skillful active manager might earn an excess return averaging 1.50 percent over that many years, but inevitably that manager would outperform in some years and underperform in others— no manager can beat the market by the same margin every single year. The actual successes of a particular investor, working with particular managers, would vary according to many factors: the time periods considered; the behavior of the markets during those periods; the skill and consistency possessed by the active managers an investor hires to oversee the portfolio; which market sectors and securities those active managers emphasize; and the investor's fortitude in staying invested during disappointing markets.

The Debate Is Timeless

The debate about active versus passive management is hardly new. Over 50 years ago, Benjamin Graham, the godfather of conservative equity investing, delivered what to some modern ears may sound like a surprising message.[2] In a November 1963 speech to the San Francisco Society of Security Analysts, Graham asserted:

> I think the ... most important reason why the investor should not be led to emphasize his selection of individual stocks, and to neglect the general level of the stock market is the fact that there is no indication that the investor can do better than the market averages by making his own selections or by taking expert advice. ...

The outstanding support for that pessimistic statement is found in the record of the investment funds, which represent a combination of about the best investment brains in the country, and a tremendous expenditure of money, time, and carefully directed effort. The record shows that the funds have had great difficulty as a whole in equaling the performance of the 30 stocks in the Dow Jones Averages or the 500 Standard and Poor's Index [sic]. If an investor had been able, by some rough across-the-board diversification to make up a portfolio approximating these averages he would have had every reason to expect about as good results as were shown by the very intelligent and careful stock selections by the investment-fund managers. But the great justification for the mutual funds is that very few individuals actually do follow such a sound and simple policy ...

The underlying problem of selection is that the "good stocks"— chiefly the growth stocks with better than average prospects— tend to be fully priced and often overpriced.[3]

It may seem curious that one of the great investment minds, and an advocate of sober, methodical investment in a selected portfolio of stocks, should steer people away from trying their hands at active investment, and instead counsel investing somehow in the market as a whole (passive investing through index funds would be invented years later). What Graham was getting at was an intuitive concept that did not yet have a name, but has since been formalized into the Efficient Market Hypothesis. To understand what that hypothesis is, and what its implications are, calls for a review of financial history.

An Elegant Theory: The Capital Asset Pricing Model

Astute investors had always had an intuitive sense that the return to be expected from an investment was related to the risk they had to incur—the greater the risk, the greater the possible return. However, the concept of risk was a subjective one, until the 1950s, when financial economists began to develop what they believed was an objective definition—that is, a way to precisely quantify and measure risk. They focused on how an investment's returns varied from one time period to another, based on the familiar statistical measures of standard deviation and variance. From this platform, economists were able to develop an expansive body of thought that came to be known as Modern Portfolio Theory, or MPT.

The first pillar of MPT is the Capital Asset Pricing Model, or CAPM, which was theorized in the 1960s by financial economists William Sharpe and John Lintner, and carried forward in the 1970s by Fischer Black.[4] (Sharpe was awarded the Nobel Prize for his efforts in 1990.) The CAPM is an elegant theory, the objective of which is to describe the relationship between risk and reward for financial assets, and it offers a simple design for thinking about markets.

We will not describe the entire CAPM structure here, but one of its key tenets is particularly relevant to the debate about active versus passive investing. The CAPM starts from the assumption that all investors define risk in the model's terms—the variability of returns. From that point, MPT demonstrates that there is one optimal portfolio of stocks which, when combined with cash, will provide the highest return possible for a given level of risk. (Alternatively, an optimal portfolio would experience the lowest possible level of risk for a given level of return.) The CAPM goes on to deduce that because all investors would hold this optimal portfolio, the market as a whole—the sum of all investors' portfolios—would be that same optimal portfolio, although on a larger scale. Viewed from the reverse angle, this means that the optimal portfolio is simply a miniature of the overall market. In essence, CAPM relies on a logical inference: investors will all want to hold the optimal portfolio, but the only portfolio that it is possible for every investor to hold simultaneously is a miniature replica of the overall market, so the market must be the optimal portfolio.

It wasn't long before investment practitioners devised products to bring theory into practice. Index funds allowing institutional investors to buy the entire stock market all in one go were invented in the early 1970s for that purpose—to meet MPT adherents' perceived need for uniform market portfolios (Chapter 12).[5]

Further Elegance: The Efficient Market Hypothesis

The second pillar of MPT is the Efficient Market Hypothesis (EMH), which grew out of research conducted by Eugene Fama at the University of Chicago in the late 1960s. (Fama, too, would eventually win a Nobel Prize for his work.) In its purest form, the EMH holds that securities prices always reflect all available information about the economy, markets and companies, and that all investors interpret that information in the same rational way, resulting in rational prices for securities.[6]

If the EMH were valid, trying to outsmart the collective knowledge of the market by forecasting prices of a select group of stocks through an active strategy would be futile. Therefore, the notion of efficient markets held great appeal to those pioneering MPT economists: it would elegantly link the stock market with the economy, simplifying the process of investing and eliminating a lot of unnecessary effort (and commissions and fees for investors).

With the development of the CAPM and the EMH in rapid succession, the late 1960s and early 1970s were a heady time in the world of academic finance. "In the decade of the 1970s, I was a graduate student writing a PhD dissertation on rational expectations models, ... and I was mostly caught up in the excitement of the time," Robert J. Shiller, a professor at Yale University, and a winner of the Nobel prize in Economics, wrote in 2003.[7]

Reality Intrudes

Reality turned out differently, however. Further research refined the questions being asked, and before long cracks started to show in the two pillars of MPT. Shiller wrote:

> One could easily wish that these models were true descriptions of the world around us, for it would then be a wonderful advance for our profession. … Wishful thinking can dominate much of the work of a profession for a decade, but not indefinitely. The 1970s already saw the beginnings of some disquiet over these models. … Browsing today again through finance journals from the 1970s, one sees some beginnings of reports of anomalies that didn't seem likely to square with the efficient markets theory, even if they were not presented as significant evidence against the theory.[8]

Some of the anomalies were quirky and minor, such as the "January effect," where stock prices tended to show better returns in the first month of the year. More troubling, Shiller notes, was the difficulty in explaining the persistently high and random level of volatility in a supposedly rational market: "The evidence regarding excess volatility seems, to some observers at least, to imply that changes in prices occur for no fundamental reason at all, that they occur because of such things as 'sunspots' or 'animal spirits' or just mass psychology." The existence of these anomalies called into question the broader framework of the CAPM. And in fact, the empirical record of the CAPM turned out to be poor.

The Achilles' heel of the CAPM is the notion of *beta,* which expresses the relationship between the expected return of an individual stock (or a portfolio), and the return of the market as a whole. In its simplest form, the CAPM assumes a systematic linear relationship, so that given a, say, 10 percent gain in the general market (over and above what is called the *risk-free rate,* usually set at the return on short-term U.S. Treasury bills), a stock with a beta of 1.5 would be expected to rise 15 percent more than the risk-free rate. Each security has an additional, unsystematic component to its return—alpha—embodying idiosyncratic factors about the stock and the underlying company. But alpha is assumed to make a small contribution over the long term, so that beta is the prime mover of a stock's returns. (Although beta is not terribly useful for projecting expected returns, it has been invaluable in measuring performance after the fact, in its ability to link a portfolio's actual returns to those of the market.)

By the 1990s financial economists had turned up a great number of theoretical arguments, as well as empirical anomalies in the markets, contrary to what the CAPM would explain. In 1993, after more than 20 years of struggle over the CAPM, the entire agenda of the prestigious annual conference of what is today known as the CFA Institute was devoted to the controversy. Yale professor Steven Ross, one of the pioneers of the CAPM and beta, presented a paper titled "Is Beta Useful?" wherein he concluded that for purposes of forecast returns, it is not:

> My first acquaintance with the conflict between theory and reality happened years ago when a company asked me to help with a cost-of-capital issue. ... We believed that, if this theory had merit, on average, over time, the stocks with betas in the bottom 10 percent would have the lowest return and those in the highest

beta class would have the highest return; an upward-sloping line would connect them. What we got was a flat line, which means that having a low, middle, or high beta does not matter; the expected return is the same. This result is very depressing. …

For many years, we have been under the illusion that the CAPM is the same as finding that beta and expected returns are related to each other. That is true as a theoretical and philosophical tautology, but pragmatically, they are miles apart.[9]

The Problem with MPT

Why have the elegant theories that make up MPT proven to be poor descriptors of the real world of markets? As with many academic models, the issue has to do with what theorists refer to as *simplifying assumptions*. MPT holds that investors evaluate potential investments in two dimensions, and two dimensions only: expected return and expected risk. (This framework is known as "mean-variance", referring to the mean of returns on securities, and their volatility as measured by the variance. The notion was developed by financial economics pioneer Harry Markowitz in the early 1950s.) MPT further assumes that all investors agree on the riskiness of a given investment or portfolio since, after all, risk is defined as a statistical measure of the volatility of returns—a number that can be calculated simply from past returns without any subjective input (or insight to the future). In addition, MPT posits that investors have a single objective: to maximize their expected return for any given level of risk.

In the past two decades, a new generation of "behavioral economists," who combined insights into human psychology with the study of economics, have cast doubts on MPT, raising questions as to whether passive investing in the broad market is optimal, either in theory or in practice.

Notes

1. Aswath Damodaran, "Investment Philosophy: The Secret Ingredient in Investment Success," 2007 presentation at New York University Stern School of Business.

2. Benjamin Graham was an investment adviser and Columbia University and UCLA instructor who, working with his colleague David Dodd, constructed a framework for investing in stocks through a conservative approach that evolved into today's "value" style. Graham and Dodd authored the classic investment text *Security Analysis* in 1934 and Graham wrote a second classic, *The Intelligent Investor*, in 1941. Among Graham's disciples are Warren Buffett, John Templeton, and Seth Klarman.

3. Benjamin Graham, "Securities in an Insecure World," speech to San Francisco Society of Securities Analysts, November 15, 1963. Accessed at: http://www.jasonzweig.com/a-rediscovered-masterpiece-by-benjamin-graham/.

4. Eugene F. Fama and Kenneth R. French, "The Capital Asset Pricing Model: Theory and Evidence," *Journal of Economic Perspectives,* Vol. 18, No. 3 (2003): 25–46. Available at: www.aeaweb.org/articles.php?doi=10.1257/0895330042162430.

5. Kate Ancell, "The Origin of the First Index Fund," University of Chicago Booth School of Business, 2012. Accessed at: research.chicagobooth.edu/fama-miller/docs/the-origin-of-the-first-index-fund.pdf.

6. Earlier, we noted that Benjamin Graham asserted that the prices of "good" stocks were efficient—or fully priced, as he put it.

7. Robert J. Shiller, "From Efficient Markets Theory to Behavioral Finance," *Journal of Economic Perspectives*, Vol. 17, No.1 (Winter 2003): 83–104. Available at: www.econ.yale.edu/~shiller/pubs/p1055.pdf.

8. Ibid.

9. Stephen A. Ross, "Is Beta Useful?" AIMR Conference Proceedings, Vol. 1993, No. 6 (October 1993): 11–15. Accessed at: www.cfapubs.org/doi/pdf/10.2469/cp.v1993.

CHAPTER 5

A More Human Description of Investors and Markets

Behavioral Finance

B ehavioral finance, emerging in the 1990s as a counter-point to Modern Portfolio Theory (MPT), pictures a world in which investing decisions are far more complex than cold trade-offs weighing only numerical measures of risk and return. "Theoretical models of efficient financial markets that represent everyone as rational optimizers can be no more than metaphors for the world around us. Nothing could be more absurd than to claim that *everyone* knows how to solve complex stochastic optimization models," wrote Robert Shiller (emphasis in the original).[1]

"... [A]lthough to err is indeed human, financial practitioners of all types, from portfolio managers to corporate executives, make the same mistakes repeatedly," wrote Professor Hersh Shefrin of Santa Clara University in 2002. Behavioral finance recognizes the influence that human emotions and reactions— hopes of earning great profits, fear of difficult choices, and inconsistent reasoning about money—exert in economic and investing decisions.[2] Accordingly, behavioral finance has grown into a rich and diverse body of knowledge, earning Nobel prizes for its researchers. We limit our discussion to a few representative aspects.

Loss Aversion

MPT dictates that all investors make identical, dispassionate evaluations of investments based solely on expected return and volatility, but this assumption ignores the impact of a phenomenon known as loss aversion. People's attitudes toward gains and losses are not symmetrical: loss aversion holds that the psychic pain an individual feels from losing, say, 10 percent on an investment is greater than the pleasure would be from gaining 10 percent. While such a reaction is asymmetrical, it's not irrational: losses are limited to 100 percent of capital, while gains can be infinite, so the opposite of the benefit of a 110 percent gain can't be a 110 percent loss.[3]

Loss aversion presents a challenge to the one-size-fits-all framework of MPT, because in the behavioral finance framework, each person's internal calculation of loss aversion is thought to be unique. One investor might see the trade-off of an 8 percent loss as equal to a 10 percent gain, while another may be more sensitive to losses, and view a 5 percent setback as sufficient to offset the benefit of a 10 percent gain.[4]

Consider the stylized example of two prospective investments in Table 5.1. Investment A has a 10 percent chance of earning 100 percent, and a 90 percent chance of losing 5 percent, and thus an expected return of 5.5 percent.[5] Investment B has a 90 percent chance of earning 15 percent, and a 10 percent chance of losing 75 percent, for an expected return of 6.0 percent.[6] And by the numbers, the volatility of Investment A is slightly higher

TABLE 5.1   Loss Aversion: Outcomes from Two Hypothetical Investments

	Outcomes	
	Investment A	Investment B
Probability		
90%	–5%	15%
10%	100%	–75%
Expected return	**5.5%**	**6%**

Source: Epoch Investment Partners

than that of B. Thus, according to the rational return-risk criteria of MPT, all investors would always prefer B (for its higher return yet lower risk). However, many investors would not give as much weight to the overall probabilities, and their attention instead would be drawn to the extremes of gain and loss—B's 75 percent loss potential, versus a 5 percent possible loss for A—and choose A over B. (We conducted a survey among Epoch's employees, and a sizable minority did in fact prefer A, in spite of B's higher expected return based on the probabilities.)

Loss aversion illustrates that MPT's two-dimensional framework of expected returns versus volatility is an inadequate measure of how real-world investors perceive risk.

Mental Accounting

Taking the notion of multiple views of risk one step further, behavioral economists have also identified ways in which one individual investor can simultaneously hold different opinions of the same investment. MPT asserts that investors view their assets as a single portfolio, but in reality many people think of their investments as being divided into different notional "accounts" (hence the name of this phenomenon). Perhaps the easiest way to see mental accounting at work is to observe people in casinos. A gambler who started the night with $1,000, and has managed to turn it into $1,500 after an hour of black-jack, will often think of the additional $500 as "the house's money"—distinct from the original $1,000 stake, even though the entire $1,500 belongs to the gambler. Faced with a deci-sion on whether to take a particular risk (for example, whether to hit or stand on a 16), many people will make a different decision depending on whether they are gambling with what they think of as their own money versus gambling with the house's money.

In the context of investing, consider the case of an investor who purchased shares in a mutual fund two years earlier for $10,000, and since then has earned a $5,000 gain. The notion of mental accounting suggests that many investors might be willing to take greater risks with the $5,000 gain portion—the equivalent of the house's money in the blackjack example—than with their own original $10,000.

The phenomenon manifests itself as well in the way that people divide their assets into multiple portfolios, not just men-tally but in reality, and adopt different levels of risk appetite in their various portfolios. An investor may perceive a particular stock as being too risky for the college savings fund, but per-fectly fine for the vacation home fund. Thus, many people do not make investment decisions by seeing their assets as an integrated whole, which runs against the assumptions that MPT makes about investor behavior.

Minimizing Regret

Another area where MPT is incomplete, by not taking into account the complexity of real-world investor behavior, is the assumption that all investors seek only to maximize their return for a given level of risk. Behavioral finance theorists argue that this is just one of multiple objectives, and that investors simultaneously seek both to maximize return and to minimize regret, objectives that often clash.[7]

Minimizing regret is another manifestation of loss aversion. In the loss aversion examples, one investment had a potential, although unlikely, loss of 75 percent. Many investors might avoid that choice, realizing that they will regret the loss if things turn out badly—even when, in MPT terms, it has a higher expected return and lower expected risk.

Regret minimization can also cause investors to hold on to investments which looked promising at the outset, but which have turned out to show poor prospects. Investors will use their purchase price as a reference point, and become reluctant to sell for less and "lock in" a loss (bringing the investment to an end, and thus feeling definite regret). Some other investment, or probably many, might offer better current return opportunities, but a regret-minimizing investor could hope that the first investment will someday recover to at least its purchase price, where it could be sold regret free.

Overconfidence

Holding too much confidence in ideas and aptitude extends to many fields of endeavor. In investing, it can lead investors, both individuals and professionals, to believe they know more than they really do about the market or individual stocks. Overconfidence can take the form of erroneous forecasts—such as false notions of where a company's revenue growth or profit margins are heading—or an investor's belief that he has learned a bit of news to which the market as a whole has not yet caught on. Professor Hersh Shefrin asserts that overconfidence hurts investors in two ways: first, having the wrong information leads them to buy the wrong securities; second, an excess of confidence causes them to trade more often than they should.[8]

Extrapolation and Reversal

Investors also are likely to see patterns where none exists. One common misconception is the extrapolation of a trend in returns—that a winning stock will keep winning, and losers will keep falling. The opposite, known as the *gambler's fallacy*, holds that what has gone up must come down, and that trends will reverse. These sorts of forecasts are constructive when they are founded in changes in the facts of fundamentals of a company or a market climate, but when they simply express a view that it's time for a change, they're likely to be biased (and wrong).

These are just a sample of the many anomalies and exceptions to the systematic, dispassionate thinking that MPT has ascribed over time to the financial markets. Through the lens of behavioral finance, it is clear that investors do not all think and act alike and that their actions are not entirely rational and optimal.

Investor Behavior in Action

To illustrate how misperceptions make their way into stock prices, we consider the impact of the markets' reactions to company earnings announcements (or post-earnings-announcement drift, a phenomenon widely studied by financial economists). If markets were efficient on earnings information, stock prices would adjust the moment that companies announce their earnings, or perhaps within a few days. Instead, researchers over 50 years or so have found that full adjustments to earnings news tend to be diffused over time. For instance, Hersh Shefrin cited studies suggesting that industry analysts—professional investors, that is—underreact to new earnings information when revising their forecasts, with the result that "one positive earnings surprise is followed by another, and then by yet another."[9]

"Think about what this pattern implies," Shefrin added: "It pays to hold stocks that have experienced recent large positive earnings surprises, because the market does not adjust fully to the good news. Instead, the market adjusts over the three quarters that follow an announcement."

This is a sign of overconfidence at work, Shefrin contended—that analysts are overconfident in their prior forecasts, and underweight evidence that disconfirms their views. He also noted that other researchers had concluded that analysts underreact to news they gathered from public sources, such as earnings reports, while overreacting to information they turned up on their own. "The result is conservatism," he concluded. "Permanent changes in circumstances get mistaken for temporary ones, at least up to a point."

While academics and investors have known about these tendencies for decades, the market apparently has not bid them away. Academics Haigang Zhou and John Qi Zhu, writing in the *Financial Analysts Journal* in 2012, developed a profitable trading strategy from stocks with large positive and negative earnings surprises, based on the trading history of 1971 through 2009. "Market participants seem largely to underreact to, or are simply unaware of, the latent 'extremely good (or bad) news' signaled by the direction of jumps around earnings announcements," they conclude.[10]

These points are important to active investment managers, as investors' reactions, overreactions and missteps lead to the mispricing of securities, and create some inefficiencies and opportunities in the markets. However, it's a long way from academic pronouncements that securities markets are efficient or inefficient to assembling actively managed portfolios that outperform the market.

MPT Still Lives

MPT's proponents have not been content to let behavioral finance steal the academic spotlight. In part, this may simply be due to the worldview of most economists. As MIT Professor Andrew Lo noted, in a paper on corporate culture:

> [T]he culture of economics ... prizes the narrative of rational economic self-interest above all else. Given two competing explanations for a particular market anomaly, a behavioral theory and a rational expectations model, the vast majority of economists will choose the latter—even if rationality requires unrealistically complex inferences about everyone's preferences, information, and expectations.

Lo concludes that the mathematical elegance of an equilibrium according to rational expectations usually trumps a "messy and imprecise narrative"—such as those founded on less formal behavioral economics.[11] Thus, when investment practitioners and skeptical academics documented the anomalies to MPT—showing that stocks failed to perform in line with the predictions of the Capital Asset Pricing Model (CAPM) and its single risk factor, beta—its adherents countered that the early CAPM had been too simplistic (or, in the technical parlance, misspecified), and responded with newer, more complex versions of MPT.

In 1992, Professor Eugene Fama, who formulated the Efficient Market Hypothesis, and Professor Kenneth French of Dartmouth College improved on the simple CAPM with their documentation of the "value effect"—an inverse relationship between how stocks are valued in the market and their subsequent returns.[12]

Fama and French devised a three-factor model, expanding the simple CAPM to include a variable on firm valuation, and another metric on company size (thus creating a three-factor CAPM). They found that the additional factors greatly enhanced the explanatory power of plain-vanilla beta based on volatility alone. Simply stated, "value stocks" that are given cheaper valuations—lower ratios of price to earnings, cash flow, or book value—tend to show better subsequent returns than stocks with higher valuation ratios. The value effect has since been studied and documented far and wide, over many time periods and in many markets around the world. Similarly, the size effect shows that smaller companies earn systematically higher returns than larger companies.[13] One plausible explanation is that investors see lower-valued companies, often selling cheaply because they are down on their luck, as well as smaller companies, as more risky, and thus demand greater returns for investing in them.[14]

Fama and French also offered crucial inferences on the risks in stocks, and the shortcomings of the rational investor views of simple beta and the CAPM: "If assets are priced rationally, our results suggest that stock risks are multidimensional. One dimension of risk is proxied by [company] size. ... Another dimension of risk is proxied by ... the ratio of the book value of common equity to its market value. ... It is also possible, however, that [the ratio of book value to market value] just captures the unraveling ... of irrational market whims about the prospects of firms."[15]

Recently, Fama and French have created yet another version of the CAPM, this time adding two more company risk factors: firm profitability and levels of investment in plant, equipment, and acquisitions.[16] They find—not surprisingly—that higher profitability tends to be associated with better stock performance. More unexpected, however, is that higher levels of investment by companies—aggressive expansions of their operations—are associated with poorer stock performance. Taken together, the returns to these two risk factors suggest that companies able to generate greater profits with lower capital investment are likely to be rewarded with higher returns on their shares. (In Chapter 10 we discuss in detail the importance of companies' return on invested capital in the investment process.)

The academic debate may go on forever, as the MPT and behavioral finance camps compete with new and improved models of investors and markets. But the dogmatic views in the 1960s and 1970s, which dictated that all investors should hold the same "market portfolio," and effectively ruled out that active investment management could add value over a passive strategy, have been greatly undermined by the development of behavioral finance.

Notes

1. Robert J. Shiller, "From Efficient Markets Theory to Behavioral Finance," *Journal of Economic Perspectives,* Vol. 17, No. 1 (Winter 2003): 83–104.
2. Important sources for this discussion are Epoch Investment Partners' white paper "The Case for Active Management," March 2015, and Hersh Shefrin's book *Beyond Greed and Fear: Understanding Behavioral Finance and the Psychology of Investing* (New York: Oxford University Press, 2002).
3. William Priest, David Pearl, Steven Bleiberg, and Michael Welhoelter, "The Case for Active Management," Epoch Investment Partners, 2015.
4. Loss aversion was developed by behavioral economists Daniel Kanehman and Amos Tversky, initially in 1970. In studies of simple financial decisions, they found that for many people the

pain of a loss is about two and one-half times the pleasure of a gain of the same amount.

5. Expected return for Investment A: (10% × 100%) + (90% × –5%) = 5.5%.

6. Expected return for Investment B: (90% × 15%) + (10% × –75%) = 6.0%.

7. Priest, Pearl, Bleiberg, and Welhoelter. *Note:* Regret is a very powerful emotion: consider how many songs have been written about regret, and then think of how many you know about optimizing risk-adjusted return on investment.

8. Shefrin, 41.

9. Ibid., 97.

10. Haigang Zhou and John Qi Zhu, "Jump on the Post-Earnings Announcement Drift," *Financial Analysts Journal*, Vol. 68, No. 3 (May/June 2012): 63–64.

11. Andrew W. Lo, "The Gordon Gekko Effect," NBER Working Paper Series, Working Paper 21267, National Bureau of Economic Research, 2015, p. 11. Available at: www.nber.org/papers/w21267.

12. Eugene F. Fama and Kenneth R. French, "The Cross-Section of Expected Stock Returns," *The Journal of Finance*, Vol. 47, No. 2 (June 1992): 427.

    Fama and French were not the first to study the value effect. The earliest academic work seems to be from Sanjoy Basu in the late 1970s, then a professor at McMaster University in Hamilton, Ontario, Canada, (see Sanjoy Basu, "Investment Performance of Common Stocks in Relation to Their Price-Earnings Ratios: A Test of the Efficient Market Hypothesis," *Journal of Finance*, Vol. 32, No. 3 (June 1977), 683–682), and he was followed by many others. While their discrepancies and inefficiencies were derived scientifically, the roots of the value effect go back much further—at least as far the 1930s, and the more intuitive writings of investment managers Benjamin Graham and David Dodd.

13. Donald Keim, "Financial Market Anomalies," in the *New Palgrave Dictionary of Economics*, 2nd ed. (New York: Palgrave Macmillan, 2008).

14. Fama and French, 428.

15. Ibid.

16. Eugene F. Fama and Kenneth R. French, "A Five-Factor Asset Pricing Model," Fama-Miller Working Paper, September 2014. Available at: SSRN: ssrn.com/abstract=2287202 or dx.doi.org/10.2139/ssrn.2287202.

CHAPTER 6

Active versus Passive Management

The Empirical Case

G iven the debate of the past 50 years, we conclude that what might have started off as an ironclad theoretical case for passive management has been worn down by the real-life insights of the behavioral economists. Today a fair observer could say that with all the possible sources of inefficiencies in stocks arising from investor behavior, active managers should be able to add value over a passive strategy—or at least that they have they the raw materials available to them. But what happens in the real world?

A large and diverse investment industry works hard to outperform the broad markets, but the historical record of returns achieved by active managers is mixed. Many times, the average manager falls short, depending on the asset categories, time periods, and market environments considered.

This underperformance is not just a recent phenomenon. At about the same time Robert Shiller was finding exceptions to the Capital Asset Pricing Model (CAPM) and the notion of efficient markets, real-world results were also challenging old beliefs that astute managers could beat the market. In mid-1975 Charles D. Ellis, the founder of Greenwich Associates, a pioneering firm of consultants in investment management, authored an article on the failure of active management, titled "The Loser's Game."[1] For the three market cycles running from September 1962 to December 1974, he pointed out that:

> Not only are the nation's leading portfolio managers failing to produce positive absolute rates of return (after all, it's been a long bear market) but they are also failing to produce positive relative rates of return. Contrary to their oft articulated goal of outperforming the market averages, investment managers are not beating the market: The market is beating them.[2]

Forty years later, not much has changed, and investment managers are still being beaten. Table 6.1 details the 1-, 3-, 5-, and 10-year performance of managers of institutional active strategies investing in U.S. large-cap core equities, all as of December 2015. For the year then ended, as well as 3 and 5 years, between 40 percent and 50 percent outperformed the S&P 500 (before the deduction of management fees). For 10 years, however, the proportion is far higher, at 69 percent (also before fees).

Shouldn't skillful managers always be able to outperform the market? It's not very likely. This chapter covers the various forces that come into play in determining whether a manager outperforms or underperforms in a given year. In many cases,

TABLE 6.1   U.S. Large-Cap Core Equity Managers versus the S&P 500, for Periods Ended December 31, 2015

	1 Year	3 Years	5 years	10 Years
% of managers outperforming	42%	48%	46%	69%
Number of observations	356	338	317	266

Source: eVestment

such market pressures can more than offset any value the manager adds from skill.

Market Regimes

Professional investment managers' task of generating excess returns for clients has never been easy, but the data suggest that the job has become more difficult in recent years. One important factor has been the nature of the market environment. There is a financial phenomenon known as a *stock pickers' market*—periods where markets reward those companies that manage their businesses well with higher share prices (and punish the opposite).[3]

That is, at certain times, there are big differences among the performance of individual stocks related to the financial performance of individual companies. Those active managers who can anticipate the likely winners and avoid the less distinguished can thus outperform the market as a whole. But there are more challenging market regimes—where companies' fundamentals seem a secondary factor, and stocks tend to move as a pack, rendering managers' processes for picking stocks on their fundamentals less effective. Markets of the past few years have worked against stock pickers, and this can be shown by a number of measures.

Correlation and Dispersion

The two best statistical measures of how widely the returns of individual stocks vary from one another are correlation and dispersion. Correlation primarily measures to what extent stocks move in the same direction, while dispersion measures how much the magnitude of returns varies across stocks.

During periods that stock prices are heavily influenced by broad macroeconomic factors—as opposed to the financial health of their individual businesses—investment managers have less to work from in generating differential performance. That is, if all stocks are moving more or less together, managers face fewer opportunities to create a return that meaningfully outperforms the market as a whole (at least in the short run).

That has certainly been the case since the 2008 global financial crisis, a period during which the world's financial markets have been propelled higher by sustained near-zero interest rates and excessive liquidity. Looking at the stocks in the Russell 1000,[4] correlations measured over rolling periods of 63 trading days averaged 0.26 in the 10 years preceding the financial crisis (1998 through 2007) but rose to 0.39 between September 2008 and December 2015.[5] During the thick of the crisis, September 2008 through December 2010, correlations averaged 0.46. Figure 6.1 plots the average correlation of every possible pairing of stocks within the Russell 1000 from 1980 through 2015, illustrating the rising trend of the past several years and the extremes in correlation reached in 2009, 2010, 2011, and late in 2015.

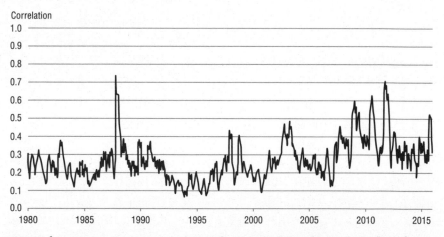

FIGURE 6.1   Average Pairwise Correlations for Russell 1000 Index Stocks, Rolling 63 Days

Source: The Vanguard Group © The Vanguard Group Inc., used with permission

This is not to say that managers are necessarily more likely to outperform in periods of high dispersion or low correlation. For the years 2003 through 2012, researchers at S&P Dow Jones Indices found that high dispersion of stocks in the S&P 500 did not increase the likelihood of outperformance for active managers.[6] This conclusion is not surprising: market characteristics alone do not make managers any more or less skillful. However, all managers, whether skilled or not, are likely to be more challenged in periods of low dispersion and higher correlation.

Company Quality

Another view of the recent unusual market conditions, and the challenge to active managers, can be seen in the behavior of stock market indices based on the quality of the underlying stocks. The USA Quality Index published by MSCI Inc. ranks U.S. companies on factors of business quality—defined by MSCI as showing high return on equity, stability in earnings growth, and low financial leverage—and includes just the top 20 percent (125 large and mid-cap companies, from a universe of about 625 U.S. companies). Over the long run, higher-quality companies have outperformed: for the 40 years ended December 2015, the MSCI USA Quality index compounded at an 11.5 percent rate, while the overall MSCI USA index returned 10.1 percent annually. For the three calendar years ended 2014, however, quality companies lagged the broad market, earning an annualized return of 19.4 percent, versus 20.4 percent for the broader U.S. market—leaving higher-quality companies at a counterintuitive annual return disadvantage of 1.0 percent.

Why did higher-quality companies fall short in those years? That is a puzzle: we assume that most active managers—although perhaps not all—follow investment methods that seek higher quality companies (as shown by those companies' tendency to earn superior returns over the very long term). Paradoxically, however, the recent winners were companies of lower quality.

Lower-quality companies may have been well rewarded in those years for several reasons. Perhaps investors assumed lower-quality names would see sharper recoveries in profits than the more resilient high-quality companies, and purchased those stocks more eagerly. Alternatively, because low-quality shares saw greater falls in prices, they may have made sharper percentage recoveries in returning to normal levels (an advantage which may be biased by the time period selected for measurement).

In our view, however, the prime mover for lower-quality stocks—and higher quality companies as well—was the overpowering force of quantitative easing (QE) undertaken by the Federal Reserve starting in November 2008. When interest rates decrease, the current value of cash flows to be received in the future rises—and all the more so when rates approach zero, as they did in the Federal Reserve's three programs of QE.[7,8] (For a general discussion of the math of valuation for financial assets, and how changes in interest rates can change asset prices, please see Appendix B.)

With lower-quality stocks, all these factors probably played some role in their strong returns, with the illogical result that managers sticking to their strategies based on quality were bound to underperform.

The Weight of Cash

Another drag on the recent performance of active managers arose from holdings of cash in active strategies. Index funds are fully invested in their markets at all times, or nearly so. Active portfolios, on the other hand, typically hold 2 percent to 3 percent of assets in cash, in order to be able to initiate new positions as opportunities present themselves without necessitating the sale of an existing position to do so. In the case of mutual funds, managers also have to be able to meet redemptions immediately, which is facilitated by having cash on hand.

While necessary for the smooth functioning of the portfolios, holding cash creates a drag on performance, because cash typically has a lower yield than the return on stocks.[9]

Over the long run, going back to 1928, stocks have returned about 10 percent annually, while three-month Treasury bills have earned about 3.5 percent. On that gap of 6.5 percent, a 3 percent cash holding would have cost an average of about 0.2 percent per year in portfolio return, or a cumulative 0.6 percent over a three-year span.

Since the global financial crisis, however, the drag of cash has been especially acute, as returns on stocks have been strong, and those on cash unusually low—essentially zero—raising the cost of not being fully invested. In the four years ended December 2015, the Standard & Poor's (S&P) 500 gained about 77.0 percent, while three-month Treasury bills earned 0.2 percent (that's not per year, but the cumulative total). Thus, the typical 3 percent cash holding of a mutual fund would have cost active managers about 2.3 percent, or about 0.6 percent per year.

Luck versus Skill

Investment managers face many challenges—complex forces in the markets and economy, which are constantly changing—so that even in favorable environments, outperforming the broad market is not a sure thing. To generate superior performance, a manager needs a capable investment process, and to be able to execute it with skill.

But beyond skill, investment management also involves luck (both good and bad), in the eyes of investment strategist and prolific author Michael Mauboussin. In his book *The Success Equation: Untangling Skill and Luck in Business, Sports and Investing*, he subjects all three human endeavors to statistical scrutiny, and rates investing as one involving a high share of luck.[10] The financial markets are highly random in their operation, particularly over short periods, and while Mauboussin ranks investing as less dependent on luck than, say, slot machines or roulette, he believes it is nevertheless a field where skill has less of an impact than, in his own ranking, professional hockey, football, baseball, soccer, basketball, or chess.

Mauboussin recognizes that attributing so much to luck is not psychologically satisfying—considering the importance of successful investment management, and all the effort that it entails:

> One of the main reasons we are poor at untangling luck and skill is that we have a natural tendency to assume that success and failure are caused by skill on the one hand and a lack of skill on the other. But in activities where luck plays a role, such thinking is deeply misguided and leads to faulty conclusions.[11]

It's not that investment management is easy, or that managers don't possess skill. He describes a concept known as the *paradox of skill,* which holds that over time, as participants in sports, investing, or whatever become more skillful, their performance becomes more consistent, making luck increasingly important to any one person's results. In professional baseball, for instance, it's been nearly 75 years since Ted Williams achieved the last .400 batting average.[12] But it's not for lack of skill: since then, training methods have advanced, teams are drawing from a wider pool of talent, and both pitchers and hitters have raised their skill levels. "[I]n statistical terms," Mauboussin writes, "...

the variance of batting averages has shrunk over time, even as the skill of the hitters has improved."[13]

Like baseball, investment management exhibits a paradox of skill. Earlier, we cited the influential 1975 article by investment consultant Charles Ellis, "The Loser's Game." During the 30 years prior to the article's publication, wrote Ellis, the investment management business had drawn large numbers of intelligent professionals, and accordingly become more competitive. The publication of Ellis's article coincided with the beginning of the Employee Retirement Income Security Act (ERISA) for corporate pension funds, which greatly expanded the scope and size not only of pension plans but also the managers needed to handle them, and prompted a second evolution of the industry's intellectual horsepower.[14] "As the population of skilled investors increased," Mauboussin observes, "the variation in skill narrowed, and luck became more important."[15]

In the field of investment management, sorting out skill and luck calls for looking at the persistence of managers' performance through time. This has been a popular topic for financial economists to examine, and with 50 years' worth of study the results are mixed. Assessing the persistence of skill in investing is complicated by measurement problems: the market environments and periods of time under study; the market segments and investment styles included; and the techniques of measurement—how performance is decomposed, and the adjustments made for the risks managers take in active portfolios.

One comprehensive study from 2010, "Performance and Persistence in Institutional Investment Management," authored by academics Jeffrey Busse, Amit Goyal, and Sunil Wahal, examined 4,617 U.S. equity portfolios from 1991 through 2008 holding $2.5 trillion in assets, and from examining past returns found little to no evidence of persistence of performance among investment managers. Like Mauboussin, they also addressed the skill-luck continuum: "We find very weak evidence of skill in gross returns, and net-of-fee excess returns are statistically indistinguishable from their simulated counterparts." Comparing their own results with the many competent studies conducted prior, they concede that some persistence can be detected over short periods, such as one year, but conclude: "To us, on balance, it is difficult to make the case for persistence."[16]

Other researchers find more constructive conclusions on distinguishing between luck and investment skill. In a 2014 report on equity investing, Willis Towers Watson, the global investment consulting firm, pointed to studies showing that going strictly by the numbers does not suffice in proving skill. Relative returns, or alpha, of investment managers are highly random, they point out, and it's often difficult to draw statistically significant conclusions on track records shorter than 15 years. Although a few firms can produce such long histories, they seldom have been truly "intact" for that long—that is, without turnover of the investment staff, or a significant increase in managed assets that might have required changes to portfolio construction.[17]

Willis Towers Watson makes the important observation that over short periods, say, three years—a time frame often relied upon by institutional asset owners—managers can apparently outperform their benchmarks, even when they don't show much skill over the long run. In their judgment, across the universe of investment managers only 10 percent can be considered truly skilled over the long term, while 70 percent show mediocre performance, and 20 percent are truly inferior. And while skilled managers are far more likely to outperform the rest, Willis Towers Watson asserts that "[even] if you only ever hire managers with good past performance, only 21 percent of your candidate managers will be skilled."

Given that historical performance alone is an unreliable guide, Willis Towers Watson advises that asset owners also consider the economic reasoning behind principles in firms'

investment philosophies, as well as the details of their investment processes, including reviews of portfolio positions to see
that philosophies are logically carried out.

J. P. Morgan Asset Management studied the question of
manager consistency for the 10 years ended June 2013. Comparing results of the two five-year intervals within that period,
they found that from 35 percent to 45 percent of active equity
managers repeated their outperformance, depending on which
market segment they worked in. However, in earlier 10-year
periods—those ending in 2009 and 2011—consistency of outperformance was significantly greater, at 50 percent to 60 percent.
Researchers did not offer an explanation for the slippage in the
later years, but concluded that "these levels indicate modest
consistency at an industry level, and do not point to either
high, reliable levels of consistent outperformance by successful
managers, or the opposite, the notion that manager outperformance is a constantly mean-reverting trend."[18]

An insightful analysis into the causes of active managers'
over- and underperformance was made by researchers at GMO
LLC, the Boston-based investment firm, in a February 2015
white paper titled "Is Skill Dead?"[19] They start with the supposi-
tion that if active managers were applying independent investment strategies, for any given period roughly half would beat
their benchmark, and the other half would fall short. Instead,
they find that the ratio of outperformance or underperformance
is consistently one-third to two-thirds, or as they say: "Almost
everyone wins, or almost everyone loses. This strongly suggests
that there are some common factors that drive the performance
of the typical manager and that these factors ultimately heavily
influence their success or failure."

They posit that missing the mark is the result of managers'
holding investments outside their benchmarks, citing managers
of large cap U.S. stocks as an example. Many take active stakes
in off-benchmark securities such as non-U.S. stocks, small cap

U.S. stocks, or cash. These other asset classes can result in performance very different from the U.S. large-cap S&P 500, depending on the time period.

To measure the difference to an active strategy, GMO built a model that assumed investment of 5 percent in non-U.S. stocks, 5 percent in small and midcap U.S. stocks and 1 percent in cash. They found that the pervasive underperformance of 2014 coincided with all three factors lagging the S&P 500, as did underperformance in 2011 and 2012, as well as in 1995 through 1999. "The conclusion to be drawn," say GMO researchers Neil Constable and Matt Kadnar, "is that a very large proportion of the historical variability of large cap managers' ability to add alpha is explained by our simple three-factor out-of-benchmark model." (The model's r-squared, that is, the proportion of variance it explains, is an admirable 70 percent.) GMO concludes that often what appears to be skill, or lack of skill, can in fact be attributed to the forces of market regimes.

Investors Voting with Their Dollars

Many forces can combine to cause investment managers to lag their benchmarks. Perhaps it is not surprising, then, that investors have migrated away from active strategies. As of March 2015, 62 percent of U.S. equities owned by U.S. institutional investors was held in active strategies, down from 74 percent in March 2010, and 79 percent in March 2005 (Figure 6.2).

Some observers have predicted that the active managers' share of institutional assets would fall to below half, but investor attitudes have not slipped quite that much.[20] Among individual investors, index funds have gained a smaller, but still substantial share. In 2000, index funds made up about 6 percent of total U.S. mutual fund assets, but by 2014 had increased to about $2.1 trillion, or 13 percent of the $15.9 trillion in mutual

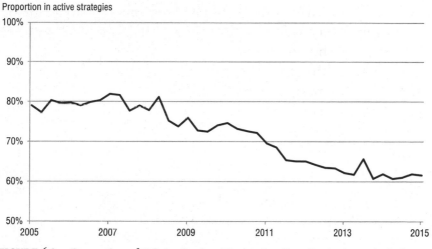

Proportion in active strategies

FIGURE 6.2   Proportion of U.S. Institutions' Large-Cap Core Equity Assets in Active Strategies, 2005–2015

Source: eVestment

fund assets.[21] Exchange-traded funds accounted for about as much—another $2.0 trillion in assets. As a group, active managers have their work cut out for them in convincing investors to stay the course for the prospect of above-market returns.

Notes

1. Charles D. Ellis, "The Loser's Game," *Financial Analysts Journal* (July/August 1975): 19–26.
2. A long bear market indeed: from its high in January 1973 to a low in October 1974, the S&P 500 fell 48 percent.
3. In addition to such an actual phenomenon, there is also a euphemism of a stock picker's market. At the beginning of any given year, the financial media feels obliged to provide market forecasts and dutifully turn to the insights of market strategists, some of whom will invariably predict that "This year will be a stock picker's market!" or "It's going to be a market of stocks, rather than a stock market," or something equally obscure and unverifiable.

4. The Russell 1000 is a stock market index that tracks the market capitalization-weighted performance of the 1,000 largest stocks in the U.S. market.

5. Average pairwise correlations were calculated for each time period by computing individual stock-pair correlations among the index constituents for the prior 63 trading days, and then averaged across all the correlations computed. Sixty-three trading days is the equivalent of three calendar months.

6. S&P Dow Jones Indices, "Dispersion: Measuring Market Opportunity," December 2013.

7. As noted earlier, an Epoch Investment Partners white paper from 2014, "The Power of Zero and The Power of the Word," considered in detail the effects of the low interest rates resulting from central banks' QE ("The Power of Zero") as well as central bankers' reassurances to the financial markets that QE would stay in force as long as necessary ("The Power of the Word").

8. "The Power of Zero and The Power of the Word," Epoch Investment Partners White Paper, 2014. Available at: www.eipny.com/index.php/epoch_insights/papers/the_power_of_zero_the_power_of_the_word.

9. However, cash is not always a drag: in markets where stock prices are falling, holding cash will actually boost a portfolio's return relative to the index.

10. Michael J. Mauboussin, *The Success Equation: Untangling Skill and Luck in Business, Sports and Investing* (Boston: Harvard Business Review Press, 2012).

11. Ibid., 89.

12. Williams hit his .406 average in 1941. On May 15, the same day Yankee great Joe Dimaggio began his famed 56-game hitting streak, Williams started his own 23-game string, the longest of his career, during which he batted an astounding 0.489. See Bill Pennington, "Ted Williams's .406 Is More Than a Number," the *New York Times*, September 17, 2011. Accessed at: www.Nytimes.Com/2011/09/18/Sports/Baseball/Ted-Williamss-406-Average-Is-More-Than-A-Number.HTML?_R=0.

13. Mauboussin, 89.

14. ERISA, or The Employee Retirement Income Security Act of 1974, is a federal law which sets standards for pension plans in private industry. For background on ERISA, see *The Financial Reality of Pension Funding Under ERISA*, by Jack L. Treynor, Patrick J. Regan, and William W. Priest, published in 1976 by Dow Jones-Irwin.

15. Mauboussin, 89.

16. Jeffrey A. Busse, Amit Goyal, and Sunil Wahal, "Performance and Persistence in Institutional Investment Management," *Journal of Finance*, Vol. 45, No. 2 (April 2010): 765.

17. Willis Towers Watson & Co. "Equity Investing: Insights into a Better Portfolio," 2014.

18. J. P. Morgan Asset Management, "A Search for Intelligent Life in the Active Equity Manager Universe," 2013.

19. Neil Constable and Matt Kadnar, "Is Skill Dead?" GMO LLC, 2015.

20. John Keefe, "Passive Performers Beat Active Cousins," *Financial Times*, July 8, 2012.

21. Investment Company Institute, "2015 Investment Company Fact Book," 55th ed., 2015.

CHAPTER 7

The Case for Active Management

I n striving for returns that beat the market averages, investment managers face many challenges—ranging from adverse economic and market climates, to a competitive battle among active managers, to a flood of low-cost passive investment products that match the returns of the market. Asset owners face their own set of demands, in having to identify managers able to carry forward their skill into future markets. This chapter starts with a front-row seat in the active-passive debate, and then details our reasoning on the merits of investing with active managers, and thoughts on manager selection.

April 2015: Investment Giants Square Off in New York City

Promoters of the active-passive struggle sponsored a championship bout in April 2015, at New York's Plaza Hotel. Two of today's more thoughtful financial minds—Jack Bogle, founder of the mutual fund giant Vanguard Group, and innovator of the S&P 500 index mutual fund, and Jim Grant, renowned financial author and editor of *Grant's Interest Rate Observer*—mounted the Plaza podium.[1] The occasion was one of the popular conferences on professional investment sponsored by *Grant's*, and the aim was to further the decades-long discussion central to the investment management business. An excerpt of their comments:

Jack Bogle: "The low-cost proposition is elemental and simple: the gross market returns shared by investors, as a group, is a zero-sum game. The cost of investing, shared by active [mutual fund] managers at a high cost, is 2 percent a year, roughly. The cost shared by index fund investors is about five basis points (or 0.05 percent). Therefore low-cost investors—collectively—must earn higher returns. ... That's why indexing is so dominant."

"The question Mr. Grant poses is: 'Is [indexing] a fad?' No, it is not a fad. It is a new way of owning America at low cost."

Jim Grant: "I disagree that the cost of investing is the determining factor in success. For the average lay public investor it may generally be true, and for the run-of-the-mill index-tracking professional it may also generally be true. But the argument I wish to make is that for the accomplished professional investor it ought not to be true. For not a few of the people in this room, it certainly isn't true. [But] Jack counsels not to try—it's almost as if one should not bother to open the paper, but instead go with the S&P 500 flow."

"[In] the market that you buy today," Grant continued, "you have 99 stocks with a short interest over 5 percent, 149 with a P/E ratio over 25 times, or no P/E ratio, and [when you invest in passive index funds] you get it all. Mr. Bogle wants you to get it all, and ... not discriminate or make judgments."

While the two opponents made strong cases in April 2015, no winner emerged, and the debate goes on. There's no clear solution: it's a complex issue, and there are many ways to pose the question, and just as many analytical routes to an answer.

Jack Bogle's rationale starts with a crucial foundation in the arithmetic of returns. For all those investing in a market such as U.S. equities, the aggregate return (before fees) has to be the return of the market. Some managers and investors might earn more than the market for a given year, but that has to be offset by others earning less. Everyone can't be above average.

This is a central point in the debate: it must be true that all managers can't beat the market at the same time. But some do, and Jack Bogle acknowledged that idea in his presentation: "Of course, some managers can win. A winner could be a value-seeking, footnote-reading, neurologically and emotionally qualified manager."

An Active-Passive Equilibrium

Could a stock market where all investors pursue active management, or all are passive, stay in equilibrium? Probably not: If all investors were active, their combined efforts would make prices highly efficient, and some investors would realize they could earn better returns than the average active manager by avoiding the costs of research and simply holding a passive index fund. Indeed, this is a good description of the conditions that prevailed when index funds got started. At the other extreme, if all investors were passive and no managers were researching company fundamentals, mispricings would abound and astute managers would realize they could earn better returns than the market by incurring the costs of research and engaging in active strategies to capitalize on those mispricings.

A more likely equilibrium would see a mix of active and passive investors that changes with market regimes—such as the current arrangement. At times when the research efforts of too many active investors make the market too efficient to beat, astute investors would move to passive at the margin. But if too many investors swing to passive management, so that the reduction in research activity led to a less efficient market—and better results from active managers—then some investors would migrate back toward active management.

Modern Portfolio Theory (MPT) encouraged the development of passive portfolios as a viable option for investors, and led to measuring active managers' returns against passive market benchmarks. But in a variation on what physics calls the "observer effect"—where a scientist cannot measure a phenomenon without altering it somehow—evaluating managers against passive indexes has brought unintended consequences to active portfolio management, in two ways.

First, many managers have come to emphasize performance relative to benchmarks over the absolute returns of their strategies, and frame their stock selection and portfolio composition relative to the indexes they are compared to. A manager may find a particular company to be highly overvalued, but if it constitutes 3 percent of the benchmark index, he likely would feel pressure to hold at least a nominal position, even against his better judgment: if he is wrong, and the overvalued stock performs well nonetheless, the decision to exclude it would hurt the strategy's relative return. (By definition, however, not holding it would not change the portfolio's absolute return, other than representing an opportunity lost.)

Second, the drumbeat of quarterly and annual returns on indexes has also caused many managers to shorten their investment horizons. A manager might believe that a company is undervalued, and that at some point over the next few years, the market would recognize and correct the disparity. But if his clients are unwilling to tolerate performance below the benchmark for more than a year, he may not be willing to chance a position in its shares, for fear that the mispricing will not be resolved soon enough. Such a focus on short-term relative performance may be steering managers away from what they believe are the best long-term investments.

In this context, the ideas of Deb Clarke, global head of research at Mercer, are again relevant. She holds that evaluating managers against a passive benchmark over short to medium time periods may induce decisions by portfolio managers that place more importance on short-term results, and wind up harming the long-term interests of investors.[2]

The Case for Active Management[3]

At this point, we have reviewed the theoretical arguments that MPT makes against active management, and we have discussed some of the empirical data that indicates that the average manager does, in fact, struggle to beat the market in most time periods. So why do we still believe that active management can add value?

MPT is an impressive achievement, and it has reshaped for the better the way that people think about investing by focusing on the relationship between risk and return. But like any body of theory, it is based on certain simplifying assumptions. When it comes to defining risk, we believe the assumptions that MPT makes are too simple. The work of behavioral economists has demonstrated conclusively that investors do not perceive risk in the way that MPT defines it, and more importantly that each investor perceives risk differently. As a result, we think MPT's conclusion that there is one portfolio of stocks—the market portfolio—that is optimal for all investors is unfounded. Each investor needs to understand his or her own perception of risk to determine which investment strategy suits them best.

That leaves the door open to pursue actively managed strategies. The empirical evidence does indicate that most active managers have failed to outperform the broad market, but we take the view that this is an indication that many of those managers are not following a sufficiently disciplined investment process. To the extent that behavioral biases create market inefficiencies, managers need to understand how and why those inefficiencies arise. Most importantly, managers need to understand that they too are subject to these same behavioral biases, and must learn to recognize and overcome them in their own thinking. Generally, the best way to achieve that is to create a process that will guide the manager toward (or away from) stocks with certain characteristics (or sets of characteristics), despite what the manager's "better judgment" might be saying, and to stick to that process rigorously.

Capturing the impact of stock-specific inefficiencies requires a disciplined process that (1) understands the forces that create an inefficiency, (2) captures it by "casting a wide net" across stocks that are likely to be affected, and (3) properly structures the portfolio so as to filter out the impact of any factors (e.g., size or industry effects) for which the manager currently has no forecast, and which might otherwise swamp the excess return generated by the inefficiency that the manager is trying to capture. We would argue that most active managers fall down at one or more of these steps. If that is true, then the fact that active managers have not generated excess returns as a group does not constitute proof that generating excess return is impossible; rather, it demonstrates that it is simply very difficult, and that most managers have not been following an approach that is likely to work.

It is important to understand, though, that even the most skillful active managers will sometimes underperform. Indeed, just as getting a hit three times for every 10 at-bats makes for a great baseball hitter, one could argue that outperforming 60 percent of the time makes for a great active manager. But that means even the best managers will underperform 40 percent of the time. And in some market environments, most active managers can be expected to underperform. The market conditions of recent years, in which unorthodox monetary policy sent a flood of liquidity into the capital markets, pushing up low-quality stocks faster than high-quality stocks and magnifying the drag from holding cash, created just such an environment.

Successful active management is difficult, and the need to identify skillful managers in advance adds to the complexity for investors. To conclude, we offer the closing passage from "Active Management in Mostly Efficient Markets," written by Robert Jones and Russ Wermers, which appeared in the *Financial Analysts Journal* in 2011. The authors—one an investment practitioner and one an academic—surveyed a wide array of academic literature on whether active management can add value and on whether investors can identify skillful managers *ex ante*. They end their article with these conclusions:

> [S]tudies suggest that investors may be able to identify [superior active managers, or SAMs] *ex ante* by considering (1) past performance (properly adjusted), (2) macroeconomic correlations, (3) fund/manager characteristics, and (4) analyses of fund holdings. We suspect that using a combination of these approaches will produce better results than following any one approach exclusively.
>
> Active management will always have a place in "mostly efficient" markets. Hence, investors who can identify SAMs should always expect to earn a relative return advantage. Further, this

alpha can have a substantial impact on returns with only a modest impact on total portfolio risk. Finding such managers is not easy or simple — it requires going well beyond assessing past returns — but academic studies indicate that it can be done.[4]

The next two chapters consider the details of fundamental analysis and security selection, and look at some of the analytical errors many active managers commit—in focusing on accounting earnings as a measure of profit (Chapter 8), and the application of valuation metrics based on earnings (Chapter 9). Chapter 10 then considers the investment process of Epoch Investment Partners, based on companies' ability to generate free cash flow, and how it is allocated to growing their businesses and rewarding owners.

Notes

1. Mr. Bogle introduced the first mutual fund indexed to the S&P 500 in 1975. As of December 2015, Vanguard Group managed $2.4 trillion in indexed funds invested in the equity and bond markets worldwide, as well as about $1 trillion in active strategies, for total assets of $3.4 trillion.
2. Deb Clarke, "A Broader View of Risk," Top1000funds.com, January 20, 2016. Accessed at: www.top1000funds.com/featured-homepage-posts/2016/01/20/transforming-decision-making-of-long-horizon-investors/.
3. This section is based on Epoch Investment Partners' 2015 White Paper "The Case for Active Management," by William Priest, David Pearl, Steven Bleiberg, and Michael Welhoelter.
4. Robert C. Jones and Russ Wermers, "Active Management in Mostly Efficient Markets," *Financial Analysts Journal* (November/December 2011): 42.

CHAPTER 8

Debates on Active Managers' Styles and Methods

"[T]he stock market] is not a *weighing machine*, on which the value of each issue is recorded by an exact and impersonal mechanism, in accordance with its specific qualities. Rather should we say that it is a *voting machine*, whereon countless individuals register choices which are the product partly of reason and partly of emotion (emphasis in the original)."[1] So wrote Benjamin Graham and David Dodd in 1940, in a discussion relating the inherent worth of companies with the prices of their shares.

Graham and Dodd went on to point out the value of systematic analysis to the investment process, and how careful research on companies—both quantitative studies on their financial health and qualitative reviews of their competitive context and strength of management—could aid investors in evaluating whether the prices investors set by their votes offer attractive investment prospects.

This chapter considers the variety of styles and techniques equity managers apply to their investing, and highlights what

Epoch considers to be at the core of companies' economic value: free cash flow.

Manager Style

Among investors, deliberating over whether to pursue active versus passive approaches may be a binary, yes-or-no question. Within the community of active managers of equities, however, there are second-, third-, and fourth-level debates over how to best earn superior risk-adjusted returns from selecting securities. The main divisions are in the dimensions of style (value versus core versus growth) and research process (fundamental versus quantitative).

Each manager likely has its own definition of where its style falls within the different categories. Stated simply, however, growth-oriented managers seek out stocks where revenues and profits will expand more rapidly than the economy or the market as whole, often in industries innovating new technologies or services. In contrast, value managers are less concerned with sheer earnings growth, and seek out companies selling at relatively low multiples of earnings or book value per share (compared either to other stocks or to their own history), typically expecting some catalyst to emerge and trigger a higher price. Core strategies draw candidates from the entire market.

Fundamental managers rely on traditional financial research techniques—in-depth financial statement analysis, supplemented by qualitative evaluations of management skill, and subjective judgments about the future of a particular industry. Quantitative managers focus on a more objective analysis of data, numerically scoring companies on characteristics that they believe are associated with outperformance. With heavy reliance on computer models, they look at financial parameters, but also factor in measures derived from market trends such as price momentum and share volatility, as well as other statistics of their own design. Fundamental managers seek to know a lot about a relatively small number of companies, while quantitative managers seek to know a little about a large number of companies.

The boundaries defining managers' styles were quite distinct a generation ago, but they have become blurred thanks to the availability of massive computing power and data resources at relatively low cost. Thus, in current practice, most managers apply some sort of quantitative technique in their investment process.

According to one comprehensive database of investment managers, published by eVestment, roughly 1,200 firms were managing strategies in large cap U.S. equities at year-end 2014. Firms pursuing growth, core and value strategies each made up about one-third of the population. Sixty-five percent of managers followed fundamental methods, while 16 percent deemed themselves heavily quantitative, and the remaining 19 percent reported a combined fundamental/quantitative process.

Epoch Investment Partners does not take a traditional view on growth versus value styles, or quantitative versus fundamental research techniques. We don't find those distinctions especially meaningful. But we do firmly advocate active management. Accordingly, we do not believe the financial markets are "efficient" in the academic sense, where all information available on a security is incorporated in its price. That's not to say that we think markets are chaotic, and that prices of individual securities are completely out of whack. In fact, the collective judgment of investors usually arrives at pretty reasonable values for most stocks in the fullness of time.

However, investors' behavior can be highly flawed over shorter periods. On any given trading day, the market is arriving at mistaken judgments of varying sizes on hundreds or thousands of stocks, resulting from the tendencies toward loss aversion, mental accounting, trend extrapolation, and overconfidence described by behavioral finance.

Free Cash Flow Is the Measure of Value

The lifeblood of an operating business is cash. Managers of a business start with cash, then convert it into assets of various kinds, such as plant and equipment and inventories. When products are made and sold they are converted into accounts receivable, which then are collected as cash, and the cycle starts all over again.[2]

Simple enough. Over time, however, as businesses have become more complex and sophisticated, keeping track of their profits has become rather intricate, and there are many ways that companies can record earnings, in an accounting sense, that are not accompanied by cash flow. Consider the hypothetical example of a construction company with a contract to put up a large building, which is expected to take three years. Payment on the contract will be made when the building is complete. This transaction could be accounted for in a number of ways: one might be to wait to recognize the revenues and profit until the end of the project, when all is done and agreed to (accountants designate this technique the "completed contract" method).

Under that approach, though, the company is not recognizing its efforts as they go along, or matching the expenses of construction with the anticipated revenues. To measure that progress, management might record the expected payments as receivables as the construction moves along, under a technique known as "percentage of completion."

Under that method, though, the company would show a profit for one-third of the project each year, but hasn't collected any cash. This is a stylized example, but it serves to illustrate the gap that can arise between what a company estimates and believes its earnings are and will be, versus what has actually been collected in cash. If no cash has come in, has the company made a genuine profit each year, and if so, how much?

The question is not new. In 1985, Leopold Bernstein of Baruch College and Mostafa Maksy of the University Chicago wrote: "Analysts of financial statements and other users have long complained that the increasing intricacy of the accrual accounting system masks real cash flows from operations and widens their divergence from reported net income. Not only do they point to net operating cash inflows as ultimate validators of profitability, they also emphasize that it is cash, and not 'net income,' that must be used to repay loans, to replace and expand the stock of plant and equipment in use, and to pay dividends."[3]

Corporate managers have many accounting techniques at their disposal, but there are three crucial areas where accounting rules can drive a wedge between a firm's reported accounting performance and its true economic value: depreciation, accruals, and the treatment of research and development costs.

Depreciation

The greatest shortcoming of earnings reported under generally accepted accounting principles (GAAP) is probably depreciation expense. Through a well-meaning notion known as the matching principle, accounting rules try to allocate the cost of an asset over its expected productive life through depreciation, deferring the recognition of the full cost by expensing a portion each year. However, depreciation is based on estimates of assets' useful lives, and if those estimates are not accurate, accounting depreciation can greatly distort the picture of their productive capacity, as well as the company's earnings. The dollar amounts can be very large relative to revenues, and because the estimates span long periods, faulty estimates can have significant and long-lasting effects.

One classic example is commercial aircraft. Accounting conventions once commonly estimated the useful lives of airplanes at 10 to 15 years, and charged their costs to earnings over that period. In actual practice, however, many planes stay in the air and churn out revenues much longer—say 30 or 40 years. That may seem like a windfall to the company in the later years, as there is no longer any depreciation expense, but it also means that the charges to accounting earnings early on were too high, so that the accounting earnings of the past were understated.

At the other end of the spectrum, consider the case of a manufacturing firm that builds a new plant with an estimated life of 30 years, only to learn a year later that the widgets it was to produce suddenly have become technologically obsolete, and there's no market for the product. In this case, the plant is not worth much in terms of future earnings, and the depreciation rate should be 100 percent.

Now, we are not faulting the accounting profession for not having perfect foresight: in estimating how long their planes or factories will be productive, companies have to start their accounting somewhere, and the accuracy of those estimates will vary. But our point is that the accumulated results of the accounting process can be highly inaccurate, so that a company's accounting earnings can present a very different picture from what is relevant to investors—economic earnings, or free cash flow.

Accruals

Accruals are a way to anticipate a transaction—recording revenues before the related cash is received, or expenses before it is paid out. At the end of a month, a quarter, or a year, companies routinely accrue sales transactions and the related accounts receivable, or payrolls and other expenses where services have been rendered but not yet settled. When the cash eventually arrives at or leaves the company, the accrual is reversed and the cash transaction takes its place.

Accruals have been part of accounting for centuries, and are an invaluable tool in the accountant's kit. However, like any sharp object they must be used with care. While revenues and expenses received and paid in cash are definite, accruals are merely conceptual, and by their nature estimates, so that companies can accrue whatever transactions management's logic, and their auditors, will allow. If companies are too optimistic with their accruals, accounting earnings will be overstated relative to the actual cash they generate, and will eventually have to be scaled back in some future period.

Reported earnings can include large non-recurring items such as restructuring charges, extraordinary expenses, and gains or losses from discontinued operations, and while all are important events to take into account, they may not be relevant to future results. Consequently, investors typically try to strip out the effects of such special one-time items when assessing the sustainable portion of reported earnings.

A more serious problem arises from the smaller-scale, yet ongoing efforts of a company's senior executives to manage their earnings. Common tactics include "channel stuffing"—artificially boosting sales to meet announced targets—or aggressive timing of the recognition of gains and losses to raise earnings in one quarter (and penalize future periods). Other examples of smaller-scale aggressive accounting are prematurely recognizing revenues before shipment or customers' acceptance; recording revenue although customers are not obligated to pay; and capitalizing, that is, recording as inventories or other assets, costs that should be expensed.[4] Additional problem areas are accounting methods used in acquisitions, assumptions applied to pension accounting, and subsidiary companies not reported as part of the parent company.[5] To the extent that managements rely on

these techniques, a company's historical accounting earnings—
even if they technically meet all required reporting principles—
become a less reliable guide to the future.

It might be tempting to think that the accruals even themselves out over time, but they don't, according to George
Christy, a seasoned corporate banker and treasurer, in his 2009
book *Free Cash Flow*. He explains:

> A viable company has no "end." Every company is continu-
> ally booking new accruals and modifying existing accruals and
> reserves. Even if there were no new accrual accounts put on
> the books, the world in which a company is operating is always
> changing as is the company itself, so the company must continu-
> ally reassess and modify its accrual assumptions.[6]

Investors are not easily fooled, however, and are able to
distinguish between the higher-quality portion of companies'
earnings transacted in cash, and the lower quality accrual
portion. The topic has been rigorously studied, but in 1996
Richard Sloan, a professor at the University of California,
Berkeley, conducted the first academic research demonstrating
that the accrual portion of earnings, as measured by increases
in companies' noncash working capital (such as accounts
receivable), is a less reliable indicator of future earnings than
the cash flow portion. Investors in his samples didn't detect
the difference instantly, but they did catch on eventually.
Sloan wrote that:

> [S]tock prices act as if investors "fixate" on [accounting] earnings,
> failing to distinguish fully between the different properties of the
> accrual and cash flow components of earnings. Consequently,
> firms with relatively high (low) levels of accruals experience
> negative (positive) future abnormal stock returns that are con-
> centrated around future earnings announcements.[7]

That is, share prices react to reported accounting earnings at first, but as the accruals are revealed, prices more often than not gravitate to levels that reflect their cash earning power.

That said, there are many companies in the market trading at nonzero prices even though they do not generate positive cash flow, as well as companies that produce little cash flow that trade at very high prices. As often as not these tend to be "concept stocks"—in the current market, Tesla Motors. Inc. is an example of the first, and Amazon.com, Inc. illustrates the second. In such cases, it seems investors look through the companies' current financial position to some long-term future year when the companies' business concepts, and free cash flow and dividends, are eventually to be realized.

In 2004, David Hirshleifer, a professor of finance at the University of California, Irvine, headed a team that undertook further research on the distinctions between cash profitability and accounting earnings. They found that when companies reached too far, and overstated their economic earnings through accruals, future profits suffered: "[W]hen cumulative net operating income (accounting value added) outstrips cumulative free cash flow (cash value added), subsequent earnings growth is weak."[8] And like Sloan, Hirshleifer's team asserted that firms with high net operating accruals are overvalued by those investors with limited attention who naively concentrate on earnings-based valuation, and ignore mounting evidence of "relative lack of success in generating cash flows in excess of investment needs."[9]

In other words, aggressive accounting may impress some investors for short periods, but ultimately the market sees through the artifice and values the company on its ability to generate free cash flow. Thus, the research of Sloan and Hirshleifer reinforce the investment aphorism, emphasized by banker George Christy, that "[Accounting] profit is an opinion; cash is a fact."[10]

Research and Development Costs

For some companies, research and development (R&D) costs pose the same challenge as depreciation expense. For the most part, generally accepted accounting principles for U.S. companies (U.S. GAAP) require that companies treat their spending on research and development as a current expense. Costs of internally developed software and web site development are handled differently, however: they are deemed to have some ongoing value for the future, and are capitalized and amortized over the useful lives that the company estimates.[11] For many old-line companies these costs typically are minor, but for the growing cohort of technology companies software development may represent a large portion of productive assets. Like the depreciation of fixed assets, amortization of capitalized software incorporates subjective estimates of the useful life of internally developed software, which result in equally subjective charges to earnings. However, companies are required to disclose such amortization: investors that base their valuation methods on cash flow can readily make the needed adjustments, but investors working from unrevised GAAP earnings are dealing with softer numbers.

Differences in accounting standards and methods can complicate the comparison of companies based in the U.S. to those overseas. One significant variation is the treatment of research and development expense under International Financial Reporting Standards (IFRS) versus U.S. GAAP. IFRS requires companies to capitalize their successful R&D efforts in some circumstances, deferring the recognition of expense, with a wide variety of results. PricewaterhouseCoopers published a study in 2010, based on financial statements from 2008, which examined the R&D capitalization practices of a variety of European technology companies.[12] It found that computer and network companies capitalized relatively little—from 0 percent to 14 percent of their R&D spending—while software and internet companies capitalized from 0 percent to 61 percent, and alternative energy companies capitalized from 23 percent to 94 percent. When more spending is capitalized, current earnings appear to be higher—less of the cost is charged against them, and future periods are left to bear the burden.

European companies in other industries capitalize their R&D as well, including a high proportion of technology spending of the automotive sector. Pharmaceuticals, on the other hand, capitalize relatively little because regulatory approval of new drugs, which determines the ultimate value of the investment in research, tends to come late in the R&D cycle.[13] Careful cash flow-oriented investors have financial disclosures at their disposal to put the results of U.S. and European companies on equal footing by looking through the accounting earnings to cash flow, but relying on unadjusted accounting earnings alone can lead to misleading comparisons of companies' economic earning power.

Why Do Accounting Figures Still Dominate the Discussion?

Beyond the issues arising from depreciation, accruals, and R&D, a more general shortcoming of accounting measures is that conventional financial statements are backward-looking.[14] They report the history of a company's successes or failures, but they say nothing about what the future might hold. This point is crucial, because the prime mover of stock prices is investors' expectations of future economic earnings, and the future dividends those earnings will be able to sustain—that is, future cash flows.

Why, then, do accounting figures get so much attention? We are not alone in recognizing the shortcomings of companies' earnings statements: many investors have incorporated cash flow techniques in their decision processes. As long ago as 1998 a survey conducted among 297 members of what is today known as the CFA Institute found that of four analytical inputs—earnings, cash flow, book value and dividends—investors ranked cash flow measures highest in importance (although earnings measures trailed just slightly).[15]

But the markets still have to pay close attention to earnings reports: they may be flawed, but are the primary source of immediate information on a company's quarterly profits. A complete analysis of cash flows can't be done until a company files its full financial statements, typically 45 days after the end of the quarter, while quarterly earnings reports, prepared according to conventional accounting principles, are released within a couple of weeks. In the interim, the markets have to react to something, and for that period the best evidence available is accounting earnings, which get plenty of immediate attention from the financial media. Later, more expansive filings of quarterly reports seldom receive much media attention, unless they disclose truly surprising corporate events.

The CFO Perspective

Companies themselves appear to place greater weight on earnings-based measures than on cash flow. F. W. Cook, a firm of compensation consultants, conducts an annual survey of executive compensation methodology among large companies, and for its 2015 report, said that 51 percent of companies relied on profits to measure performance, while just 11 percent looked to cash flow metrics. (However, most companies combine multiple statistics in setting compensation.) The leading gauge of performance, however, has become total shareholder return, cited by 55 percent of companies in 2015, up from 48 percent in 2012.[16]

A revealing survey conducted in 2006, by academics John Graham, Campbell Harvey, and Shiva Rajgopal, polled chief financial officers of about 350 U.S. companies—public and private, large and small.[17] "We asked CFOs to rank-order the perceived importance of several competing measures of value: earnings, pro forma earnings, revenues, operating cash flows, free cash flows, and economic value added," the authors reported: "Earnings are king. . . . Nearly two-thirds of the respondents ranked earnings as the #1 metric; fewer than 22 percent chose revenues or cash flow from operations."

Executives' preferences differed by company characteristics: private companies placed greater emphasis on cash flows, "which suggests that perhaps capital market motivations drive the focus on earnings." The authors went on to say that CFOs in the study emphasized the importance of reporting steady, predictable patterns in earnings, and how crucial meeting market expectations of quarterly earnings is to share prices, as well as to CFOs' current and futures career prospects: "The common belief is that a well-run and stable company should be able to 'produce the dollars' necessary to hit the earnings target, even in a year that is otherwise somewhat down. In other words, because of the common belief that everyone [manages accounting earnings], missing earnings indicates that a company has no available slack to deliver earnings . . . and must have already used up its cushion."

It's curious and indirect, but such a finding suggests that those companies that are forthright, and don't manage their earnings, could place themselves at a disadvantage with investors. Accounting earnings are by their nature smoothed, while cash flows are more erratic: if executives believe investors will mark down their companies' share prices for volatility in their results, a steady path of earnings is a natural choice, especially when condoned by generally accepted accounting principles.

Graham, Harvey, and Rajgopal, joined by Ilia Dichev, extended their survey research on earnings quality in 2013, polling 375 chief financial officers of U.S. companies. "CFOs endorse the sustainability notion of earnings above all else," they concluded. "[This result] dovetails nicely with the well-documented importance of earnings for valuation, because most valuation models view a company as a stream of earnings and cash flows, and sustainability in profits is the key to projecting such variables."[18]

CFOs were asked to provide a list of red flags for identifying poor earnings quality: "Lack of correlation between earnings and cash flows was the top choice. … The presence of lots of accruals and one-time charges and consistently beating analyst forecasts also scored highly." One CFO in the survey said: "I think if earnings are not backed by actual cash flows, then they are not good earnings."

The researchers also found that CFOs as a group believe that as many as 20 percent of companies intentionally misrepresent their earnings in any given year, through discretionary application of generally accepted accounting principles. Moreover, the CFOs surveyed believed that the misrepresentations were quite large—about 10 cents on every dollar. Two-thirds of the misstatements were thought to overstate actual earnings, while the balance underreported profits.

Although earnings management may be fairly common, detecting it from public sources is challenging, but worth the effort, in the researchers' view. "The takeaway for analysts is that the identification of poor earnings quality has potential for significant rewards," they wrote. "Companies with deteriorating earnings quality incur substantial price declines, lower price multiples, and higher costs of capital."

To their credit, many companies are now reporting pro forma free cash flow measures when they release accounting earnings. And while it would be extremely helpful, in our opinion, for companies to publish free cash flow figures on a per share basis in their financial statements, it's actually forbidden under GAAP:

> Financial statements shall not report an amount of cash flow per share. Neither cash flow nor any component of it is an alternative to net income as an indicator of an enterprise's performance, as reporting per share amounts might imply.[19, 20]

We disagree. Cash flow may not be easy to interpret, but it's not all that complicated, and the effort is worthwhile as it provides far better measures of companies' successes in creating value. However, we are not eager to see the abandonment of GAAP earnings reports: the system has to have rules, but to the extent that accounting profits exaggerate true economic profits, they create inefficiencies in share prices, and open opportunities for earning excess returns through active portfolio management.

Notes

1. Benjamin Graham and David Dodd. *Security Analysis,* 6th ed. (New York: McGraw-Hill, 2009): 70.
2. Leopold A. Bernstein and Mostafa M. Maksy, "Again Now: How Do We Measure Cash Flow from Operations," *Financial Analysts Journal* (July/August 1985): 74
3. Ibid.
4. Diane Brady, "Schilit's Guide to Accounting Shenanigans," *Bloomberg BusinessWeek,* April 3, 2002. Accessed at: www.bloomberg .com/bw/stories/2002-04-03/schilits-guide-to-accounting-shenanigans.
5. Ilia Dichev, John Graham, Campbell Harvey, and Shiva Rajgopal, "The Misrepresentation of Earnings," *Financial Analysts Journal,* Vol. 72, No.1 (January/February 2016): 22–35.
6. George Christy, *Free Cash Flow: Seeing through the Accounting Fog Machine to Find Great Stocks* (Hoboken, NJ: John Wiley & Sons, 2009), 23.
7. Richard G. Sloan, "Do Stock Prices Fully Reflect Information in Accruals and Cash Flows about Future Earnings?" *The Accounting Review,* Vol. 71, No. 3 (July 1996): 289–315.
8. David Hirshleifer, Kewei Hou, Siew Hong Teoh, and Yinglei Zhang, "Do Investors Overvalue Firms with Bloated Balance Sheets?" *Journal of Accounting and Economics*, Vol. 38, No. 1 (December 2004): 297-331.
9. Ibid.

10. Alex J. Pollock, "The Government Should Not Try to Promote Investor Confidence," American Enterprise Institute, 2005. Accessed at: www.aei.org/publication/the-government-should-not-try-to-promote-investor-confidence/.

11. PricewaterhouseCoopers, "Accounting for Innovation: The Impact on Technology Companies of Accounting for R&D Activity Under IFRS," March 2010.

12. Ibid.

13. Ibid.

14. In recent years, company managements have been providing the investing community with "guidance"—glimpses into their estimates of revenues and profits for the year ahead. But there are no detailed forecasts—accounting rules don't allow them. Crucial forecasts of the future are left to investors, and to analysts at brokerage firms who study companies and industries.

15. Stanley B. Block, "A Study of Financial Analysts: Practice and Theory," *Financial Analysts Journal,* Vol. 55, No. 4 (July/August 1999): 86.

16. Frederic W. Cook & Co., "The 2015 Top 250 Report: Long-Term Incentive Grant Practices for Executives," December 2015. Accessed at: fwcook.com/research_reports.html.

17. John R. Graham, Campbell R. Harvey, and Shiva Rajgopal, "Value Destruction and Financial Reporting Decisions," *Financial Analysts Journal,* Vol. 62, No. 6 (November/December 2006): 27.

18. Dichev, 22–35.

19. Christy, 33.

20. Financial Accounting Standards Board, Statement of Financial Accounting Standards No. 95, Statement of Cash Flows, November 1987, Stamford, Connecticut.

CHAPTER 9

The Jump from Company Earnings to Stock Prices

Reports on a company's earnings, whether reported in terms of accounting earnings or cash flow, are by their nature historical. Investing, on the other hand, looks to the future. What economic profit is a company likely to create? What internal profit growth can it sustain, and what dividends and other returns will those profits afford to the owners of the business? And what do all these components imply in today's market for the value of the company's shares? A company's history is often the best guide to its future, and deciphering past results and building them into a forecast of cash flows, and then into a prospective valuation, is the beginning of the investment process.

Flaws in Traditional Valuation Measures

Over time investors have devised many measures for turning up attractive stocks, by deriving the potential value of a share and comparing that estimate to its current price. One classic is a comparison of a stock's price to its current or projected earnings per share—the price-earnings (P/E) ratio. Another is comparing the current price to the book value, which is the portion of a company's net worth, according to the financial statements, that is attributable to each share. Both the ratios of price to earnings and price to book value per share can be easily calculated, and are widely used as shorthand measures of a stock's price versus its true value.

But the P/E ratio and price-to-book value per share fall short for a number of reasons. One is that they try to compress information on a company's past, present, and future into one statistic, at one point in time, and are too simple as a result.

Additionally, P/E or price-to-book ratios are not absolute measures: faster-growing companies typically show higher ratios than laggards, and in a favorable market ratios for all firms will generally be higher. In effect, each sector and market regime requires a different measuring stick, and price-earnings and price-to-book value ratios thus call for a lot of interpretation.

These criticisms are not new: in 1972, Jack Treynor, an investment scholar, former editor of the *Financial Analysts Journal*, and one of the great thinkers in the financial world, criticized both simple measures of valuation that took reported earnings without adjustment as gospel, and the investors who rely on them: "Needless to say, if the analyst insists on being provided with a single number so simply related to market value, then he is delegating away to whoever provides that number most of the real task of security analysis."[1]

But in our view, the underlying reason for rejecting such simple valuation measures is that they typically are derived from accounting measures of profits and assets, as reported and without adjustments. Even though corporations employ brigades of accountants to prepare financial statements, and turn them over to regiments of auditors who evaluate their fairness, reported results in many cases are simply not representative either of companies' current financial health or their prospects.

Net book value, for example, measures the assets of the corporation net of debt, but it does so from the accounting perspective of historical cost—the amounts originally recorded for assets and liabilities. For assets in particular, net book value seldom reflects current value, and can thus present a misleading estimate—either overstated or understated, depending on the case—of a company's value per share.

The P/E ratio is severely limited as well, even apart from the distortions created by the accounting rules that go into the calculation of the earnings figure. The P/E ratio compares earnings per share for a given period—typically the latest 12 months, or a forecast of the coming year—to a share's price. This calculation yields a number that an investor has to subject to a complex comparison. Long ago—in the early decades of the last century—stock valuation was fairly simple, as investors tended to apply a standard price-earnings ratio of 10 times to all stocks. Then in the late 1920s, investors became more inventive with valuations, and higher and higher multiples were applied to stocks thought to have superior prospects for profit growth (in the market of the time, these included public utilities and chain retail stores).[2]

In the aftermath of the U.S. stock market crash in 1929, John Burr Williams, a Harvard-trained investment manager, developed a method for valuing stocks that was similar to the valuation of bonds—taking into account the stream of payments, that is, dividends, an investor receives into the future. This method has both greater practical and theoretical appeal than the P/E ratio. For one thing, it looks further ahead in time than the one-year forecast typical for P/E valuation, trying to take account of a changing future. For another, it addresses the valuation question more directly: the investor doesn't receive earnings per share every year—just that portion that is paid out in dividends.[3] Such dividend discount models are elegant solutions, but are highly detailed, and rather than cover them here, we present a review in Appendix B.

In summary, both P/E ratios and price-book ratios are badly flawed and long outmoded, so that many professional managers have replaced them with alternative measures. In the case of Epoch, those measures are based on free cash flow. We define free cash flow for a given period as the company's cash available for distribution to shareholders after the investment in all planned capital expenditures and the payment of all cash taxes.[4]

Why is free cash flow so important? We'll be discussing many aspects of companies' cash flow, but to reiterate our earlier point, a company's free cash flow is the origin of the value of a company. In the normal case, companies pay dividends from free cash flow, so understanding how much free cash flow a company might be able to consistently generate, and its ability to pay future dividends, is essential.

Accounting versus Finance: A Case Study

For an illustration of the shortcomings of accounting principles, and the potential peril of measuring a company's performance solely on accounting earnings, we turn to a classic case study: "Feathered Feast," appearing in the November-December 1993 edition of the *Financial Analysts Journal*, and authored by Jack Treynor. The case study is reproduced in Appendix C.

"Feathered Feast" tells of a fictional pension portfolio manager, Shephard Saunders, who is about to face his investment board to account for the fund's unsuccessful investment in Feathered Feast, Inc., a chain of fast food restaurants, also fictional, where the signature dish is the Featherburger.[5] Saunders typically preferred to invest in solid companies possessing tangible assets, but he had fallen prey to a broker's story that Feathered Feast shares, already trading at a lofty 40 times earnings, were headed higher on the back of the company's steady earnings growth (10 percent per year) and generous dividend payout (85 percent or so of annual net income). All was on track in December 1991, but in the following year profits rapidly turned to losses, due to cutthroat competition and excess capacity in the fast food business. By the end of 1992 the company was selling its trademark restaurants— 30-foot high chickens sculpted from stainless steel—for scrap.

The central question in the case study is what defines the value of those restaurants. The company recognized their cost in earnings through annual depreciation, spread over 12 years to match the term of lease contracts—an estimate thought to be fairly conservative, as the physical life span of the steel structures was 40 or 50 years.

By the end of 1991 Feathered Feast had invested over $700 million in its restaurants, and net of depreciation, they were on the books for about $600 million. For 1991, they earned the company a net income of $85 million, but as noted, by the end of 1992 the restaurants showed large losses.

Through this example, Treynor successfully contrasts accounting measures with financial valuations, particularly for fixed assets with long lives. In accounting terms, the restaurants seemed to be a valuable asset, with a remaining cost of hundreds of millions yet to be depreciated. However, their ability to generate positive net cash flow had disappeared in the competitive battle. Shephard Saunders, the case study's portfolio manager, consults an accounting oracle during his post mortem investigation of the failed investment, who observes: "A brick wall is nothing but mud on edge if its capacity to render economic service has disappeared; the molecules are still there, and the wall may be as solid as ever, but the value has gone."[6]

In a company's financial statements, plant and equipment are stated in terms of historical cost, net of depreciation. "Net book value" is how that measure is known, but that is a misnomer: as any well-trained accountant would explain, net book value is not—and not meant to be—a representation of an asset's market value. Instead it is the result of a systematic allocation against earnings of an asset's purchase price over time. But what meaning does it have? Only by coincidence would it equal the asset's economic value. Thus accounting measures are usually a poor foundation to use in estimating future value of an enterprise. Even so, out of habit or insufficient knowledge, many investors rely on net book value and other accounting measures as primary metrics of what an asset or company is worth.

Instead, as "Feathered Feast" demonstrates, the economic value of an asset, or an entire company, is determined by the future cash flow an asset will be able to generate. Valuing companies on their free cash flow offers a superior method, incorporating the entire value chain—revenues, margins, working capital requirements, and capital expenditures—into one consistent analysis.[7] Thus, it is able to answer crucial questions on a company's "story": how and why have revenues grown over time? What has been the cost, in materials and capital expenditures, of producing those revenues? Has management's past capital spending provided the company with profitable growth opportunities? Generally accepted accounting principles (GAAP) measures of earnings, in contrast, are highly condensed, and provide too little of the information needed for competent forecasts.[8]

The distinction between the opinion of accounting profit and the fact of cash creates opportunities for investors attentive to the difference, and is the basis for the investment philosophy of Epoch Investment Partners.

Notes

1. Jack Treynor, "The Trouble with Earnings," *Financial Analysts Journal,* Vol. 28, No. 5 (September/October 1972): 41–43. *Author's Note:* Jack Treynor was the single most brilliant financial

mind I have known in my long career. For further work by him, see *Treynor on Institutional Investing*, published by John Wiley & Sons.

2. Benjamin Graham and David Dodd, *Security Analysis*, 6th ed. (New York: McGraw-Hill, 2009), 496–497.

3. Nicholas Molodovksy, "A Theory of Price-Earnings Ratios," *The Analysts Journal,* Vol. 9, No. 2 (November 1953): 65–78.

   Nicholas Molodovsky, an early financial scholar, pointed out the important distinction between what a company earns and what it pays out as dividends in a 1953 article. "Imagine ... the extremely and purely hypothetical case of [Frozen Corporation,] controlling considerable wealth, but prohibited by its by-laws from paying any dividends. ... In its successive reports, its growth could look impressive. However, [its common stock] will have a value and command a price only as long as potential buyers hope that its property will eventually be sold [and distributed to shareholders in liquidation]. ... [But if we insert a clause in its bylaws] prohibiting the sale of the property ... [that] would effectively seal the fate of Frozen common. By extinguishing all hope of future payments it would be rendered completely worthless despite the enormous assets behind it."

4. Enrique Arzac, *Valuation for Mergers, Buyouts and Restructuring*, 2nd ed. (Hoboken, NJ: John Wiley & Sons, 2008), 8.

5. Noah Hill, "A Chicken Autopsy," The Motley Fool web site, October 1998. Accessed at: www.fool.com/EveningNews/foth/1998/foth981007.htm.

   The resemblance between Feathered Feast, Inc. and Boston Chicken, another failed chain of poultry purveyors, may today seem prescient but is more likely coincidental: Boston Chicken (now called Boston Market) had just completed its initial public offering at the time of publication of Treynor's fictional case study in 1993, and filed for Chapter 11 bankruptcy in October 1998.

6. Jack Treynor, "Feathered Feast: A Case," *Financial Analysts Journal,* Vol. 49, No. 6 (November/December 1993): 9–12.

7. William Priest and Lindsay McClelland. *Free Cash Flow and Share-holder Yield: New Priorities for the Global Investor* (Hoboken, NJ: John Wiley & Sons, 2007): 19.

8. Bradford Cornell and Wayne R. Landsman, "Accounting Valuation: Is Earnings Quality an Issue?" *Financial Analysts Journal,* Vol. 59, No. 6 (November/December 2003): 20–28.

CHAPTER 10

Epoch's Investment Philosophy

This chapter pulls together the theory and practice of markets and investors, and discusses, at a high level, Epoch's process for selecting individual stocks for investment. To sum up the foundation of the past several chapters: first, we respectfully depart from the theoretical arguments of Modern Portfolio Theory, and substitute the observations of behavioral finance—that real-world investor behavior is complex and leads to inefficiencies in stock prices, creating mispricing in securities and opportunities for active managers. Second, we believe that the reliance by corporate managements, as well as by many investors, on backward-looking financial measures derived from generally accepted accounting principles (GAAP) financial statements distorts the financial picture many companies present. Moreover, accounting-based investment decisions can give rise to their own category of mispricings and inefficiencies. Accordingly, we believe that cash flow is the origin of value in stocks, and that forecasts of cash flows should be the basis for security selection.

In the next few pages we discuss Epoch's framework for evaluating the cash flows of individual companies. We emphasize the importance of managements' decisions in allocating their available cash flow—either by adding value to their businesses through capital reinvestment, or returning capital to the owners through share repurchases and dividends.

The Starting Point: Generating Free Cash Flow

Epoch seeks to invest in companies with business models that are transparent, and can be readily understood from the sources and uses of their free cash flow. As noted above, we define free cash flow as the cash provided by the company's operations, less planned capital expenditures and cash taxes.[1] Management can thus deploy this uncommitted cash at its discretion.

Once a company has reckoned its free cash flow for a given period, how will management allocate it? Epoch outlines five possible destinations: reinvesting capital in the business through corporate acquisitions and capital spending on internal projects, as well as distributing cash to the owners through dividends, buying back outstanding shares, and repaying debt (Figure 10.1).[2] Of the companies Epoch chooses to research and monitor, we fully investigate their capital allocation process. Some companies turn out to be unappealing investments, for reasons such as a weak competitive position, low profitability, a poor growth outlook, or

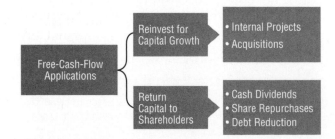

FIGURE 10.1   Applications of Free Cash Flow

Source: Epoch Investment Partners

unwise capital application, and thus we reject them from further consideration. For those companies with attractive strategies and strong operating cash flow, if their share prices fall within Epoch's estimates of reasonable value, we will add them to our portfolios. And if they are sound businesses but seem too expensive at the current price, we monitor their progress until their share prices move to a point where we think they can be capitalized upon.

Reinvesting capital for further growth and returning excess capital to the firm's owners are not mutually exclusive. Depending on the economic and competitive environment, most companies are likely to find profitable projects for new investment, but not enough to consume all the free cash flow they create. In such cases a sensible capital allocation policy devotes some resources to expanding the business, and the rest to rewarding its owners.

Choosing to Reinvest

In order to grow, companies must reinvest in their businesses, but simply expanding the size of operations does not ensure an increase in the firm's value. Basic principles of finance and investment hold that a company should invest only in new opportunities that are expected to earn a return higher than a firm's marginal cost of capital (that is, the cost of an incremental issue of debt or equity). John Maynard Keynes formalized this notion in 1935, and called it the "marginal efficiency of capital."[3] Keynes was a peerless economic thinker and writer, but his definitions on this topic are roundabout and complex, so we will not quote them here. To paraphrase, however, the marginal efficiency of capital is a breakeven rate of return, which equates the present value of the expected benefits from investing in a new plant or company to the cost of the new investment.

Capital Investment: Returns and Capital Costs

For management of a current-day corporation, the challenge in qualifying new projects is to identify the prospective free cash flow they might generate, anticipating as best it can future changes in revenues, costs, and the competitive environment. This amount, which Keynes called the "prospective yield," is then compared to the cost of the new investment, including financing. If the project is expected to generate more cash than it consumes, including the marginal (that is, incremental) cost of financing the new project, then undertaking the investment in the project can increase the value of the business.

It is crucial that managements evaluate projects on their cash flow merits, rather than projections of accounting-based earnings. Some investments that generate apparently positive accounting earnings may in fact reduce the value of a firm when considered through the lens of cash flow, primarily due to the accounting mechanism of depreciation. Depreciation defers the cost of an investment over time, rather than recognize the full cash outflow at the start, and thus reduces the cost of the investment in present value terms. Therefore a project may appear to have a positive net present value from an accounting view of the associated costs and revenues, while at the same time its net present value calculated from the expected cash flows could be negative.

When looking at prospective returns on invested capital (ROIC) versus the cost of capital, it is essential to distinguish between marginal and average measures, and to make an evaluation based on the marginal figures. Weighted average cost of capital (WACC) measures the proportional cost of a company's total existing base of capital, for both debt and equity combined. The weighted average cost of the debt portion simply measures the interest rates the company has to pay on each form of debt, weighted to reflect the size of the borrowings.

The cost of equity capital, however, is harder to observe directly. A firm is not required to make cash distributions to shareholders, but that does not make equity capital free: even if equity holders do not receive cash dividends from the company, they expect to earn a return on their investment through the appreciation of the stock price. Thus, the cost of equity capital is usually thought of as the expected return on equities in general, adjusted for the volatility of the equity returns of the individual firm (as measured by the beta coefficient in the CAPM—firms with higher betas are thought to have a higher cost of equity capital, and vice versa).

Suppose the capital structure of the mythical Griffin Corporation consists of 80 percent equity and 20 percent debt, and its total enterprise value (equity plus debt) is $1 billion. The debt carries a weighted average interest rate of 5 percent, while the equity cost of capital is assumed to be 10 percent. The firm's WACC will therefore be 9 percent.[4] The firm operates one business line, earning a 14 percent return on its invested capital—500 basis points over the WACC.

Suppose further that the firm is considering an investment in a new line of business, estimated to cost $200 million, which is to be funded entirely with newly issued debt. Management believes that the new business will earn an ROIC of 8 percent. On the cost side, interest rates have fallen, and the firm can now borrow at 3 percent, rather than the 5 percent it pays on its debt borrowed in the past. Should Griffin's management go ahead with the investment?

From the perspective of average cost of capital, the answer would be no. The existing WACC is 9 percent, and an 8 percent return would fall short by 100 basis points. Against a 9 percent hurdle rate, the project would not earn its keep and destroy value.

But the project will not be funded by the firm's existing capital; instead, it will be funded by an incremental $200 million in debt costing 3 percent. The 8 percent expected return on the project would be 500 basis points higher than the cost of the capital to fund the project. Therefore, on its own merits the new project would be profitable, and the company would create value by taking on the investment, notwithstanding the apparently unfavorable comparison against the averages.

Similarly, on the return side of the calculation, what matters is the marginal ROIC, rather than the average ROIC the firm earns on all of its businesses. Suppose that instead of earning a projected 8 percent, the proposed new business was expected to earn only 2 percent. If the firm goes ahead with the investment, its average ROIC on all businesses would drop from 14 percent to 12 percent. (Equal to $1 billion times a 14 percent average ROIC, plus $200 million times a 2 percent marginal ROIC, divided by total assets of $1,200.) In addition, adding $200 million in debt costing just 3 percent would reduce the firm's WACC. As a first approximation—ignoring any impact on the cost of equity capital—the lower cost of the new debt would reduce the WACC from 9 percent to 8 percent. However, adding the new debt might make the enterprise look more risky to equity holders, so we assume that the cost of Griffin's equity capital would rise to 11 percent. All in, the net effect on WACC would then be a reduction to 8.7 percent. (Equal to $800 times an 11 percent cost of equity, plus $200 times a 5 percent average cost on existing debt, plus $200 times a 3 percent marginal cost of debt, divided by total liabilities and equity of $1,200.)

Since the new average ROIC of 12 percent would still be higher than Griffin's new 8.7 percent WACC, does the investment makes sense? In this case the answer is no because the cost of the new borrowing, 3 percent, would be funding an investment earning just 2 percent. That's a formula for destroying value.

What matters in evaluating new projects are not the averages of capital costs and investment returns, but instead the marginal costs and returns they generate.

Once More: Cash Flow-Based Measures Are Superior

We'll take one more look, in depth, at how decision making on the financial measures of free cash flow and ROIC is superior to relying on accounting-based techniques.

Consider the five-year records of two hypothetical companies, Green Enterprises and Red Corporation (Table 10.1).[5] In the initial year, both companies earn revenues of $1,000, and generate accounting earnings of $100. And for both, revenues and earnings grow 5 percent annually. On the basis of accounting earnings alone, the two enterprises would appear to be of equal value.

But Green is actually worth far more than Red, as revealed by a comparison of their cash flows. Green has a higher ROIC, and is able to maintain its 5 percent growth in revenues and

TABLE 10.1   Hypothetical Financial Summaries, Green Enterprises and Red Corporation

	Years				
	1	2	3	4	5
Green Enterprises					
Revenues	$1,000	$1,050	$1,103	$1,158	$1,216
Earnings	$100	$105	$110	$116	$122
Investment	($25)	−$26	−$28	−$29	−$30
Free cash flow	$75	$79	$83	$87	$91
Red Corporation					
Revenues	$1,000	$1,050	$1,103	$1,158	$1,216
Earnings	$100	$105	$110	$116	$122
Investment	($50)	−$53	−$55	−$58	−$61
Free cash flow	$50	$53	$55	$58	$61

Source: McKinsey & Company, Tim Koller, Marc Goedhart, and David Wessels, *Valuation: Measuring and Managing the Value of Companies,* 5th ed. (Hoboken, NJ: John Wiley & Sons, 2010), 19.

earnings by investing just 25 percent of its earnings, while Red needs to reinvest 50 percent of its cash flow to keep growth steady. Accounting earnings of the two are equal, but Green generates $75 in free cash flow in year 1, while Red generates only $50 in free cash flow. In years 2 through 5, the respective free cash flow figures then grow at 5 percent per year, in line with revenues and accounting earnings.

In choosing between the two companies as investment candidates, comparing accounting earnings would be a constructive start, but would not go far enough: they provide no insight on the resources required to keep the business going. The additional dimension of cash flow provides a more complete view, showing how much will be claimed by reinvestment, and what will be left over for the owners at the end of each year. In this example, the simple sum of the free cash flow for Red over the five years is $276, while the higher ROIC at Green generates $415. In present-value terms, assuming a growth rate for both companies of 5 percent in perpetuity and a cost of capital of 10 percent, Green is worth $1,500, while Red is worth $1,000.

Table 10.1 conveys two messages. First, a company's value originates not in its accounting earnings, but instead from its free cash flow. Second, a higher ROIC leads to a higher valuation, holding other factors equal.

Consider what the traditional earnings-based valuation metrics that most investors rely on would say about these two companies. Both companies have the same $100 in earnings, but because of its higher ROIC and lower reinvestment requirements, Green is worth $1,500, while Red is only worth $1,000. That means that if both companies were trading at their fair value, Green would have a P/E of 15, while Red would have a P/E of 10. Investors who rely on P/E as a measure of value would say that Red is more attractively priced than Green, yet both are in fact fairly priced. Now suppose that Green was trading at $1,400 and Red was trading at $1,100. Green's P/E would be 14, and Red's would be 11. The P/E investor would still say Red is priced more "cheaply," yet now Green is actually undervalued and Red is overvalued. A P/E ratio simply doesn't tell the investor anything about a company's underlying ROIC, and as a result its usefulness is limited.

Some investors believe that they can overcome this short-coming of the P/E ratio by looking at what is known as a "PEG ratio," which divides the P/E ratio by the rate of the company's expected growth. Companies with higher expected growth will trade at higher P/E ratios, the thinking goes, and a P/E-to-growth ratio will enable an investor to make an apples-to-apples comparison. A company with a P/E of 10 and expected growth of 5 percent will have the same PEG ratio as a company with a P/E of 20 and expected growth of 10 percent, implying that they are similarly valued. But our example shows that the PEG ratio can also be misleading. Both Green and Red are growing at 5 percent per year, so if they were trading at their fair values, Green would have a PEG ratio of 3 (P/E of 15 divided by 5 percent growth) while Red would have a PEG ratio of 2 (P/E of 10, growth of 5 percent). This implies that Red is somehow the better value relative to its growth rate, yet we know that both companies are fairly priced. And in the situation where Green trades at $1,400 and Red is at $1,100, Green would have a PEG ratio of 2.8 (P/E of 14 divided by 5 percent growth) and Red would have a PEG ratio of 2.2. As we saw when we used the P/E ratio alone, Red looks cheaper than Green, yet Red is overvalued and Green is the one that is undervalued, even with its higher P/E and higher PEG ratio.

From the perspective of investors in the stock market, the superior framework for evaluating a company's worth is a focus on capital allocation—how the company deploys the money it has already made. Accounting-based measures such as earnings per share, book value and the price-earnings ratio aren't designed to estimate what the company's business is expected to earn over the life of its investments, and thus offer information far less valuable than the dynamics of return on investment and the cost of capital.

To summarize, company managers maximize returns to shareholders by allocating capital toward its most profitable use. The first step is investing only in opportunities that can earn an ROIC higher than the marginal cost of the capital needed to fund the investment. When projects cannot justify an ROIC higher than the marginal cost of capital, managers should instead return capital to shareholders, who may have a higher-return alternative for the funds.

Trends in Capital Allocation

Managements of U.S. corporations have shown a significant shift in their approach to capital allocation over the past 20 years. Prior to 2005, free cash flow invested in capital expenditures and acquisitions swamped distributions to shareholders in dividends and share buybacks (Figure 10.2): from 1994 through 2005,

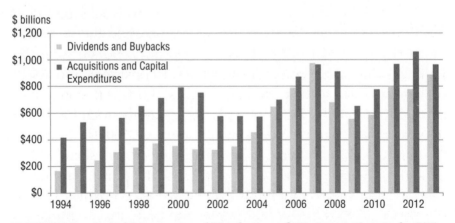

FIGURE 10.2   Capital Investment and Distributions of U.S. Corporations in the S&P 1500, 1994–2013

Source: S&P Dow Jones Indices

corporations in the broad S&P 1500 index carried out $7.3 trillion in new investment, while returning $4.1 trillion to owners. More recently, cash flow allocation has been more balanced: from 2005 through 2013 new investment still claimed a greater share, at an aggregate $7.1 trillion, but share buybacks and dividends were not far behind, at $6.1 trillion.[6] (Discretionary debt paydowns are not included in distributions to owners, as we have not found an authoritative source for them.)

Dividends

Dividends are the traditional means of rewarding shareholders. They also can provide important insights into the thinking of a company's managers: dividends typically reflect the ability to earn an economic profit with consistency, and many investors see steady dividend increases as an indicator of current financial health. Dividends also can serve as a signal from management: companies are reluctant to cut their dividends, so that steady increases can speak to insiders' confidence in the future prospects for the business.[7]

While dividends are a hot topic among investors today, they have gone in and out of favor as a force behind the valuation of share prices. For most of the history of corporate America, investors cherished companies that paid consistent and rising dividends. Going back 20 or 30 years, however, companies slowed the growth of distributions (although the total paid continued to rise).[8] For the companies in the S&P 500, for example, 94 percent of companies distributed dividends to shareholders in 1980,[9] paying out about 40 percent of annual earnings.[10] Through the 1980s and 1990s, the share of companies paying dividends fell steadily (reflecting in part that companies increased their share buyback activity). The share of S&P 500 companies paying cash dividends hit bottom at 70 percent in 2002, but has since steadily recovered—with a few years' break after the 2008 financial crisis—to 83 percent of companies in 2015.[11] Compared to a recent low of $47.2 billion in third quarter 2009, dividends to shareholders had doubled to $94.4 billion by second quarter 2015, and forecasts called for a record year for 2015, notwithstanding cutbacks by energy and commodities companies necessitated by sharp drops in commodities prices.[12]

Seeking companies paying attractive dividends can indeed deliver superior returns. S&P Dow Jones Indices publishes a passive index made up of companies in the S&P 500 that have consistently raised their dividends over 25 years; it earned total annual returns through January 2016 of 14.0 percent over five years (vs. 10.9 percent for the S&P 500) and 9.8 percent over 10 years (vs. 6.5 percent for the broad index).[13] Risk-adjusted returns over those periods were higher as well.

One line of traditional investment thinking asserts that those companies paying out large proportions of their earnings in dividends may limit their future growth by starving the enterprise of needed cash, while those that retain a greater portion of profits can promote faster growth. It's a logical possibility, but the notion was refuted a few years back in a study by investment managers Robert Arnott and Clifford Asness, motivated by the low payouts for the five years ending in 2001.

Rather than confirming the conventional thinking that dividends and earnings growth tended to move in opposite directions, they found instead a positive relationship:

> The historical evidence strongly suggests that expected future earnings growth is fastest when current payout ratios are high and slowest when payout ratios are low. ... Our evidence thus contradicts the views of many who believe that substantial reinvestment of retained earnings will fuel faster future earnings growth. Rather, it is consistent with anecdotal tales about managers signaling their earnings expectations through dividends or engaging, at times, in inefficient empire building.[14]

Since the time of that study, many corporations have in fact increased their distributions, whether through dividends or share repurchases, often in response to prodding from activist shareholders. In 2004, for instance, Microsoft Corporation paid from its large cash hoard an epic special dividend of $32 billion, or about $3 per share, and doubled its usual dividend. (At the time the move was thought to be the largest such distribution on record.[15]) Payouts have only become more generous, however: Apple Inc. distributed $56 billion to shareholders in fiscal 2014, through a combination of dividends and share repurchases (Apple's 2015 fiscal year saw smaller, but still large, dividends and repurchases of $46 billion.[16])

Share Repurchases

During the past 10 years, distributions through dividends have been surpassed by corporations' repurchases of their shares (Figure 10.3). Notwithstanding their popularity, however, financial thinkers, both academics and investment practitioners, are split on the merits of share repurchases. Critics assert that repurchases divert crucial capital from new investment; that companies funding repurchases with debt are adding unnecessary leverage; and that some managements undertake repurchases to drive up earnings per share in order to artificially hit their compensation targets. These criticisms notwithstanding, repurchases now are in nearly every chief financial officer's toolbox, and during third quarter 2015 more than a fifth of companies in the S&P 500 reduced their share counts by at least 4 percent from a year earlier.[17] For the year ended September 2015, S&P 500 corporations repurchased $559 billion of their own shares, a year-over-year increase of 1.6 percent.[18]

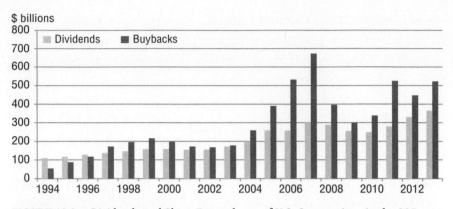

FIGURE 10.3   Dividends and Share Repurchases of U.S. Corporations in the S&P
1500, 1994–2013

Source: S&P Dow Jones Indices

Epoch is squarely in favor of share repurchases as a capital allocation tool—assuming they are carried out under the
right conditions. First, a share repurchase is reasonable only
in cases where the company cannot find sufficient profitable
investment opportunities. Second, to be effective a buyback
must represent a true reduction in the share base, and any con-
temporaneous share issuances must not be so large as to offset
the effect of the repurchase. When these requirements are met,
share repurchases are functionally equivalent to cash dividend
payouts of the same magnitude, and thus can bring the same
value to shareholders as a cash dividend.[19]

Now, repurchasing shares by itself does not increase a company's free cash flow, and thus does not itself create a higher
value for the enterprise as a whole. (To be precise, a company
would likely see an increase in cash flow from the dividends it
wouldn't have to distribute on the repurchased shares, but such
amounts would typically be minor.) Instead, it's a question of
proportion. From the perspective of the remaining shareholders, each share of stock becomes more valuable—with fewer

shares outstanding each owner has a claim on a greater share of the company's future cash flows. The box "Share Repurchase Example" provides a simple but representative example.

Share Repurchase Example

The hypothetical Rex Corporation has 10 equal shareholders, carries no debt, and at the start of Year 1 has an enterprise value of $1,000. Assume the business generates $250 of free cash flow during Year 1, all of which will be distributed to the owners.

Case 1: Assume the $250 of free cash flow will be used to repurchase the ownership interests of two shareholders.

Prior to the repurchase, each shareholder's stock is valued at 1/10 of the enterprise value, or $100. The two departing shareholders each are paid $125 to relinquish their claims on future cash flows.

After the repurchase, eight people hold 1/8 of the $1,000 enterprise value. It remains at $1,000 because there is no change in the future stream of income after Year 1. Accordingly, each of the eight remaining owners sees the value of his stake rise by $25, from $100 to $125.

Case 2: Assume the $250 of free cash flow will be paid as a dividend.

After the dividend, the enterprise value remains at $1,000: once again, the distribution of Year 1's income does not alter the stream of future cash flows. The 10 owners retain 1/10 of the $1,000 enterprise value, placing their stakes at $100 each.

In the share repurchase case, the continuing eight owners did not receive a cash distribution, but they have a larger claim on the future cash flow stream from the business. The two departing owners received their proportionate shares of the year's income, and the present value of the future income stream from the business.

(Continued)

(*Continued*)

In the dividend case, all 10 owners receive 1/10 of this year's income and retain a 1/10 share of the business's future earnings stream.

Summary:

	Share repurchase	Dividend
Cash distribution	2 × $125 = $250	10 × $25 = 250
Continuing interest	8 × $125 = 1,000	10 × $100 = $1,000
Total value	$1,250	$1,250

Source: William Priest, David Pearl, John Tobin, and Eric Sappenfield, "Dividends by Another Name," Epoch Investment Partners White Paper, 2015. Special thanks to Kera Van Valen.

Going back 30 years and more, share repurchases were uncommon, and dividends were the primary means for distributing cash to shareholders. Then in 1982, the U.S. Securities and Exchange Commission enacted Rule 10b-18 of the Securities Exchange Act of 1934, which provided companies trading in their own securities a safe harbor from charges of manipulating their stocks' prices. With this protection, U.S. corporate buybacks surged for a few years in the late 1980s, but really took off around 1995, and in 1997 they surpassed dividends as means of distributions to shareholders (Figure 10.3, above). Among all publicly traded U.S. companies, the proportion paying dividends fell off from 78 percent in 1978 to 40 percent in 2013, while those repurchasing shares increased from 28 percent to 43 percent.[20] (However, the trend among U.S. companies in the aggregate toward not paying dividends runs counter to the rising proportion of S&P 500 companies paying dividends cited above.)

Academic studies reach varying conclusions on whether stock prices benefit from share repurchases, but one comprehensive paper, authored in 2008 by Jeffrey Pontiff and Artezima Wood-gate, respectively of Boston College and the University of Washington and Russell Investment Group, made several favorable findings.[21] Their work examined both share issuance and repurchases over very long periods, and shows that stocks' future returns are strongly related to changes in shares outstanding. Overall, it's not a large effect, but it does indicate that repurchases are associated with positive future returns. Pontiff, working with R. David McLean and Akiko Watanabe of the University of Alberta, extended the research to international markets in 2009, and found a similar strong effect in countries with developed and active markets for share issuance.[22]

Recent market results confirm the academic work. S&P Dow Jones Indices presents an index focused on the 100 companies in the S&P 500 most active in repurchasing their shares (the S&P 500 Buyback Index), and it has outperformed the broad market. For the five years ended January 2016, the buyback index returned 13.1 percent annually versus 10.9 percent for the S&P 500, and for the 10 years then ended, the buyback subset earned 9.0 percent against 6.5 percent.[23]

To be sure, not all share repurchases are constructive, and some of the objections expressed by market observers are valid. A well-researched 2015 paper from investment manager Research Affiliates, "Are Buybacks an Oasis or a Mirage?," contends that some of the largest recent buybacks were not productive because the companies issued new shares that overwhelmed the effect of the share repurchase, particularly in fulfilling employee stock option compensation programs. Other significant new issuances were made to pay for mergers and acquisitions. The authors also criticize repurchases paid for with newly issued debt: "Dilution of earnings can also occur because a company issues debt, funneling earnings away from dividend payments to shareholders and toward principal and interest payments to the company's lenders. ... Five of the largest debt issuers [in 2014] were also among the largest repurchasers of equity." They conclude that in 2014, notwithstanding all the headlines about buybacks, managements of U.S. corporations in the aggregate diluted their equity base by 1.8 percent.[24]

Along similar lines, Epoch does not regard all share repurchases favorably. A critical part of our approach to identifying candidates for investment calls for regular visits with management teams—to gain a sense of their capital allocation philosophies, of which share repurchases are a key component, and how their views compare to the actual record in different market and economic environments.

Debt Buydowns

A corporation's buying back of its own debt is another application of free cash flow that can increase the value of shareholder equity. To illustrate this idea we look to the pioneering research, dating back to 1958, of financial economists Franco Modigliani and Merton Miller, then professor and associate professor, respectively, at the Carnegie Institute of Technology (now Carnegie Mellon University). Each was ultimately awarded a Nobel Prize in Economics recognizing their many contributions to the field (Modigliani in 1985, and Miller in 1990).

Prior to that time, there had been little systematic academic study of corporate finance, and Modigliani and Miller set out to measure enterprises' cost of capital and risk in a world of uncertain returns on their investment. In their initial paper, they theorized that what determined the value of a firm was not its capital structure—that is, the proportions of debt and equity that funded a company's operations—but rather the cash flows generated by its assets. In turn, they asserted, changing a company's capital structure—shifting debt to equity, or vice versa—would not change its value, unless the capital change altered the cash flows as well. Thus, a company's value is not determined by whether management raises funds as debt or equity; instead, value comes from the quality of managers' decisions on investment, and the resulting cash flows.[25]

Observers are not unanimous on the merits of the early repurchase of debt. "Assuming there is no need to pay down debt to target levels, managers should probably consider share repurchases or extraordinary dividends, since these send a favorable signal to capital markets," according to the authors of *Valuation: Measuring and Managing the Value of Companies*: "Voluntary debt repayments do not represent a positive signal, unless the company is close to or in financial distress."[26] In their view, increasing the proportion of cash flow paid as dividends sends the strongest signal to investors.

We at Epoch respectfully disagree, and see debt repayments as a constructive application of free cash flow—but as before, assuming the company is unable to identify business investment opportunities to advance growth in value.

The practical implication for equity investors is this: when a company applies free cash flow to repay debt, the transaction transfers proportional wealth from bondholders to stockholders. Assuming free cash flows from the company's underlying business hold steady, the total value of the firm is unchanged. Accordingly, when claims of bondholders are reduced, the future free cash flow attributable to stockholders is increased, as is their proportionate value in the firm.

Capital Allocation: What's the Right Mix?

Assuming they have earned the luxury of free cash flow, corporate managers have many levers to pull—investing in their businesses when that investment is expected to be profitable, and distributing capital to shareholders when it's not.

For the outside observer, and the practical matter of selecting stocks for portfolios, the analysis has many dimensions.

Understanding the starting point—how a company generates its free cash flow, and its likely growth rate—is the most straightforward. It can be understood, measured, and forecast through fundamental analysis, including the microeconomic dynamics of industries and the interpretation of companies' financial statements.[27]

Grasping a company's capital allocation policy is more complicated and subjective. A critical initial step in Epoch's investment approach is to interview senior management teams on their capital allocation philosophy (and return to the topic frequently, to learn how the story may have changed). From there we validate their thinking, examining the historical record to see that the company's free cash flow has been put to its highest and best use—that they have identified investment opportunities that enhance the value of the firm for the long run, and that distributions to owners have been productive (rather than focused on short-term manipulation of accounting earnings).[28]

We have found no universal constant for the best mix of investment and return of capital: Each company's investment set, capital structure, and opportunity costs are unique. Among the five potential uses of free cash flow, we believe all to be effective, although each may add more or less value at different companies, and at varying points in an economic cycle.

The portfolio management and analyst team at Epoch has considerable training, practical knowledge and market experience. But the investment world grows increasingly complex and gains velocity each year. In the final section of our book, we look at the role of technology in informing and expanding the investment world generally, and how Epoch has pushed an evolution in the firm's investment process through the infusion of technology.

Notes

1. Enrique Arzac, *Valuation for Mergers, Buyouts and Restructuring*, 2nd ed. (Hoboken, NJ: John Wiley & Sons, 2008), 8.

2. Together we call the latter three factors "Shareholder Yield." The notion of Shareholder Yield was covered in depth in our 2007 book *Free Cash Flow and Shareholder Yield: New Priorities for the Global Investor*, published by John Wiley & Sons.

3. John Maynard Keynes, *The General Theory of Employment, Interest and Money* (New York: Harcourt Brace Jovanivich, 1935), Book IV, Chapter 11.

4. Equal to $800 times a 10 percent cost of equity, plus $200 times a 5 percent cost of debt, divided by total liabilities and equity of $1,000.

5. The principles for this example are drawn from *Value: The Four Cornerstones of Corporate Finance*, 5th ed., by McKinsey & Company (Tim Koller, Richard Dobbs, and Bill Huyett), published in 2010 by Wiley Finance.

6. Liyu Zeng, "Examining Share Repurchasing and S&P Buyback Indices for the U.S. Market," S&P Dow Jones Indices LLP, January 2015.

7. William Priest, Eric Sappenfield, and Michael Welhoelter, "Dividends: Beautiful, and Sometimes Dangerous," Epoch Investment Partners White Paper, 2011. Available at: eipny.com/index.php/epoch_insights/papers/dividends_beautiful_and_sometimes_dangerous.

8. Michael Mauboussin, "Clear Thinking about Share Repurchase," Legg Mason Capital Management, 2006, 3.

9. S&P 500 Dividends and Payers, S&P Dow Jones Index Services, 2016. Accessed at: us.spindices.com/documents/additional-material/sp-500-dividends-payers.xls.

10. Robert J. Shiller, "Stock Market Data Used in *"Irrational Exuberance."* Princeton University Press, 2000, 2005, 2015, updated. Accessed at: www.econ.yale.edu/~shiller/data/ie_data.xls.

11. S&P 500 Dividends and Payers.

12. "S&P DJI: S&P 500 Q2 Buybacks Decline 8.7 Percent over Q1 2015, Up 13.2 Percent Year-Over-Year," Press release, S&P Dow Jones Indices, 2015.

13. S&P Dividend Aristocrats Fact Sheet, S&P Dow Jones Indices, 2016. Accessed at: us.spindices.com/indices/strategy/sp-500-dividend-aristocrats.

14. Robert Arnott and Cliffird Asness, "Surprise! Higher Dividends = Higher Earnings Growth," *Financial Analysts Journal,* Vol. 59, No. 1 (January/February 2003): 70–87.

15. Robert A. Guth and Scott Thurm, "Microsoft to Dole Out Its Cash Hoard," *The Wall Street Journal,* July 21, 2004. Accessed at: www.wsj.com/articles/sb109035431245368850.

16. Form 10-K for the fiscal year ended September 26, 2015, Apple Inc.

17. Maxwell Murphy. "Buybacks Up 9 Percent in 1Q, Will Drive EPS Growth," *The Wall Street Journal,* June 25 2015.

18. "S&P DJI."

19. William Priest, David Pearl, John Tobin, and Eric Sappenfield, "Dividends by Another Name," Epoch Investment Partners White Paper, 2015. Available at: www.eipny.com/index.php/epoch_insights/papers/dividends_by_another_name.

20. Liyu Zeng, "Examining Share Repurchasing and S&P Buyback Indices for the U.S. Market," S&P Dow Jones Indices LLP, January 2015.

21. Jeffrey Pontiff and Artezima Woodgate, "Share Issuance and Cross-Sectional Returns," *The Journal of Finance*, Vol. 63, No. 2 (April 2008). 921-945.

22. R. David McLean, Jeffrey Pontiff , Akiko Watanabe, "Share Issuance and Cross-Sectional Returns: International Evidence," *Accessed at:* http://ssrn.com/abstract=1008312

23. S&P 500 Buyback Index fact sheet, S&P Dow Jones Indices, 2016. Accessed at: us.spindices.com/indices/strategy/sp-500-buyback-index.

24. Chris Brightman, Vitali Kalesnik, and Mark Clements, "Are Buybacks an Oasis or a Mirage?" Research Affiliates White Paper, 2015.

Accessed at: www.researchaffiliates.com/Our percent20Ideas/ Insights/Fundamentals/Pages/385_Are_Buybacks_an_Oasis_ or_a_Mirage.aspx.

25. Franco Modgiliani and Merton Miller, "The Cost of Capital, Corporation Finance and the Theory of Investment," *The American Economic Review*, Vol. 48, No. 3 (June 1958). *Note:* In their initial formulation, Modigliani and Miller ignored the effect of the deductibility of interest payments from a company's taxes.

26. McKinsey & Company, Tim Koller, Marc Goedhart, and David Wessels, *Valuation: Measuring and Managing the Value of Companies,* 5th ed. (Hoboken, NJ: John Wiley & Sons, 2010), 509.

27. Priest, Sappenfield, and Welhoelter.

28. Priest, Pearl, Tobin, and Sappenfield.

PART III

Technology

In this section we look at the rapid evolution of information technology and innovation in general (Chapter 11); consider how investment managers have applied it over the past several decades (Chapter 12); discuss Epoch's own applications of technology where people and computers combine their efforts (Chapter 13 and 14); and offer a few ideas on how future interactions with information technology will further strengthen the investing process and the investment management business (Chapter 14). Epoch Investment Partners is well versed in the technological aspects of investing, and the firm and its people have published papers on such topics as trading costs,[1] a proprietary free cash flow screening model,[2] and rigorous portfolio construction techniques.[3]

Notes

1. Gilbert L. Beebower and William W. Priest Jr., "An Analysis of Transaction Costs in Equity Trading," presented at the Seminar on the Analysis of Security Prices, Center for Research in Security

Prices, Graduate School of Business, University of Chicago, November 3, 1978.

2. Kenneth N. Hightower, David Pearl, William W. Priest, and Michael Welhoelter, "Free Cash Flow Investing," Epoch Investment Partners White Paper, April 2011. Available at: www.eipny .com/index.php/epoch_insights/papers/free_cash_flow.

3. Jack L. Treynor, William L. Priest Jr., Lawrence Fisher, and Catherine A. Higgins, "Using Portfolio Composition to Estimate Risk," *Financial Analysts Journal,* Vol. 24, No. 5 (September/October 1968): 93–100.

CHAPTER 11

High-Speed Technology

We begin our discussion of investment and information technology with a personal story from Bill Priest. As a junior analyst in the late 1960s, my first assignment was to take a look at the railroad industry. Interesting things were happening: an industry consolidation of rail lines was underway, and a recent ruling allowing "fireman off" pointed to significant savings in labor costs. In the days of coal-powered steam locomotives, the fireman was an essential part of a train's crew, tending to the engine. When rail technology switched to diesel locomotives, however, many of the fireman's duties disappeared, but union rules required that the position be maintained, and the fireman was often an engineer in training. Ultimately, the position was eliminated—hence "fireman off"—reducing the team needed to run a train.

The most important part of the project was to understand what drove the demand for rail services—the linkages between economic activity and the revenues generated by the railroads. As a regulated business, the railroads published a plethora of data about themselves: the history of demand as measured by ton-miles (a unit of measure expressing one ton of goods carried one mile), as well as statistics on employment, labor costs, debt costs, capital consumption allowances, and other data that was seemingly useless. It was overwhelming.

One readily available clue to estimating ton-miles was a statistic called rail car loadings, but I judged it to be too uncertain and unreliable. I decided to build a stepwise regression program linking key elements of the economy to rail demand that could reliably estimate year-to-year changes in the industry's growth rate as measured in ton-miles.

The tools at my disposal were articles, papers, and books—particularly at the rich transportation library at Northwestern University—as well as a "state of the art" Smith Corona Marchant electromechanical calculator into which I loaded data by hand, drawn from charts and tables often prepared by hand as well. It took nearly 10 weeks to complete my analysis, the centerpiece of which was the regression equation. It showed, after many iterations with multiple variables, two important conclusions.

First, changes in aggregate railroad ton-miles could be explained by three macro factors: the Federal Reserve's index of industrial production, coal production, and grain shipments. The model's coefficient of determination (or r^2) was 0.97. Given those three variables, I could accurately explain and predict future unit growth for the railroad industry. Second, the data showed that the demand for rail services was essentially inelastic, and that the industry had unrecognized pricing power.

The point is not that I was a good analyst—I had a lot of help from the strength of the underlying data—but rather that the job took 10 weeks. Today, with data readily available online, fast computers, and spreadsheets loaded with regression programs, it could be done in a busy afternoon. That is the power of technology.

Starting in the 1950s, significant insights into the working of the stock market were being theorized by academics—many of whom have won Nobel Prizes. Harry Markowitz was one of the first, with a pioneering 1952 study of a novel way to view investment risk and return, and a framework for building efficient portfolios. In the early 1960s, building on Markowitz's ideas, the Capital Asset Pricing Model (CAPM) was first drawn up by academics William Sharpe and John Lintner, and developed further in the 1970s by Fischer Black.

The concurrent evolution of computer technology allowed these theories to be tested and refined and put to practical use. I worked on one of the first applications of these theoretical ideas with Jack Treynor, Lawrence Fisher, and Catherine Higgins, and our results were published in the *Financial Analysts Journal* in 1968[1] (the article is reprinted in Appendix A).

Our concept was a simple one. If an investor knew the risk parameters for individual stocks, he could estimate the risk character of a portfolio. To test this idea we examined all the common stocks held by a mutual fund, of which I was a co-manager, for a period of over two years. The price history of each stock was traced back as far as possible (40 years, in some cases).

We wrote:

From the price and dividend histories for the common stocks, we made running estimates of the risk parameters for each common stock held. Then, once a month for each month during the test period, we made an instantaneous estimate of the risk character of the mutual fund portfolio, based on its composition at the end of that month. Our estimate of the "market" risk for the portfolio enabled us to predict how rapidly the value of the fund would change as the market level fluctuated. Our estimate of "residual" risk for the fund gives an estimate of the amount by which the true market value of the fund will differ from our predictions.

The article demonstrates our early adoption of insights derived from the CAPM, but more to the point, it highlights the primitive state of the analytical tools then available. The sample size was small—just 133 stocks, covering a scant two years of a fund's history—and the research took four researchers two weeks. Today, one grad student could accomplish a much more robust and comprehensive study in a day or two.

Evolving information technology has allowed broader testing of financial theories, and resulted in the expansion of investment strategies managed by quantitative methods. According to eVestment, 16 percent of U.S. institutional managers follow investment processes they deem highly quantitative, and another 19 percent rely on methods are combinations of quantitative and fundamental approaches.

Information Technology: Three Relentless Forces

Computers were introduced into the business world in the 1950s and 1960s, and the first computers for personal use were developed in the late 1970s, allowing the Internet to see wide use starting around 1995. Today, information technology runs through every aspect of personal and business life, pretty much all around the world. (According to the Mobile Marketing Association Asia, of Earth's 6.8 billion people, 5.1 billion own a cell phone, while 4.2 billion own a toothbrush. It's hard to imagine, however, how they were able to measure those figures with any reliability.)[2]

How did we get to this advanced state, where everyone carries around the equivalent of a 1990s supercomputer? In their book, *The Second Machine Age*, Erik Brynjolfsson and Andrew McAfee, professors at the Massachusetts Institute of Technology, draw on a number of theories and observations about how technology will propel rapid change in the twenty-first century. They cite the interaction of three major forces in today's technology economy: relentless gains in the speed of computing, with similar decreases in its cost; massive digitization of the world's data; and recombinant technology that moves them both forward. And wrapped around these three forces is cloud computing, which accelerates and broadens their joint development, also at declining cost.[3]

Moore's Law

Computer technology has managed a stunning pace of growth in speed and power for 50 years—essentially doubling every two years, or less, with corresponding reductions in costs. This trajectory has been expressed in the form of Moore's Law.

"The original Moore's Law came out of an article I published in 1965," recalled computer pioneer Gordon Moore, at that time Director, Research and Development Laboratories, Fairchild Semiconductor, and later cofounder of Intel Corporation, in a 2005 interview. "This was the early days of the integrated circuit, [when] we were just learning to put a few components on a chip. I was given the chore of predicting what would happen in silicon components in the next 10 years, for the 35th anniversary edition of *Electronics* magazine."[4]

The main point, Moore said, was to get across the idea that electronics were going to become cheap. Fairchild's engineers had managed to put 30 transistors on one silicon chip, and were working out how to fit 60. Moore blindly extrapolated those two points out 10 years, and arrived at a forecast of 60,000 components per chip by 1975. "I had no idea this was going to be an accurate prediction but amazingly enough," Moore said, "we got nine [doublings] over the 10 years, [and] followed pretty well along the curve. And one of my friends, Dr. Carver Mead, a Professor at Cal Tech, dubbed this Moore's Law."[5]

Whether insightful or lucky, Gordon Moore's prediction 50 years ago of the path of the cost and performance of computing has held quite steady. Moore's Law was later refined, by Moore's Intel colleague David House, to posit that computer performance would double every 18 months.

At that 18-month pace, the computing power of an integrated circuit has doubled 33 times or so over the past 50 years. In *The Age of Spiritual Machines,* Ray Kurzweil illustrates the scale of the growth with an often-told story about the origins of chess: a clever fellow living in sixth-century India invented the game and, figuring there might be a market for it, traveled to the capital and offered it to the emperor. He was so pleased that he granted the inventor any reward he wished. "All I want is some rice to feed my family," he replied, and suggested that the chessboard determine the quantity—placing one grain on the first square, two on the second, and so on, doubling each time. The power of compound growth is such that 64 such doublings works out to more than 18 quintillion grains of rice in total—which would weigh more than 600 trillion pounds.[6] The emperor obviously could not make good on the reward, and in some versions of the story the inventor is executed for embarrassing the boss. (A more contemporary telling of the legend features an investment banker as the inventor, who asks for pennies on the chessboard instead of grains of rice.) Writing at the turn of the twenty-first century, Kurzweil says, "we are heading into the second half of the chessboard. And this is where things start to get interesting."[7]

Martin Ford, the author of *Rise of the Robots,* presents the acceleration of computers in terms of speed. Say a driver starts a road trip, and travels the first minute at five miles per hour, then doubles his speed the next minute, and so on. The first minute takes him just 440 feet, but in the fifth minute he would cover over a mile. Following Ford's reckoning of Moore's Law, in the 28th minute he's moving at 671 million miles per hour— quick enough to reach Mars in five minutes.[8]

Accordingly, the boundaries of computer technology are ever expanding in many directions: Google has developed a driverless car; IBM's Watson supercomputer has beaten human experts on *Jeopardy!*; and Google's AlphaGo computer program has beaten the human world champion of the complex game of Go. Even cheap smartphones can see, hear, and feel the environment around their owners. All of this has happened in just the last 10 years.

And yet, with 33 doublings of computer power since 1965, we have only reached the middle of the chessboard. Technologists regularly predict the repeal of Moore's Law, and Intel Corporation has acknowledged that in the past two transitions, the cycle has lengthened to about two and a half years.[9] Even at a slower pace, however, other enhancements to computers and software over the next few years should bring technological marvels that seem improbable and bizarre even today.

Massive Digitization

Brynjolfsson and McAfee's second force, massive digitization, combines the computing power arising from Moore's Law with the ease of gathering and manipulating information in digital formats. The nature and extent of the shift is pretty well known: social media, text messages, and e-mails dominate our personal and business communication; online banking has left branches empty; and digital formats have become acceptable for many formal documents (contracts, court filings, and the like). Journalism is increasingly digital, and in 2013 more than half of Americans (and nearly three quarters of those aged 18 to 29) called Internet publications their primary source for news.[10] Nearly two-thirds of North American Internet traffic in first half 2015 was occupied with entertainment data, with Netflix drawing 37 percent, and YouTube eating up another 17 percent.[11]

In scholarly endeavors, the Social Science Research Network offers digital versions of half a million academic papers, while in economics the Federal Reserve Bank of St. Louis provides free, downloadable time series on about 400,000 variables through its FRED database.

Less visible, but large and growing, is the "Internet of Things," where all sorts of devices in the physical world—livestock, parking meters, lighting and water systems, trucks and locomotives to name a few—are equipped with sensors for temperature, motion, acoustics, electric charges and moisture, and report data back to the ranchers, municipalities, utility companies, and logistics companies that own them. The Internet of Things has a personal dimension as well, through sensors for physical activity and health monitoring. Cisco Systems equips such networks, and has forecast such machine-to-machine connections in 2019 at three times the world's population.[12]

In order to meet all this demand, Cisco Systems forecasts total Internet traffic of 168,000 petabytes per month by 2019, representing compound growth of 23 percent annually from the 51,000 petabytes per month recorded in 2014.[13] (A petabyte equals one quadrillion bytes—said to be sufficient to map the DNA of everyone in the United States three times.)

In the financial world, commercial databases from sources such as Bloomberg, Thomson Reuters, and FactSet compile trading data in all the world's financial markets, as well as the details of issuers' financial statements and all sorts of economic data points. For years these information companies have fashioned newsfeeds that can be read and interpreted by automated trading systems, triggering instant trade reactions to data releases such as monthly employment reports and quarterly gross domestic product (GDP) data. Recently, the ability to interpret more complex news, such as Federal Reserve minutes, has also been built into automated trading systems.[14] The world is already massively digital, and bound to become more so.

Recombinant Technology

While Brynjolfsson and McAfee's forces of geometric growth in computer speed and mass digitization are fairly new, the third—the power of recombinant technologies—has been a feature of innovation and progress for many years, and perhaps ever since man started inventing things. Martin Weitzman, a professor of economics at Harvard University, authored an article on recombinant growth and innovation in 1998, writing: "Recombinant innovation refers to the way that old ideas can be refigured in new ways to make new ideas."[15] He followed the idea to the writings of economist Joseph Schumpeter in 1934, as well as to mathematician Henri Poincaré in 1908, and even traced it back to the nineteenth century, in the Edison System for domestic electric lighting, which Thomas Edison himself described as a combination of his then-novel "electric candle" with the established idea of a gas distribution system.

"[T]he true work of innovation is not coming up with something big and new, but instead recombining things that already exist. ... Each development becomes a building block for future innovations," say Brynjolfsson and McAfee. Thus, several strong ideas can result in something new that is different from and greater than the parts alone. One such recombination is the World Wide Web itself—an established data transmission network (TCP/IP), plus a language to organize the words and pictures (HTML), and a program to tie them together (browser software). "Progress doesn't run out," Brynjolfsson and McAfee say, "it accumulates."[16]

In his 1998 article, Martin Weitzman compared recombinant technologies to the techniques that move agriculture forward:

[S]uppose that we liken the development of innovations to the breeding of new plant varieties. The first step ... might be a systematic cross-pollination of parent material that had not previously been combined. The second step … [nurtures] the viable seedlings to the status of grown plants. The third step would insert the new mature plants into the population as fresh breeding stock that might allow the process to continue forward into the future.[17]

Increasingly powerful computers, mass digitization, and recombinant technologies reinforce each other, and greatly expand the prospects for innovation. Faster and cheaper computers make more data available, which can be analyzed more rapidly, in greater depth and across more disciplines. Digital communication allows for broader collaboration and more rapid development, thus increasing both the quality and quantity of candidates for innovation.

Racing with the Machine: The Human-Computer Interface

As information technology has become more capable and cheaper to use, it has taken on a greater role in the global economy, displacing conventional employment for millions of people in the process. In his analysis of the progress of robotics innovations, Martin Ford makes a bleak assessment, and not only for jobs based in physical work that can be automated— manufacturing, agriculture, and services businesses such as food service and general retail. He also contends that "[the] machines are coming for the high-wage, high-skill jobs as well."

Brynjolfsson and McAfee are more constructive, and emphasize the differences in aptitude that computers bring to the workplace versus those of humans. Coming up with new ideas is an area where computers are lacking, at least for the present: "Ideation in its many forms is an area today where humans have a comparative advantage over machines. … This is good news for human workers," they continue, "because thanks to our multiple senses, our frames are inherently broader than those of digital technologies."[18]

They contend that in professional services such as medicine and law, human skills of intuition and creativity will complement the speed and consistency of information technology. This combination they have named *racing with the machine*— a term that we believe aptly describes the opportunity facing investment managers, and have adopted for Epoch's initiative to leverage the skills of our analysts and portfolio managers.

Notes

1. Jack L. Treynor, William L. Priest Jr., Lawrence Fisher, and Catherine A. Higgins, "Using Portfolio Composition to Estimate Risk," *Financial Analysts Journal,* Vol. 24, No. 5 (September/October 1968): 93–100.

2. Jaime Turner and Jeanne Hopkins, *Go Mobile: Location-Based Marketing, Apps, Mobile Optimized Ad Campaigns, 2D Codes, and Other Mobile Strategies to Grow Your Business* (Hoboken, NJ: Wiley, 2012), xxi–xxii. See also Jamie Turner, "Are There REALLY More Mobile Phones than Toothbrushes?" 60 Second Marketer blog, October 18, 2011. Available at: 60secondmarketer.com/blog/2011/10/18/more-mobile-phones-than-toothbrushes/#disqus_thread.

3. Erik Brynjolfsson and Andrew McAfee, *The Second Machine Age: Work, Progress and Prosperity in a Time of Brilliant Technologies* (New York: W.W. Norton, 2014).

4. Intel Corporation, "Excerpts from 'A Conversation with Gordon Moore: Moore's Law,'" 2005.

5. Gordon E. Moore, "Cramming More Components onto Integrated Circuits," *Electronics*, Vol. 38, No. 8 (April 19, 1965). Accessed at: *web.eng.fiu.edu/npala/eee6397ex/gordon_moore_1965_article.pdf*

6. Ray Kurzweil, *The Age of Spiritual Machines: When Computers Exceed Human Intelligence* (New York: Penguin Books, 2000), 636–637.

7. Ibid.

8. Martin Ford, *Rise of the Robots: Technology and the Threat of a Jobless Future* (New York: Basic Books, 2015), xii.

9. Tim Bradshaw, ""Intel Chief Raises Doubts over Moore's Law," *Financial Times* (July 15, 2015). Available at: next.ft.com/content/36b722bc-2b49-11e5-8613-e7aedbb7bdb7.

10. Andrea Caumont, "12 Trends Shaping Digital News," Pew Research Center, October 16, 2013. Available at: www.pewresearch.org/fact-tank/2013/10/16/12-trends-shaping-digital-news/.

11. Global Internet Phenomena, Sandvine Incorporated LLC, December 2015.

12. Cisco Systems, "The Zettabyte Era: Trends and Analysis," May 2015.

13. Ibid.

14. Jeremy W. Peters, "From Reuters, Automatic Trading Linked to News Events," *The New York Times*, December 11, 2006. Available at: www.nytimes.com/2006/12/11/technology/11reuters.html.

15. Martin L. Weitzman, "Recombinant Growth," *The Quarterly Journal of Economics*, Vol. 113, No. 2 (May 1998): 331.

16. Brynjolfsson and McAfee, 81.

17. Martin L. Weitzman, May 1998.

18. Brynjolfsson and McAfee, 191–193.

CHAPTER 12

Technology in Investing

Economists and investment practitioners have been trying to make sense out of the financial markets for many years. Much of the early work, such as the dividend discount model and the Capital Asset Pricing Model (CAPM), was accomplished with little if any support from computers, and it continues to provide a foundation for current views of the world of markets. More recently, however, information technology has become an integral part of the academic study of investing, and is essential to investment managers in their analytical work and trading. In this chapter we consider a few high points of the role of technology in investment theory and practice. For readers interested in a detailed discussion of financial innovation, we recommend two authoritative books, both authored by the late market scholar Peter Bernstein: *Capital Ideas,*[1] published in 1992 and covering the work from 1900 through the 1980s; and *Capital Ideas Evolving,*[2] from 2007, which begins with the development of behavioral finance in the 1990s. For more general ideas on investing, we also point out Jack Treynor's *Treynor on Institutional Investing,*[3] and *A Bibliography of Finance,* edited by Richard Brealey and Helen Edwards.[4]

Information at Work

For much of the last century, financial analysis went begging for computational power. In Chapter 9, we noted the pioneering work in the 1930s of John Burr Williams, a Harvard-trained investment manager who devised a formula for determining the value of stocks from their expected future dividends (to then be compared to their prices, toward a decision on investment). Most of Williams's formulas are quite complex, requiring forecasts of companies' dividends far into the future (which in turn call for long-term forecasts of those companies' earnings and dividend policies, as well as projections of the economy, etc.). As a second and probably more crucial step, investors also have to arrive at a discount rate appropriate to the company in question for calculating the present value. Digital computers were still in the invention stage at that time,[5] so all the burdensome work had to be done by hand, or with the help of mechanical calculators. Williams submitted his doctoral thesis to the publishers Macmillan and McGraw-Hill in 1937, but both returned it, objecting to the algebra it contained. Harvard University Press eventually published it as *The Theory of Investment Value*, but forced Williams to pick up some of the printing costs.[6]

Williams's book *The Theory of Investment Value* is a classic, and the concept behind it is brilliant, but until computers became available to handle all the computational work, it's unlikely that many investors actually followed the Williams doctrine. The computational challenges also help to explain the reliance by so many investors, then and now, on shorthand measures such as price-earnings and price-to-book ratios.

Order from Chaos: Applying Scientific Frameworks

Before the waves of hypotheses and theories developed specifically for finance in the 1960s and 1970s, other early efforts to make sense of the stock market applied the understanding of the physical universe. An example is three papers authored by M. F. M. Osborne, a physicist at the U.S. Naval Laboratory, on Brownian motion in the stock market. (Brownian motion describes the random movements of particles in a fluid, as they collide with other particles.) His work appeared in the journal *Operations Research*, rather than the few journals of the day dedicated to theoretical finance.

Osborne conducted extensive research on the distribution of movements in stock prices, supplemented by the results of marathon coin tosses. To a reader without a background in physics and astronomy, the papers themselves are impenetrable. But a few of his observations are helpful: in a 1959 paper, he noted that prices of individual shares were correlated with the general market at about 0.70.[7] And in a 1962 effort, Osborne helpfully concluded:

> The picture of chaotic or Brownian motion does not imply that there can be no underlying rational structure [to the stock market]. We have tried to show that there is some underlying structure associated with what appears superficially to be the epitome of bedlam.[8]

In more familiar terms, imagine a table covered with dust. When a window is opened and the dust flies around the room, the resulting chaos looks like the erratic movement of prices in the stock market. Once the system is in action, the movements may appear to be unpredictable or random, but there is a definite cause.

Borrowing from the scientific world has not been limited to the theoretical side, however: brokers and asset managers have been hiring physicists since the 1980s, seeking to bring fresh insights of "econophysicists" to increasingly dynamic markets and financial instruments.[9]

Development of a rigorous theoretical framework custom-designed for investing had actually begun a few years earlier, with the pioneering 1952 work of Harry Markowitz, at the time a graduate student at the University of Chicago. (M. F. M. Osborne seems to have been unaware of these early efforts, as his early paper cited only books on astronomy and the behavior of gases.)[10]

Rather than examine the behavior of prices of individual securities, Markowitz considered the relationships among securities held in portfolios. He posited that investors should diversify, and that they should seek a maximum expected return. He offered a systematic solution for finding an efficient portfolio—one that provides the maximum output (return) for a given input (risk), or minimum input needed to achieve a given output.[11]

Markowitz's key insight was that portfolio risk was determined by the variance and covariance of the returns on securities—the extent to which the returns moved together—and not just the riskiness of the individual securities. His "mean-variance" framework provided a foundation for the formulation of the CAPM in the following decade (Chapter 4).

Computers to the Rescue

By themselves, Markowitz's creation of portfolio math and the CAPM research that followed required in-depth knowledge of statistics but were not computationally complex. However, implementing those ideas required extensive number crunching. "In order to follow Markowitz's prescriptions, investors must analyze every possible combination of assets, searching for the efficient portfolios among them," wrote Peter Bernstein.[12] For each security, investors need reliable estimates of expected return and variability. "But that is the easy part," Bernstein added: "They must then determine how each of the many securities under consideration will vary in relation to every one of the others. This is not something you can figure out on the back of an envelope."

Fortunately, Markowitz possessed skill with computers, in particular linear programming. The output of all this work—scrutinizing combinations of securities—was a set of efficient portfolios, which were ranked according to their expected return or riskiness, named by Markowitz as the "Efficient Frontier."

Computer technology was not a crucial part of the development of the theory of the CAPM, which dictated that all investors own, in some fashion, the market portfolio containing all available assets. However, it was essential to its implementation, in managing such a broad portfolio. Into the early 1960s, the use of computers had been limited to accounting, but in 1964 an ambitious mathematics student, John McQuown, set out to mechanize investing, or at least parts of it.[13] He found his way to Wells Fargo Bank in San Francisco, which granted him a generous budget, and McQuown was able to recruit a large and talented team—many of whom later became financial legends, among them Fischer Black, Myron Scholes, William Sharpe, Eugene Fama, Merton Miller, and even Harry Markowitz.

Three years of effort yielded no meaningful results, but Wells Fargo management was dedicated to the project, telling McQuown to start again from scratch. In 1971, six years in, a bank client—the pension fund of the luggage maker Samsonite—asked for a diversified portfolio of $6 million that spanned the entire stock market. The group developed a program for a portfolio that held all 1,500 or so issues listed on the New York Stock Exchange, in equal dollar amounts. The feature of equal weighting called for an enormous number of transactions to keep the positions at their proper weights, and the additional requirement of tracking all the transaction costs. But the fund worked, and forever changed the course of investing.

A Virtuous Circle

The expansion of information technology in the investing world resembles the general tech notion set out by Erik Brynjolfsson and Andrew McAfee: computers became cheaper, more powerful and easier to use; the increasing capacity and usefulness led to the amassing of digital financial data; and innovative ideas, both theoretical and practical, became easier to combine and cross-fertilize. Today, every corner and aspect of the markets is highly computerized: long-term equity investing, which is our main focus; as well as short-term trading and brokers' processing of orders; custody and financial recordkeeping; financial media; and the pricing of securities that ties them all together. Typically, new ideas have emerged on the investing side, leading to a demand for new types of data, and forcing the transaction processing and custody side to catch up.

Wells Fargo provides a second early example. Once the innovators at Wells Fargo had gotten started in index funds, in 1973 they devised a more practical approach to a passive portfolio, with a commingled fund that tracked the S&P 500 and weighted stocks by their market capitalization. This product had greater appeal to institutional investors, as the S&P 500 had become an accepted performance benchmark. The scheme of market weighting also required less frequent rebalancing, and thus incurred much lower transaction costs.

In a process that today seems prehistoric, orders for the initial transaction to establish the fund were hand-carried by messenger from Wells Fargo to the broker Salomon Brothers, who traded the portfolio over several days, charging then-standard commissions that amounted to about one percent of the value of the fund assets. Wells Fargo's trust accounting systems were overwhelmed by the sudden trade volumes, so that implementation of the new fund represented the start of a new era not only for investment management, but for trading and back office operations as well.[14]

Expansion of Index Funds

The large, liquid market segment of S&P 500 stocks in the 1970s was a logical starting place for index funds, but it failed to address the one-third or so of U.S. stock market capitalization in smaller companies. Index fund managers therefore established small-cap index funds. The large number of small-cap stocks, as well as their illiquidity, made owning all small companies infeasible and expensive, so the quantitative wrinkle of sampling was applied to select a portfolio that would generate a return representative of the small-cap universe.

"The development of the non-S&P 500 index fund [tracking a small cap stock index] placed active management performance at a greater disadvantage than before," wrote investment practitioner William Jahnke. The S&P 500 index fund would deliver strong returns in years favoring large cap stocks, while the non-S&P 500 index fund did well when small stocks were in favor; together, they presented tough competition for old-line active managers.[15] The development of index funds for international stock markets and bond markets was not far behind.[16] By 1990, assets in indexed funds were reported at $270 billion, one-third of which was managed by Wells Fargo.[17] After several business combinations, today that business resides with investment management giant BlackRock Corporation.

Betting Against the CAPM

While meeting the early demand from asset owners that were devotees of the CAPM, quantitative managers saw other opportunities in computer-managed strategies that defied the CAPM's assumptions of market efficiency and optimal market portfolios. Soon to follow were funds that took advantage of the many anomalies and inefficiencies observed by academics.

Robert Hagin, who migrated to the brokerage firm Kidder, Peabody & Co. from teaching at the Wharton School, explained the opportunity to the ICFA Continuing Education Series in 1984: "The era of the two-parameter CAPM is quietly drawing to a close. In its place we are seeing a newly emerging era—an era of multifactor valuation models."[18]

"Two things have happened to trigger disillusionment in the CAPM," Hagin continued: "First, there is the increased evidence of excess returns associated with factors other than beta. ... Specifically, evidence of 'abnormal' returns associated with factors such as a stock's P/E ratio, its size, and its yield has brought the CAPM into question. ..." As discussed in Chapter 5, these sorts of factors later emerged in the rehabilitation of the CAPM by Eugene Fama and Kenneth French in the 1990s.

The CAPM, Hagin conceded, had provided the valuable insight into how stocks were influenced by the market, but "with an increased understanding of the shortcomings of the CAPM, many practitioners are looking for relationships between returns and the classical attributes that we use to describe securities." Computer-assisted quantitative analysis allowed investors to scan the market widely for positive effects, and then test their reliability in producing outperformance over time and in different market conditions.

In 1979, Wells Fargo pioneered a Yield-Tilt Fund that started with a broad index, but tilted the portfolio toward those stocks offering higher dividend yields. This was the beginning of another branch of quantitative investing—"enhanced indexing." Rather than select its own portfolio from scratch, the methodology starts with the full index, and over- and underweights securities to emphasize the desired risk exposures. Wells Fargo's insight evolved into the highly successful Alpha Tilts products of Barclays Global Investors, which are today managed by the Scientific Active Equity group of BlackRock and claim managed assets of $60 billion.

Selecting stocks on fundamental factors—through computer intelligence—continues to be the core of quantitative management. It is the central idea behind systematic strategies investing in value, growth, momentum, and low volatility, which are widely available in the institutional world, and are accessible to individual investors as well, through mutual funds and exchange-traded funds. The current generation of "smart beta" strategies is refined from the early days of selecting stocks by computer, but also has fundamental thinking behind it.

Concurrent Developments

Quantitative active management received a significant, although indirect, boost from the 1974 passage of the Employee Retirement Income Security Act (ERISA). Prior to ERISA, investment managers had been bound by the "prudent man" rule, which required each holding in a portfolio to stand on its own merits, but the new law introduced the "portfolio standard" which considered securities holdings in a portfolio context. "With ERISA a defense could be made for owning a diversified portfolio of low P/E stocks, where many of the individual holdings would be considered imprudent investments by the earlier standard," wrote William Jahnke.[19] The institutional market's embrace of quantitative strategies lay years ahead, but the provisions of ERISA removed an important obstacle.

Another important advance to come out of the late 1970s was the commercialization of risk models and the portfolio optimizer, generally credited to Barr Rosenberg, who opened a firm consulting to investment managers in 1975, known as BARRA. "Before the optimizer, managers bought 30-stock portfolios and hoped they went up," says Laurence Siegel, a financial scholar and the Gary P. Brinson director of research at the CFA Institute Research Foundation. "But with Rosenberg's model, and other commercial optimizers, they had insights into

building portfolios that were mean-variance efficient. Optimizers allowed managers to keep track of more diverse portfolios,
tracking the overweights and underweights versus indices, and
the consequences of those decisions."[20]

Trained as an econometrician, Rosenberg was attuned to non-
systematic patterns and extreme observations in data. Echoing
the earlier views of M. F. M. Osborne, Rosenberg told author Peter
Bernstein:

> Randomness is not a mystery. Instead it is the poorly described
> aspects of a process. ... This sets me off from most people in
> finance who say that randomness is just what their model does
> not capture. ...[21]

His models aimed to look beyond how individual stocks
varied with the market, to predict risk that arose from industry
effects and the broader economy. "Economic events give rise
to ripples through the economy, but individual assets respond
according to their individual, or microeconomic characteristics,"
he explained, such as company size, cost structure, customer
groups, and record of growth. In a 2005 interview, Rosenberg
elaborated: "The thrust ... was to associate investment returns
with investment fundamentals; the goal was to model expected
returns, variances, and covariances in this manner. In other
words, to represent the mean-variance world in terms of the
influence of fundamentals."[22]

Acceptance of risk models by investment managers was
grudging at first, but their power and utility became obvious.
Today, they are universal in investment management, as well
as with investment consultants and asset owners, who apply
them to judging the individual performance of asset managers
as well as asset managers in combination. In 1985, Barr Rosenberg went into competition with his risk model clients, and

opened Rosenberg Institutional Equity Management, a quantitative management firm. (In 2010 Rosenberg's firm encountered regulatory challenges, forcing him to leave the investment industry.)

The Spread of Quant

Quantitative management grew in several directions. Laurence Siegel offers an evolutionary description: "The image I think of is speciation—it started with one organism, and pretty soon you had all these different animals and plants competing with each other in the garden. A few survive." Early on, the brokerage firms led the quant effort, Siegel says, because they could afford to pay high salaries to large teams. But the buy side was interested as well, both at large firms and smaller specialists. Clusters of quant activity sprung up around the financial academic centers of Boston and Chicago, as well as the West Coast and New York.

William Jahnke, in 1990, saw the evolution differently:

> The innovation in the use of computers to manage active investment strategies has come for the most part from new entrants in the business without large established interests. This is true even within the established organizations that have permitted quantitative investment management to develop and coexist. . . .[23]

Computing and Data, Neck and Neck

The evolution of the data side of finance has been just as impressive and important as trading and investing. One crucial, early resource was the Center for Research in Securities Prices at the University of Chicago's Booth School of Business. The university had collected prices and dividends on stocks listed on the New York Stock Exchange since 1926, but in 1959 a $300,000 grant from the brokerage firm then known as Merrill, Lynch, Pierce, Fenner & Smith funded computerization of the database—a boon to academics and investment practitioners, greatly increasing the accuracy and scope of their research.[24]

In 1981 a company called Innovative Market Systems opened its doors, providing pricing services for the inscrutable fixed income markets. By 1983 the firm had attracted $30 million of financing from Merrill Lynch, and in 1986 was renamed Bloomberg LP after one of the founding partners. The Bloomberg terminal is now ubiquitous in the financial world, and provides not only pricing data on all the world's markets, but high-powered analysis as well, and has become a superhighway for financial and conventional news and communication among securities traders and their clients.

At about the same time arrived what is probably the biggest advance in finance, and for that matter any other field that relies on organized data—the electronic spreadsheet. VisiCalc (for visible calculator) was introduced in 1978, and improved upon by Lotus 1-2-3, which added graphing and database functions. Other contenders such as Symphony and Quattro Pro added new and important features, but all were eventually trumped by Microsoft Excel, which has evolved to a very powerful and versatile state, and today sees universal applications to all sorts of financial tasks.[25]

The expanding digitization of data has offered astute traders and investors important, if fleeting information advantages. One case is analysts' estimates of companies' earnings per share—a crucial input to valuation models for both fundamental and quantitative investors. Plenty of individual estimates were available, but discerning any useful trends would involve gathering large samples from many brokerage firms, and tracking the data and trends by hand. But starting in the mid-1970s, Lynch,

Jones & Ryan, an innovative New York brokerage firm, began collecting earnings estimates in scale, and offered monthly summaries, on computer tapes, to institutional investor clients in a service known as I/B/E/S.

Available so broadly and quickly, earnings estimate revisions became an entirely new sort of information, and emitted a very strong—although short-term—signal that generated considerable excess returns. Some investors were so eager to plug each month's new data into their models that rather than wait a day for delivery of the fresh tapes, they would travel to downtown Manhattan and jostle for position at Lynch, Jones & Ryan's mailroom. Over time competing firms offered similar services and more rapid delivery, as well as consulting services interpreting trends, so that both the data and revision-based strategies became a standard ingredient for many investment firms' offerings. Momentum in earnings estimates is still closely followed, and still works as a quantitative factor, but its power has diminished over time as more investors have refined their analyses.

Big Data—Beyond Bloomberg

The entire investment community has benefited from massive digitization—the digital compilation and delivery of data on the global economy, markets, and company financials. Through the conduit of the Internet, information of all sorts is available more rapidly, much of it free of charge. While the main use of technology in the 1970s and 1980s was the development of quantitative management techniques, today's investors don't have to be serious quants.

The nature and quality of information has changed as well. Not only is economic information widely and instantly reported from conventional sources, the world offers real-time feedback, such as indexes of economic surprise compiled by Citibank and HSBC, measuring daily the differences between actual reports on various data points and economists' expectations. Adobe Systems now publishes several indexes on economic activity— although limited to the digital world—for prices of electronics and groceries, as well as trends in housing and employment, drawn from an extensive flow of online transactions.[26] And since July 2014, the Atlanta Federal Reserve Bank has issued what it terms a "nowcast" of U.S. gross domestic product (GDP) growth, named GDPNow, updated five or six times each month. Forecasts are refreshed after successive releases of significant U.S. economic data such as personal income, purchasing managers indexes, retail trade, and home sales.[27]

With so much information available to so many, and so quickly, it might seem that any information advantage from public sources may have been eroded. However, some investment managers see new promise in two areas of current development: big data and artificial intelligence. Much ink has been spilled on the topic of investment applications, discussing the potential for systems in trading, regulatory compliance and reporting, asset custody, and risk management, as well as our focus—the investment management function. Proponents describe the "Four Vs" of big data: volume, velocity, variety and veracity.

As it pertains to portfolio management, we define big data as assembling systems to gather and interpret the massive amounts of information available that might offer insight on securities prices—conventional information such as analysts' research reports, corporate news and financial statements, management conference calls, and media comments. Brokerage firms issue an average of 4,000 research reports per day, in 53 languages, according to a September 2015 paper from the Scientific Active Equity Group of BlackRock Corporation. They observe that while humans can make better sense of the messages in such research, they can't possibly look through it all, making advanced text analysis a requirement for managers of global portfolios hoping to stay ahead.

Big data relevant to securities prices also extends to granular, less organized, real-time information—postings to Facebook, Twitter, and other social media that could hold breaking information on consumer preferences and reactions. Motivated by academic research that links employee satisfaction to superior share performance, BlackRock reports it has devised an automated system that informs stock selection by seeking out employee sentiment on particular companies from job search web sites and social media.[28] We can envision similar systems tailored to measure economic developments and sentiment at the level of industries and companies as well.

Goldman Sachs has posited a highly nuanced opportunity to exploit research analysts' changes in earnings estimates, by anticipating revisions before the fact through close interpretation of the language in their reports. "[I]nvestment research analysts may sometimes be reluctant to raise or lower a price target or rating too rapidly," the firm writes: "Analysts may instead opt to reflect new views incrementally, by changing the tone and view of the text they write in their reports. ... [I]dentifying an analyst's evolving views prior to the release of higher ratings potentially can provide investors advantages in the decision to buy or sell a stock." That is, analysts tend to telegraph their punches, and observant investors may be able to benefit.

Goldman also cites the tactic of looking for unintuitive relationships in the share behavior of companies in disparate industries, based on the impact of influences such as oil prices, changing weather, or new regulations: "[These examples entail] the linkage of data which cannot be downloaded from standard market-data terminals."[29]

Investment managers are understandably guarded about their views and efforts on big data: it's a new area with an uncertain and far-off payday. From the few public reports, early adopters of big data techniques have been hedge funds, especially those with a quantitative bent (and large tech budgets). Traditional asset managers have been slower to move. At Epoch, we see significant potential in big data, and are researching the topic with some of the many consultants that have sprung up.

One project that is particularly interesting to us, although still aspirational, is a more granular analysis of the stocks we select for our portfolios. Traditional analytics have focused only on the securities that portfolio managers have purchased, and compared the return of that group to the total return of a benchmark for a quarter or year. We believe there is tremendous insight to be gained from more thorough analyses—a sort of Moneyball for portfolio managers and research analysts. (The practice started in baseball, conducted by managers diligently gathering and analyzing each at bat, run, hit, and RBI, through a science called Moneyball. It's more properly known as sabermetrics, and the acknowledged founder is Bill James, who in 1974 established the statistical analysis committee of the Society for American Baseball Research, along with Pete Palmer and Dick Cramer.)

Ultimately, our goal is to reckon not only our "errors of commission"—our results on the securities purchased—but also our "errors of omission"—the record on those that we should have bought but did not. Likewise, for our research analysts, a system can be devised to rigorously evaluate the choices of stocks recommended or discarded, which will enable us to better focus their coverage.

Big data takes investment research in a new direction—compiling thousands or millions of transactions, consumer opinions, and weather observations in real time. And it's available now, in various forms of development. Individual investors can access a rough-and-ready source of new data, for free, from Google Trends, and plot the prices of individual stocks against the frequency of various searches (such as "durable goods," "auto sales," or "mobile and wireless").

Artificial Intelligence

The last technological topic we consider represents a quantum leap for investing and technology—computers that can guide themselves and learn from the experience, or artificial intelligence (AI). The notion of computers that can operate outside preset programs and think on their own has been around for a long time. (Depending on the source, artificial intelligence may reach back to myths of ancient Greece, Frankenstein's monster (1818), or the Babbage difference engine (1822).) A web site dedicated to computer pioneer Alan Turing presents a 22-page paper, written in 1948 but not published, titled "Intelligent Machinery"—laying out principles resembling today's conception of AI, and discussing how the various computing machines available at the time measured up to the challenge.[30] Current efforts at AI have received plenty of attention through their accomplishments beating the best human opponents at several sorts of games, but while complex, they operate in environments that are defined and relatively well controlled. They're not subject to constant bombardment by new information such as China's purchasing manager index, or a quick turn in the price of crude oil. What role does AI have in investment management?

For Epoch the development and implementation of such systems are well beyond our technical capabilities at this time, but we are interested observers nevertheless. The major AI proponents as of early 2016 seem to be large and technically inclined asset managers, in particular hedge funds. That is what press reports say, at least: it's likely that most firms working on AI are not willing to share their involvement, for fear of losing whatever proprietary edge the effort can produce.

The interest that has been reported is remarkable, however. Point72 Asset Management, a Connecticut-based hedge fund manager, is said to have hired a team of 30 in 2015 (although, as described by Bloomberg, their objective seems more oriented to big data than AI). Bridgewater Associates, currently the world's largest hedge fund manager, in 2012 hired David Ferrucci, who led the team of engineers at IBM Corporation who developed the *Jeopardy!*-winning Watson supercomputer.[31] In early 2016 the firm also hired as president Jon Rubinstein, said to be the primary developer of Apple Inc.'s innovative iPod music player.

"[T]he human mind has not become any better than it was 100 years ago, and it's very hard for someone using traditional methods to juggle all the information of the global economy in their head," said David Siegel, co-head of Two Sigma, another leading computer-powered manager, quoted in the *Financial Times*. "Eventually the time will come that no human investment manager will be able to beat the computer.[32]

At Epoch, we disagree, and our money is on the human-computer combination: *racing with the machine*.

Notes

1. Peter L. Bernstein, *Capital Ideas: The Improbable Origins of Modern Wall Street* (New York: The Free Press, 1992).
2. Peter L. Bernstein, *Capital Ideas Evolving* (Hoboken, NJ: John Wiley & Sons, 2007).
3. Jack L. Treynor, *Treynor on Institutional Investing* (Hoboken, NJ: John Wiley & Sons, 2007).
4. Richard A. Brealey and Helen Edwards, eds. *A Bibliography of Finance* (Cambridge, MA: MIT Press, 1990).
5. "History of Computing," Iowa State University College of Engineering. Available at: www.ece.iastate.edu/the-department/history/history-of-computing/.
6. Bernstein, *Capital Ideas*, 151.

7. M. F. M Osborne, "Brownian Motion in the Stock Market," *Operations Research* (March-April 1959): 170.
8. Ibid.
9. Stephen Foley, "Physicists and the Financial Markets," *FT Magazine* (October 18, 2013). Accessed at: https://next.ft.com/content/8461f5e6-35f5-11e3-952b-00144feab7de
10. Bernstein, *Capital Ideas*, 140.
11. Ibid., 53.
12. Ibid., 57.
13. Kate Ancell, "The Origin of the First Index Fund," University of Chicago Booth School of Business, Available at: research .chicagobooth.edu/fama-miller/docs/the-origin-of-the-first-index-fund.pdf.
14. William W. Jahnke, "The Development of Structure Portfolio Management: A Contextual View," in *Quantitative International Investing: A Handbook of Analytical and Methodological Techniques and Strategies*, Brian Bruce, ed. (New York: McGraw-Hill, 1990), 160–161.
15. Jahnke, 169.
16. Bernstein, *Capital Ideas Evolving,* 128.
17. Bernstein, *Capital Ideas*, 249.
18. Robert Hagin, "Quantitative Routes to Better Security Selection," ICFA Continuing Education Series, 1984.
19. Jahnke, 169.
20. Laurence Siegel, personal interview, April 2016.
21. Bernstein, *Capital Ideas*, 249.
22. "From Concept to Function: Converting Market Theories into Practical Investment Tools, Discussion with Barr Rosenberg, PhD," *The Journal of Investment Consulting*, Vol. 7, No. 3 (Winter 2005–2006). Available at: www.imca.org.
23. Jahnke, 169.
24. "CRSP Reaches 90-Year Milestone," Center for Research in Securities Prices, University of Chicago Booth School of Business. Available at: www.crsp.com/crsp-reaches-90-year-milestone.

25. D. J. Power, "A Brief History of Spreadsheets." Available at: www
    .cs.umd.edu/class/spring2002/cmsc434-0101/MUIseum/applica-
    tions/spreadsheethistory1.html.

26. Adobe Systems, Inc. "New Digital Price Index by Adobe Uses
    Fisher Ideal Price Index for Highly Accurate Inflation Measure-
    ment," Press release, March 16, 2016. Available at: www.adobe.
    com/news-room/pressreleases/201603/031616AdobeDigitalEco
    nomyProjectLaunch2016.html.

27. Federal Reserve Bank of Atlanta Center for Quantitative Eco-
    nomic Research. "GDPNow." Available at: www.frbatlanta.org/
    cqer/research/gdpnow.aspx?panel=2.

28. BlackRock Corporation, "The Evolution of Active Investment:
    Finding Big Alpha in Big Data," September 2015.

29. Goldman Sachs Asset Management, "The Data Revolution,"
    2015. Available at: assetmanagement.gs.com/content/gsam/us/
    en/advisors/market-insights/gsam-insights/2015/the-data-
    revolution.html.

30. Alan Turing. "Intelligent Machinery," National Physical Laboratory,
    1948. Available at: www.alanturing.net/turing_archive/archive/l/
    l32/l32.php.

31. Imone Foxman, "Cohen's Point72 Hires 30 People for Big Data
    Investing," Bloomberg LP, March 10 2015. Available at: www
    .bloomberg.com/news/articles/2015-03-10/cohen-s-firm-said-to-
    hire-30-seeking-edge-in-public-data.

32. Robin Wigglesworth, "Fintech: Search for a Super-algo," *Finan-
    cial Times* (January 20, 2016). Available at: www.ft.com/intl/cms/
    s/0/5eb91614-bee5-11e5-846f-79b0e3d20eaf.html#axzz45dJoiqX6.

CHAPTER 13

The Epoch Core Model

Epoch manages a variety of equity strategies, differing by the markets where they invest (in the United States, outside it, or globally) and by the size of companies they target. What they all have in common, however, is the firm's active investment philosophy detailed earlier, which selects companies on their ability to generate free cash flow, and allocate that capital wisely.

Considerable effort goes in to the decision to add a stock to the Epoch portfolios. A part of the process is a thorough understanding of the drivers of each company's business, and forecasts of what is likely for the future. Every sector has its own set of economics, and within sectors, companies' business models can vary widely. Each of Epoch's fundamental research analysts is responsible for maintaining complete financial models for 100 or so companies per sector—a workload that rapidly becomes voluminous.

The work is also complex: the evaluation of companies is highly subjective and requires detailed handwork, so to speak, on the part of our analysts. In some cases companies' free cash flow is revealed with simple adjustments to the financial statements they present, while in others more subjective interpretation is necessary. For instance, in their deployment of capital investment some companies pursue a higher proportion of internal opportunities in existing business lines while others grow through acquisitions. Putting them all on an equal footing requires the insights of experienced analysts. At times the analysis of the finances has to be tempered by interpretations of the message coming from companies' managements.

Fortunately, some of the initial steps of identifying suitable companies can be handed off to information technology. One such application is the Epoch Core Model, developed in 2007, and since enhanced with minor refinements. It's a powerful quantitative tool that "casts a wide net," sorting through and ranking thousands of stocks across global markets and industries, examining a group of factors focused on the sources and uses of cash flow (both historical and forecast) as well as company quality.

Factors in the Epoch Core Model

The Epoch Core Model does not apply in-depth knowledge of companies' business models or the industries they operate in. Rather, it looks through financial statements to identify and rank a large number of companies with a preliminary set of desired financial and valuation characteristics. By ranking individual companies against their peer groups—rather than setting the bar at absolute levels of statistics—the model remains flexible and adaptable to a range of market environments. The primary factors in Epoch's analysis are described in the following pages.

Historical Free Cash Flow Yield

The starting point of the Epoch Core Model, and receiving a significant weight in the rankings of companies, is historical free cash flow yield. Free cash flow is defined as a company's cash flow from operations—cash available for distribution to shareholders after all planned capital expenditures and the payment of all cash taxes.[1] Free cash flow is therefore the amount of cash available for immediate, discretionary and strategic use. For a statistic in ranking companies, the model uses a company's free cash flow generated over the latest 12 months as a percentage of the market value of its equity.

In addition to the quantity of free cash flow a company generates, the Epoch Core Model considers the behavior of free cash flow through time. In analyzing the past, we explicitly consider stability and growth, taking into account trends over the previous five years.

Forward-Looking Free Cash Flow

Free cash flow of the future is equally important, and the model includes several crucial variables looking at the likelihood of sustained growth. Based on the consensus estimates of sell-side industry analysts, the model looks at the trend of recent changes in the median estimated earnings per share for the coming year. It also includes the forecast year-ahead earnings yield, that is, a company's median forecast earnings per share divided by its price. In addition, the model ranks stocks on forecasts of their dividend yields and dividend payout ratios.

In view of our strong opinions on the low reliability of accounting-based measures (Chapter 10), how do we justify incorporating earnings per share into the Epoch Core Model? First, as starting points, we assume, reasonably in our view, that Wall Street analysts are forecasting "true" earnings uncontaminated by accruals, and that depreciation expense and capital expenditures can be considered roughly equal. Thus, what we target is the expected change in earnings, rather than the absolute levels; this growth, combined with our earnings quality factor, serves as a proxy for improving free cash flow.

Second, as a practical matter, some Wall Street analysts—although not all—forecast free cash flow, and among those who do, their methods are not consistent. As a result comprehensive forecasts of cash flow are not available, while reasonably well-informed forecasts of earnings are (and we rely on those instead). Finally, before further fundamental analysis is conducted on candidates, analysts check the data for reliability.

Leverage

The Epoch Core Model measures financial leverage by comparing a company's net debt to its total assets. Our rationale is simple and classic: companies with large debt loads are committed to pay out cash flow in higher fixed interest charges, which can be burdensome in difficult economic times when the business is under pressure and cash flow is tight. Additionally, firms that rely heavily on the debt markets have less flexibility in their financing, and are viewed by investors as more risky (often for good reason). Borrowed money usually has to be replaced at some point, and during hard times, a company with a heavy debt load may be able to refinance only at high interest rates (although for the past several years, corporations have had a rather easy time of raising and replacing debt capital). In the extreme, lenders can require companies to apply all available cash to meeting the debt, and suspend dividend payments to shareholders.

Accruals and Earnings Quality

In Chapter 10 we contrasted the approaches to measuring companies' economic profits derived by accountants with the cash flow approach of investors, highlighting the misleading results that can arise from conventional accounting principles, particularly through accruals. Accordingly, a company's accruals inform the Epoch Core Model in two respects. The first deducts the portion of noncash accrual-based earnings to arrive at free cash flow from operations, serving to penalize those firms with less sustainable earnings, and reward those with higher earnings quality.

The second interprets the extent of accruals as a measure of quality. The model looks at operating accruals that are short term in nature, which tend to result in growth in noncash working capital. Thus, the model measures changes in accruals as a percentage of total assets, and a higher ratio of accruals to assets results in a lower score in the model.

The Epoch Core Model also considers growth in firms' long-term operating assets, such as property, plant and equipment, as well as capitalized software development costs. Researchers have noted a negative relationship between companies' accumulations of long-term assets and earnings quality: "We find that, after controlling for current profitability, both components of growth in net operating assets—accruals and growth in long-term net operating assets—have equivalent negative associations with one-year-ahead return on assets," wrote Patricia Fairfield, Scott Whisenant, and Teri Lombardi Yohn, of Georgetown University and the University of Houston, in 2001, adding: "We also find that, after controlling for current profitability, the market appears to equivalently overvalue accruals and growth in long-term net operating assets. ...."[2] This sort of build-up was termed "balance sheet bloat" by David Hirshleifer et al. of Ohio State University in 2004.[3]

In Chapter 8 we mentioned the important early research on accruals in 1996 by Richard Sloan of the University of California, Berkeley. More recently, Sloan, working with Berkeley colleagues Patricia Dechow and Natalya Khimich, noted that other researchers had found that starting in 2000, the potency of accruals as a strategy factor had started to decline. But they also cited good news in their fresh conclusions:

> What Sloan did [in 1996] is very easy to copy, so it stands to reason that investors caught on to it and arbitraged it away. But his results serve to highlight the potential gains from more thorough fundamental analysis that can distinguish between 'bad' accruals that will reverse and 'good' accruals that correctly anticipate future benefits. ... Thorough fundamental analysis involves getting to know a firm and conducting a detailed evaluation of its financial statements. Such analysis, properly conducted, will never go out of style and is essential for keeping securities markets reasonably efficient.[4]

Results of the Epoch Core Model

Our goal for the Epoch Core Model was not to assemble a typical quantitative "black box" that mines market and company data to identify a long list of factors associated with positive returns. Instead, we wanted to develop a model that expressed and reinforced, in quantitative terms, the economic logic behind Epoch's fundamental research—seeking out companies earning strong free cash flow, and headed by capable management. Moreover, we desired a model made up of relatively few factors, thinking that the simplest techniques are often the most effective.

We like to think of Epoch's combined fundamental and quantitative investment process as being a mile wide, and a mile deep. Breadth comes from the model's ability to rapidly sort through thousands of companies, while depth is achieved by the knowledge of Epoch's research analysts on the dynamics of industries and companies.

One benefit from the hybrid process is a significant increase in productivity of our analysts, through identifying candidate companies in advance. (In a sense, the Epoch Core Model serves as a sort of *Consumer Reports*, prequalifying individual stocks from the entire market.) The combined approach also has pointed out blind spots in research coverage—highlighting businesses which fit Epoch's investment philosophy, but had been overlooked by our analysts (and in the cases of some smaller-cap and non-U.S. stocks, overlooked by sell-side analysts and other institutional investors as well).

Another benefit is the creation of an analytical "sweet spot" from combining the quantitative and fundamental insights, as our analysts leverage the capabilities of the Epoch Core Model. The model's screens have succeeded over time in finding winning stocks, so the companies it identifies have a higher-than-average probability of being winners from the start. In turn, those cases that are identified as attractive both by the model and Epoch's research analysts stand an even higher chance of outperformance.

In addition to providing an initial screen of stocks across many markets and industries—casting a wide net—sometimes the model is called upon to refine lists of stocks that our portfolio managers have already identified on fundamental grounds. For example, given an expectation of a strong rebound in housing construction in the United States, the model could be applied to a group of companies that are favorably exposed, resulting in better-informed portfolio choices from those earning the highest model scores. Finally, the discipline of constantly monitoring stocks through the model's lens can also bring to light dislocations within an industry that lead to high-quality companies becoming temporarily undervalued.

All these advantages square with the Fundamental Law of Active Management, an idea posited by investment practitioner Richard Grinold in 1989, relating a manager's outperformance to the level of his skill at selecting securities and the breadth of his strategy. As Grinold put it: "You can think of [breadth] as how often you play (number of times a year) and [skill] as

a measure of how well you play."[5] The Epoch Core Model is
a tool for increasing both. It raises analysts' skill through better and more consistent investment processes, but importantly,
the model also increases breadth by increasing the number of
stocks an analyst can research—without diminishing the ability
to apply skill by having to reduce the time spent researching
each idea.

The effort has worked. Over a long investment horizon, the
Epoch Core Model has consistently identified sets of stocks that
fit our fundamental investment criteria. Stocks that rank highly
have earned better returns than those which show less favorably.
More important, portfolios of high-scoring stocks have tended
to outperform market indices over long periods. Figure 13.1
shows the Epoch Core Model's ranking of stocks over time:
including backtests from 2002 through taking the model live in
2007, the model's first and second quintiles (the highest scoring

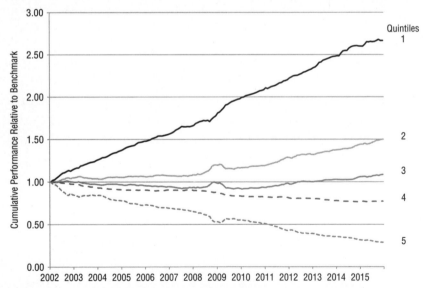

FIGURE 13.1   Cumulative Relative Return of the Epoch Core Model, January 2002–
November 2015

Source: Epoch Investment Partners

securities) have outperformed the fourth and fifth quintiles (the lowest scoring).

Notes

1. Enrique Arzac. *Valuations for Mergers, Buyouts and Restucturing*, 2nd ed. (Hoboken, NJ: John Wiley & Sons, 2008), 8.
2. Patricia M. Fairfield, Scott Whisenant, and Teri Lombardi Yohn, "Accrued Earnings and Growth: Implications for Earnings Persistence and Market Mispricing," working paper, 2001.
3. David Hirshleifer, Kewei Hou, Siew Hong Teoh, and Yinglei Zhang, "Do Investors Overvalue Firms with Bloated Balance Sheets?," *Journal of Accounting and Economics*, Vol. 38, No. 1 (December 2004): 297–331.
4. Patricia M. Dechow, Natalya V. Khimich, and Richard G. Sloan, "The Accrual Anomaly," Working Paper, March 2011. Available at: ssrn.com/abstract=1793364.
5. Richard C. Grinold, "The Fundamental Law of Active Management," *Journal of Portfolio Management*, Vol. 15, No. 3 (Spring 1989): 30–37.

CHAPTER 14

Racing with the Machine

Investing Is Too Important for Robots Alone

We noted in Chapter 8 that among active equity managers in the United States, about one-sixth considered their investment styles to be heavily quantitative—that is, selecting securities for their portfolios from preset rules based on company and market history, typically carried out by computers screening thousands of stocks. Quantitative strategies have delivered solid returns, given the right market climate: as a general rule, quant approaches outperform fundamental managers in market regimes of low to moderate volatility in returns, and, most important, when the future turns out to be similar to the past.

But in more dynamic markets, such as the weakness following the tech bubble (1999 through 2001) and surrounding the global financial crisis (2007 through 2009), fundamental strategies tend to see better relative results.[1] That advantage stands to reason, as fundamental portfolio managers may have greater flexibility in reacting to turns in the market, as well as anticipating market moves with informed forecasts.

Thus, the two contrasting methodologies develop insights that complement each other, and Epoch believes that combining them can result in better-informed judgments. The holy grail of investing may be the realization that there is no holy grail.

As a result, Epoch's investment strategies feature varying mixes of fundamental and quantitative methodologies. Most of our strategies lean more heavily on fundamental analysis. This approach is akin to examining a large haystack—the global stock markets—in search of a few needles. In other words, the analysts and portfolio managers focus their attention on finding stocks to include in the portfolio, each of which may be attractive for a different reason. But in our more quantitatively driven strategies, the process is reversed: we are essentially trying to filter out the needles and buy the haystack. We develop criteria for determining what makes a stock attractive, and by screening companies' financial and market data we produce a group of stocks that all have these favorable characteristics (i.e., the haystack). At that point, research analysts and portfolio managers scrutinize the individual names and decide which names to exclude (i.e., the needles)—due to changing circumstances at the company, or misleading data that gives a false positive reading. In Epoch's Shareholder Yield strategies, for example, the quantitative tools select candidate companies demonstrating the desired levels of cash dividends, share repurchases, debt buybacks, and growth in cash flow, after which the analysts and portfolio managers use their knowledge of the companies and their judgment to decide whether those distributions to owners are sustainable.

Racing with the Machine

While Epoch's investment process has always relied on information technology, since early 2015 we have formalized and expanded its role into an initiative we call *racing with the machine* (a phrase borrowed from Brynjolfsson and McAfee's book *The Second Machine Age*). This program is still in its early days, but our aim is to assemble a series of new techniques, with the goal of increasing our efficiency as an investing organization and improving the risk-adjusted performance of our strategies. In Epoch's case, *racing with the machine* is not giving over decision making to software algorithms, but instead recognizing the strengths of information technology and how it can inform the investment decision-making process. We want the machine to serve the analyst—not the other way around.

Just as with artificial intelligence, the potential of the man-machine combination has been an ambition of computer scientists since the early days. A 1960 paper on cooperation between humans and computers authored by J. C. R. Licklider held that:

> The main aims are 1) to let computers facilitate formulative thinking as they now facilitate the solution of formulated problems, and 2) to enable men and computers to cooperate in making decisions and controlling complex situations without inflexible dependence on predetermined programs.[2]

Licklider predicted that the "anticipated symbiotic partnership" would entail humans doing the thinking—establishing goals and hypotheses, and evaluating criteria and results—and computers executing tasks that could be automated. As a result of this cooperation, the machines would provide data to support human insight and decision making.

For Epoch, one tactic will be refining our existing tools–in particular the Epoch Core Model, increasing its flexibility to accommodate the special characteristics of industries, and to incorporate a broader range of market-based signals. Another is to leverage the work of our research analysts with tools for making better predictions, and to help them avoid cognitive biases.

We also aim to adapt big data techniques that read trends in the financial markets, corporate information, and other real-time data sources. Epoch does not invest for the short term—no trading algorithms for us—and we do not intend to increase our trading frequency simply because new data is available. But even for long-term investors, it's essential to pay attention to what's happening in the short term, because that is when the inefficiencies arise—when investors under- or overreact suddenly to corporate, economic or market events. A new generation of analytical tools should help uncover them.

Seeking High Return on Capital

In a more recent application, Epoch has developed and built a set of strategies that might not have been possible—and certainly not practical—without *the machine*—the combination of mass digitization of financial data and rapid computing power. (We have named the central idea Capital Reinvestment Opportunities.) However, they are not conventional quantitative models, or looking for new ephemeral bits of market information: instead, they apply the capital allocation concepts discussed in Chapter 10, backed by academic and market research. While our Shareholder Yield strategies seek out companies making the right distributions to businesses' owners, this new branch of strategies addresses the earlier stages of the capital allocation process—how effectively managers invest their capital, whether through internal projects or acquisitions of other companies.

In recent years, financial researchers have documented that profitability exerts an important influence on stock returns. Robert Novy-Marx, professor at the University of Rochester, has identified a gross profitability premium, noting in a 2012 article that "profitable firms generate significantly higher returns than unprofitable firms, despite having significantly higher valuation ratios."[3] He defined gross profitability as the ratio of a firm's gross profit (revenues less cost of goods sold) to assets.

Similarly, investment practitioners Cliff Asness and Andrea Frazzini, working with academic Lasse Pedersen, concluded that the market rewards "quality," defined as a combination of characteristics including profitability (measured several ways), growth, safety (measured on dimensions such as beta, volatility, leverage, and earnings stability), and dividend payout.[4]

What is more, in their 2014 five-factor formulation of the Capital Asset Pricing Model (CAPM), academics Fama and French also found that profitability has a positive impact on stock returns (noted in Chapter 5). Importantly, they show that stocks of companies operating with smaller capital investments—implying that they have a correspondingly higher returns on invested capital (ROIC)—earn better returns than those of companies with higher, less efficient investment.

These studies' results are intuitively appealing, but like all academic research they are based in past market experience. For the conclusions to be useful in active management, investors need to be able to identify in advance those companies with the highest profitability. That is, does past profitability provide reliable forecasts of future profitability, and do those translate into high stock returns?

The experience of individual companies is idiosyncratic: a technology company's competitor might release a revolutionary new product, or a pharmaceutical company's drug might be shown to cause previously unknown harmful side effects. For the market as a whole, however, profitability tends to be consistent over fairly long periods, making a focus on profitability and ROIC the basis for an attractive strategy. Tim Koller, Richard Dobbs, and Bill Huyett, all consultants with McKinsey & Company, looked at trends in ROIC among U.S. companies over the 11 years from 1995 to 2005. They found significant persistence: for companies where ROIC was greater than

20 percent in 1995, 67 percent were still earning ROIC above 20 percent in 2005; 14 percent had an ROIC between 10 percent and 20 percent; and 19 percent had seen their ROIC fall to below 10 percent at the end of the period. Similar persistence held at the other end of the spectrum: among the companies whose ROIC was below 10 percent in 1995, 57 percent of them still earned an ROIC less than 10 percent in 2005, while 28 percent had seen ROIC move to between 10 percent and 20 percent, and just 15 percent had improved to an ROIC greater than 20 percent.[5]

Investment strategist Michael Mauboussin studied persistence in ROIC from 1997 to 2006 for a universe of 1,000 nonfinancial U.S. companies. He sorted companies into quintiles on their ROIC in 1997 and again in 2006. Of stocks in the top ROIC stratum in 1997, 41 percent appeared in the top quintile again in 2006. At the other extreme, 39 percent of the bottom quintile companies based on 1997 ROIC remained at the bottom in 2006. Broadening the analysis, 64 percent of the stocks that made the top quintile in 1997 were in the top two quintiles in 2006, while only 25 percent had fallen into the bottom two quintiles.

A More Practical Study

While the persistence in these studies is promising, both are a few years out of date. Moreover, most investors, including Epoch, are unlikely to hold stocks for such long periods. We undertook our own analysis of persistence in ROIC on a shorter time frame, studying the companies in the MSCI World Index for each of the 10 years ending in 2015. We also added one more wrinkle—estimating each firm's weighted average cost of capital (WACC) based on its debt costs and equity beta. We then subtracted WACC from ROIC to arrive at each firm's return on invested capital over its cost of capital. (Our discussion in Chapter 10 posited that companies be measured based on their marginal ROIC and WACC, but instead we are working with firms' average ROIC and average cost of capital. First, we are evaluating companies overall, rather than the impact of new capital investments at the margin. Second, data on marginal rates of ROIC is not generally available.)

On average, 70 percent of the companies in the top quintile in a given year remained in the top quintile the next year (shown by the upper left cell in Table 14.1). Moving one cell to the right, an average of 14 percent of the companies in the top quintile in one year fell to the second quintile the next year. (If ROIC minus WACC exhibited no persistence whatsoever, every cell in this table would show a proportion of about 20 percent; that is, of the stocks in any given quintile in year X, roughly 20 percent would end up in each of the five quintiles in year X + 1.)

The averages of year-to-year changes in Table 14.1 yield several interesting observations. One is that the most likely outcome for a company's ROIC minus WACC in any quintile is to

TABLE 14.1   Average Persistence of ROIC-WACC for MSCI World Index Companies, 2006–2015[a,b]

		ROIC-WACC Quintile in Year X + 1				
		1	2	3	4	5
ROIC-WACC Quintile in Year X	1	70%	14%	3%	2%	3%
	2	16%	50%	18%	5%	5%
	3	4%	20%	42%	20%	8%
	4	2%	6%	21%	44%	21%
	5	3%	6%	10%	22%	51%

[a]Shaded cells are the highest in each column.
[b]Figures in the table do not add to 100 percent, because some companies drop out of the sample each year due to mergers or bankruptcies.

Source: Epoch Investment Partners

remain in that same quintile the following year (shown by the shaded cells, which are the highest proportion in each row). Another is that few companies migrated from one extreme to the other in a single year: on average only 3 percent of companies in the top quintile one year fell to the bottom the next year, and only 3 percent of companies in the bottom quintile one year rose to the top.

Also important is that persistence was greatest in the top quintile (the 70 percent figure at top left), ranging from a high of 76 percent between 2014 and 2015 to a low of 55 percent between 2007 and 2008. As for the latter years, the global financial crisis surely disrupted many companies' profitability, so the faster turnover is not surprising. Nevertheless, more than half of the top-quintile firms stayed at the top even during that challenging time.

Is Persistence Contradictory?

Basic economic principles would argue against ROIC remaining high for long periods. Companies earning premium ROICs would attract competitors eager to earn similar returns; the competition would cut into profitability; and over the long term, high returns on capital should revert to some average. But what constitutes the long term? Based on the evidence in Table 14.1, a year seems not to be long enough for ROIC to revert completely. And the earlier studies showed that even over 10 years, high and low levels of ROIC would persist.

ROIC itself is a simple measure, calculated as:

$$\text{ROIC} = \frac{\text{Operating profit}}{\text{Invested capital}}$$

But understanding persistence in ROIC can be complex, due to the many factors that determine a company's profitability.

Companies that earn a higher ROIC are either able to charge higher prices, incur lower costs, or run their businesses with less invested capital. The first two factors raise the numerator, while the third lowers the denominator. Of course, a combination of these factors may be at work.

ROIC varies widely across companies, and the biggest source of variation arises in the numerator, from how the structure of different industries affects companies' ability to raise prices and lower costs. These differences are well explained by the five forces framework advanced by Michael Porter, professor at Harvard Business School: threat of new entrants; threat of substitutes; bargaining power of buyers; bargaining power of suppliers; and rivalry among firms in the industry[6] (Figure 14.1).

The first three factors bear most directly on a company's sales and pricing flexibility, while the fourth is most germane to costs. Rivalry, the fifth factor, addresses pricing as well as capital investment: if exiting a business is difficult because operating assets are expensive or challenging to repurpose, firms are less likely to quit, and instead will compete more vigorously. The classic example is railroads versus airlines: if an airline route becomes unprofitable, the company could switch its planes to another market. But a railroad couldn't readily tear up its tracks and lay them somewhere else, so management would likely fight harder to preserve its established business.

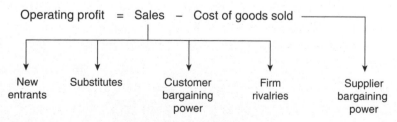

FIGURE 14.1   Factors Determining Operating Profits

Source: Harvard Business Review

ROIC can also be driven by special characteristics of a company or product. A firm may possess a unique low-cost manufacturing process or enjoy patent protection. Additionally, some products simply require less capital to produce: forging steel requires a greater physical investment than writing software (where the biggest investments are foosball tables and climbing walls). Thus, if a software company can succeed in generating revenue, it is likely to have a higher ROIC than a steel company.

For many reasons, some companies earn a higher ROIC and can sustain that advantage over time. But business history is filled with names such as Montgomery Ward, Bethlehem Steel, Polaroid, Eastman Kodak, and Xerox, whose fortunes fell due to changes in technology, competition, and customer taste.

Reversion to a mean level of ROIC can take many years—so long that for investors, the economist's insight on competition eroding profitability yields little relevant information. John Maynard Keynes wrote in 1923 that:

> [T]his long run is a misleading guide to current affairs. In the long run we are all dead. Economists set themselves too easy, too useless a task, if in tempestuous seasons they can only tell us, that when the storm is long past, the ocean is flat again.[7]

That call for more actionable conclusions probably applies to a large portion of financial research as well.

Applying Keynes's point to our topic, we can say with confidence that the dominant firms of the current era—Google, Apple, Microsoft, Facebook—are unlikely to be as dominant 25 or 50 years from now as they are today, or may no longer exist. But that doesn't necessarily mean that investors won't be able to earn superior returns by holding those stocks over, say, the next few years, if the companies can hold on to a dominant position that affords high levels of ROIC.

An ROIC Strategy

We have seen that that certain companies that achieve a high level of ROIC can be expected to sustain it over periods of at least a few years, and that the ROIC companies earn is transmitted into their share prices. Can this backward-looking information be fashioned into an profitable investment strategy—based on owning companies that have experienced high ROIC in the recent past, on the assumption that enough of them will continue to do so that their returns will outperform the general market?

Michael Mauboussin followed up his study of ROIC persistence with a look at stock performance from 1997 through 2006. He found that owning the stocks in the highest quintile for the full 10 years did not generate the best returns. The bottom quintile group did show noticeably lower returns, but for quintiles 1 through 4 there was little variation. Even though stocks in the top two ROIC quintiles were more likely than average to maintain a high standing in the ending year, and even though the stocks that did maintain high ROIC outperformed the market, enough stocks had fallen into the bottom two quintiles—and their shares had performed badly enough—to offset the strong returns of the high-ROIC stocks.

Epoch's study, however, shortened the investment period to just one year, and saw an increase in persistence of ROIC (versus Mauboussin's earlier work). Did the same hold true for stock performance? That is, would owning the stocks in the top ROIC quintile for a year, and then rebalancing the portfolio to reflect the latest membership in the top quintile, result in better performance?

Our research shows that it did—calculated on monthly capitalization-weighted performance of each quintile from 2006 through 2015. To avoid foresight bias, we assumed that ROIC data was unknown until 90 days after the end of a company's annual reporting period. For example, in measuring the performance of quintile 1 for January 2010, membership is based on the data available as of September 30, 2009. Table 14.2 shows the capitalization-weighted returns for each quintile annually over the ten years. Each year's highest return is shaded in dark gray, while the lowest return is shaded in lighter gray.

Holding the quintile of companies earning the highest ROIC-WACC would have been a winning strategy over these 10 years, as it earned the highest annualized return among quintiles, and outperformed the 4.98 percent annualized return of the MSCI World Index (including dividends net of taxes). In fact, the cumulative returns fall into nearly the same order as the ROIC quintiles (quintile 5 outperformed quintile 4 by 0.03 percent per year). Note, however, that the top quintile did not generate the best returns in each year—although it did earn

TABLE 14.2   Annual Returns of MSCI World Index stocks, in Percent, Ranked by ROIC-WACC Quintiles[a]

	ROIC-WACC Quintiles				
Year	1	2	3	4	5
2006	17.6%	21.7%	25.1%	23.5%	18.6%
2007	21.0%	12.8%	2.8%	6.2%	2.8%
2008	−39.0%	−36.2%	−45.9%	−42.5%	−41.1%
2009	38.6%	34.4%	29.0%	24.3%	22.2%
2010	12.0%	10.4%	11.6%	18.2%	15.8%
2011	4.1%	−2.8%	−8.7%	−19.2%	−13.9%
2012	15.4%	16.3%	18.0%	19.4%	20.2%
2013	24.6%	27.5%	29.1%	25.9%	32.0%
2014	9.0%	2.9%	4.3%	1.8%	0.5%
2015	2.0%	1.3%	−3.5%	−1.3%	−2.7%
10 years annualized	8.4%	6.9%	3.4%	3.1%	3.1%

[a]Dark shading indicates the highest return; light shading indicates the lowest.

Source: Epoch Investment Partners

the highest return in five of the ten years, more than any other quintile.

One other interesting result echoes the point made earlier on quantitative easing's impact on the markets: in both 2012 and 2013, the prime years for quantitative easing, quintile 5—composed of those companies doing the worst job of generating ROIC—rose the most, while quintile 1—with the companies showing the best ROIC—gained the least. Only in those two years did the bottom quintile see the best results, highlighting the distorting effect that QE had on the stock market.

As an aside, Epoch's CEO, Bill Priest, examined a similar question in a 1965 article in the *Financial Analysts Journal*,[8] although from the perspective of companies' return on equity (ROE) rather than ROIC. He examined whether investing in companies earning high ROE over the period from 1947 to 1953 produced better-than-average returns over the ensuing 10 years through 1963 (similar to Mauboussin's methodology mentioned earlier). He then examined results over a five-year holding period as well. At the time, data collection was completely manual, necessitating a small sample size, and making it difficult to draw authoritative conclusions. But the message was like that of Mauboussin: holding shares of firms that have previously earned high operating returns for a full decade may not be a winning strategy, as many of the companies will experience regression to the mean in their returns on investment over that time. A shorter holding period, however, offers hope of capturing excess returns.

In one sense, this result is not surprising. The academic research indicates that the market rewards high profitability and punishes excess investment, meaning that companies earning the highest ROIC should perform well. And given that high levels of ROIC show a high degree of persistence from one year to the next, it is not unreasonable to think that stocks with the highest levels of ROIC-WACC in very recent history should therefore perform well over short periods, because they are more likely to experience above-average levels of ROIC-WACC over the ensuing year.

In another sense, however, the results are puzzling, because they imply that investors are not fully pricing in the value of high ROIC-WACC. The market seemed to be continually surprised that companies that have experienced high ROIC in the recent past turn out to be more likely to do so the following year, despite the historical evidence about ROIC persistence. One possible explanation may be that too many investors continue to rely on traditional valuation metrics such as price-earnings (P/E) and PEG (which divides the P/E ratio by the rate of the company's expected growth) ratios, and do not take into consideration the role that ROIC plays in creating value. Another possible reason is behavioral—as noted in Chapter 5, investors tend to under- and overreact to earnings surprises, so that stock prices can take long periods to adjust to new fundamental information.

The Value of Judgment

The ROIC-based investment strategy that we have outlined seems promising. First, the underlying economic premise is sound—that investors would be attracted to companies earning higher profits from a more efficient capital base. Second, the hypothetical portfolios built from simple rules, and readily available information, not only earned a positive return, but also outperformed the broad market they were drawn from.

However, favorable results like these are not uncommon for backtests of investment strategies. They are a natural outcome of efforts to find novel strategies: a financial researcher or investment practitioner develops a hypothesis, looks for suitable data sources, and then links the behavior of the data with the related returns on stocks. Unfortunately, these sorts of conclusions often turn out to be biased for a number of reasons.

One cause for bias is that the signals are valid and indeed produce high returns, but were drawn from an unusual period where the effects were only transitory. For example, in Chapter 6 we noted that over long periods, companies that demonstrate higher quality in their financial results have tended to outperform the broad market, but that following the global financial crisis lower-quality stocks prevailed for several years. One possible explanation cited was the excess liquidity poured into the global financial markets by central banks, which had the effect of lowering the discount rate for cash flow streams, driving up the prices of all assets, particularly those with long-duration characteristics. (For further discussion, see Epoch's white paper "The Power of Zero + The Power of the Word," included in Appendix A.)

The influence of quantitative easing has been noticeable and pronounced, but over time many other transitory forces shape the markets in less obvious ways. An investment strategy model that worked well during times of, say, falling inflation and interest rates, or rapid technological change, may not fare well when those benefits or pressures are reduced.

Another cause for the declining success of strategies is the presence of inadvertent flaws in models. "Selection bias results when the researcher employs the best performing signal or signals from among multiple candidates, and fails to account for doing so," wrote scholar Robert Novy-Marx in 2015.[9] He did not deny the value of multiple signals but pointed out that the value of each signal should stand on its own: "This is not to say that one should not use multiple signals that one believes in. Signals that work well individually will work even better together. One should not, however, believe in multiple signals because they backtest well together." (Think of a stepwise regression program that over time finds critical variables that explain results.

The insight may be an "explain" list, but it also may fail to show causality. Moreover, what worked over decades may fail for long periods outside the sample, thus causing investors to lose faith in the process.)

A third cause for declining power in strategies is investor adaptation. From time to time, new data sources become available which offer innovative investors an edge, but only temporarily. One example is the factor of trends in revisions to analysts' earnings estimates (mentioned in Chapter 12).

Investors also apparently pay great attention to the work of financial academics, according to a 2015 paper from R. David McLean and Jeffrey Pontiff of Boston College. They examined 97 variables cited in 80 academic studies, and found that the average return of profitable strategies fell 32 percent after the publication of the relevant paper, noting: "These findings are consistent with the idea that academic research draws attention to predictors. ... [A]cademic publications transmit information to sophisticated investors."[10]

So-called "smart beta" strategies are not immune from the forces that can reduce the efficacy of a strategy. As investment practitioners Peter Hecht and Zhenduo Du point out, investors interested in smart beta strategies need to be particularly alert to the possibility that what appears to be an exploitable factor may instead be the result of unintentional data mining. In addition, there is the possibility that smart beta factors, once made known, will be arbitraged away. Hecht and Du's paper presented evidence to indicate that some of the more well-known smart beta factors, such as company size and book-to-price ratios, are only about 40 percent to 70 percent as effective in generating excess returns in recent years as they were before receiving widespread attention starting in the early 1990s.[11]

We make these points not to say that quantitative models don't work, or that their power is necessarily fleeting, but rather that they stand a greater chance of success with the application of judgment from skilled analysts and portfolio managers. The need for judgment is not limited to investment management: Google's well-known driverless cars still require an awake and alert human behind the wheel, just in case.[12] And while super-computers have been beating human champions at chess since 1997,[13] the combination of human plus machine can still beat the machine alone.

That's the value of judgment. In an investment setting, as Epoch applies technology, the quantitative models "collect the dots"—efficiently gathering and sorting the raw information—while the analysts and portfolio managers "connect the dots" and conduct the security selection. Judgment can be greatly informed by technology, but technology will never be a substitute for judgment.

Notes

1. R. Dino Davis, Matthew W. Krummell, and Jonathon W. Sage, "A Blended Approach: Combining Quantitative and Fundamental Investment Indicators," MFS Investment Management White Paper, November 2013, 3.
2. J. C. R. Licklider, "Man-Computer Symbiosis," *IRE Transactions on Human Factors in Electronics*, Vol. HFE-1 (March 1960): 4–11. Available at: www.cs.rit.edu/~rpretc/imm/project1/biography.html.
3. Robert Novy-Marx, "The Other Side of Value: The Gross Profitability Premium," *Journal of Financial Economics,* Vol. 108, No. 1 (2013), 1–28.
4. Clifford S. Asness, Andrea Frazzini, and Lasse H. Pedersen, "Quality Minus Junk," Working Paper, 2013. Available at: papers.ssrn.com/sol3/papers.cfm?abstract_id=2312432.
5. Tim Koller, Richard Dobbs, and Bill Huyett. *Value: The Four Cornerstones of Corporate Finance* (Hoboken, New Jersey: John Wiley & Sons, 2011).

6. Michael E. Porter, "How Competitive Forces Shape Strategy," *Harvard Business Review* (March–April 1979). Accessed at: https://hbr.org/1979/03/how-competitive-forces-shape-strategy.

7. John Maynard Keynes. *A Tract on Monetary Reform*. (Original publication London: Macmillan, 1923), 80.

8. William W. Priest Jr., "Rate of Return as a Criterion for Investment Decisions," *Financial Analysts Journal* (July-August 1965): 109.

9. Robert Novy-Marx, "Backtesting Strategies Based on Multiple Signals," Working Paper, University of Rochester, June 2015. Available at: rnm.simon.rochester.edu/.

10. R. David McLean and Jeffrey Pontiff, "Does Academic Research Destroy Stock Return Predicatbility?" Available at: papers.ssrn .com/sol3/papers.cfm?abstract_id=2156623.

11. Peter Hecht and Zhenduo Du, "Smart Beta, Alternative Beta, Exotic Beta, Risk Factor, Style Premia, and Risk Premia Investing: Data Mining, Arbitraged Away, Or Here To Stay?," Evanston Capital Management, March 2016. Available at: www.evanstoncap .com/docs/news-and-research/evanston-capital-research— smart-beta.pdf.

12. David Shepardson, "Google Expanding Self-Driving Vehicle Testing to Phoenix, Arizona," Reuters, April 7 2016.

13. Dana Mckenzie, "Update: Why This Week's Man-Versus-Machine Go Match Doesn't Matter (and What Does)," *Science*, March 15, 2016. Available at: www.sciencemag.org/news/2016/03/update-why-week-s-man-versus-machine-go-match-doesn-t-matter-and-what-does.

EPILOGUE

Our goal in writing this book has been to describe the qualities that we think are essential in the creation and perpetuation of successful asset management firms. We have also tried to describe Epoch Investment Partners, and to map out our place in an industry undergoing rapid change in its strategies, its channels of distribution, and its use of technology.

In the end, all of the ideas we have discussed in this book are encapsulated, in one way or another, in Epoch's aspiration statement:

> To provide superior risk-adjusted results using a transparent approach based on our free cash flow philosophy;
> To serve investors who seek and value Epoch's investment approach;
> To continue as a thought leader and innovator in global investment management.

First is Epoch's recognition of its charge: deliver positive risk-adjusted results through a transparent methodology—judging and selecting companies for investment based on their ability to generate free cash flow and to allocate that cash flow properly, rather than on their earnings as calculated under accounting principles (those that are generally accepted, or the more flattering non-GAAP variations many companies have devised). Cash flow is the true measure of a company's economic profit. This is not only our intellectual and theoretical viewpoint: the durability of cash flow as a positive factor in stock returns has stood up to rigorous academic analysis. Our analysts and portfolio managers have developed an expertise in seeking out free cash flow—a significant advantage that distinguishes our investment process, and provides us with a "cash flow arbitrage" opportunity in generating returns.

Our second aspiration addresses our relationship with our clients. It is critical that our clients understand our philosophy and approach. In other words, we strive to ensure that our clients understand the financial architecture and the rationale behind our methodology: we identify companies which appear to offer long-term value propositions for the owners, and have management teams who understand how successful capital allocation drives value creation.

The classic distinction between investment and speculation states that true investors look at their holdings as evolving businesses, and intend to benefit from an increase in value through profits earned and dividends paid over time, while speculators are more focused on near-term changes in share prices. We seek to build relationships with clients who think of themselves as owners of attractive businesses through their investment portfolios, not as participants in some sort of statistical game.

Our third aspiration expresses our goal to be constantly evolving with the markets and the state of the investment art. The final four chapters of this book have shown how information technology runs through every aspect of investing. We noted in Chapters 11 and 12 that the markets and investing techniques will change every year, and if the recent past is a reliable indicator, they will be light-years ahead of today's speed, complexity and intelligence in 5 or 10 years' time. Accordingly we are investing considerable resources in expanding technology's role in the firm, to inform the judgment of our analysts and portfolio managers, and to support our investment process.

Put simply, one must think ahead. That challenge is motivation for the ongoing development of new investment strategies, publication of white papers and investment perspectives the firm develops, and for authoring this book.

We are proud of the firm Epoch has grown to become in just a dozen years. But as we've stated in these pages, our goal is to evolve on all fronts. In fact, we have found an unusual inspiration for our culture—the National Transportation Safety Board, which is the U.S. government's investigative authority for aviation, marine, rail and highway accidents. The NTSB operates with small, experienced teams, and each of its reports is approved by a senior board of five, creating a culture of accountability, collaboration, empowerment and pride. Among safety agencies the NTSB enjoys a worldwide reputation as "the best in the business," and for most employees, a position at the NTSB is a capstone to a successful career.[1,2]

We aspire for Epoch's culture to be regarded one day as one of the best in the investment business—by our clients, their consultants, and our colleagues in the industry. For our investment teams, we emphasize and reward individual effort and accountability, and we strive for Epoch to be a destination for investment talent. And for our clients, we are dedicated to innovation and the pursuit of outstanding performance over the long term.

Thank you for sharing your time to consider our thoughts.

William W. Priest
Steven D. Bleiberg
Michael A. Welhoelter

Notes

1. Eric Fielding, Andrew Lo, andJian Helen Yang."The National Transportation Safety Board: A Model for Systemic Risk Management," November 14, 2010. Available at SSRN: ssrn.com/abstract=1695781 or http://dx.doi.org/10.2139/ssrn.1695781.
2. Cynthia C. Lebow, Liam P. Sarsfield, William L. Stanley, Emie Ettedgui, and Garth Henning, *Safety in the Skies: Personnel and Parties in NTSB Aviation Accident Investigations* (Santa Monica, CA: Institute for Civil Justice, RAND, 1999).

Selected Articles and White Papers of Epoch Investment Partners

Using Portfolio Composition To Estimate Risk

This article, authored by Jack L. Treynor; William W. Priest, Jr.; Lawrence Fisher; and Catherine A. Higgens, originally appeared in the September–October 1968 issue of *Financial Analysts Journal*.

In recent years a number of financial scholars have commented on the marked degree of co-movement in the prices of securities. Statistical techniques have been applied to measuring the character and degree of co-movement by Donald Farrar, Hester and Feeney, and Benjamin King. Perhaps the best known model of stock prices which recognizes and incorporates the co-movement phenomenon is that of William Sharpe. In Sharpe's model fluctuations in the price of a particular common stock have two causes: (1) fluctuations in the general market level and (2) fluctuations unique to the stock in question. More complicated models than Sharpe's have been proposed and the Sharpe model has occasionally been criticized as being too simple to fit reality (see for example Benjamin King's discussion).[1,2] Nevertheless, its simplicity gives it great appeal.

We are not the first to apply simple financial models to practical problems involving risk measurement. Marshall Blume tested the applicability of the Sharpe model to the problems of predicting the risk character of simulated rather than actual portfolios.[3] James Fanning, now of Rockefeller Brothers, and Marc Steglitz of Bankers Trust have measured risk in actual common stocks defined in terms of a related, but different, model and applied the results to estimating the risk character of actual portfolios containing these stocks. Although the present paper has benefited substantially from the work of Fanning and Steglitz, in terms of model and approach we are much closer to Blume than Fanning and Steglitz.

Sometimes it is possible to identify stock price changes with particular news events. Even though the events which cause price changes sometimes seem to be unique, it is nevertheless useful to think of the events which affect prices as drawn at random from a large population, some of which can cause large price changes and some small, many of which have a high degree of uniqueness or individuality, but which, taken as an entire population, have a character which demonstrates some continuity over time. Labor unions will continue to strike; countries will continue to declare war or to make undeclared war; the Fed will continue by turns to tighten up and loosen the money supply; and so forth. Some of these events are felt throughout the economy and have their impact in greater or lesser degree

[1] "Market and Industry Factors in Stock Price Behavior," *Journal of Business*, Volume 39, Number 1, Part II ("Supplement," January, 1966), pp. 139–190.
[2] It should be noted that in conversation with one of us (Fisher) in 1964 or 1965, Harry Markowitz expressed the opinion that the degree of clustering of fluctuations found by King would not cause portfolios to show riskiness substantially different from that estimated using the Sharpe model.
[3] Unpublished monograph, The Empirical Adequacy of Portfolio Theory, submitted to *Journal of Business,* July 1968.

on prices of most common stocks. The impact of other events is specific to at most a few companies or industries.

The Sharpe model specifies that price fluctuations in a particular common stock will be the sum of fluctuations due to fluctuations in the market index and fluctuations unique to the stock in question.[4] The risk character of the stock is completely specified under the assumptions of the Sharpe model by specifying two parameters: The first is sensitivity of the stock to market fluctuations. It is common knowledge, however, that price fluctuations in individual common stocks are not completely explained by a market index. We call the portion of price changes left unexplained by a market index the residual price changes. The second risk parameter in the Sharpe model is a number that expresses the average magnitude of the residual fluctuations. In Sharpe's model, residual fluctuations are assumed independent from one security to another.

Some companies are more sensitive to the impact of events affecting the market index than others. Rapidly growing companies, companies which manufacture capital goods, companies with high fixed costs, and highly levered companies all tend to be more sensitive than companies for which these factors are absent. Companies for which several of these factors are present simultaneously are likely to be particularly sensitive.

The second parameter in the model—the measure of the magnitude of residual fluctuations—tends to be larger for companies in which technological changes in products or processes are taking place very rapidly. It also tends to be larger for one-product companies, companies for which style is an important factor and for companies whose fortunes depend on a single

---

[4] Sharpe's model was nearly anticipated by M. F. M. Osborne in his celebrated paper "Brownian Motion in the Stock Market" (*Operations Research*, Vol. 7, March-April, 1959). Osborne considered an "ensemble consisting of 1,000 pennies and one gold piece." The outcome of the toss of the gold piece affected the prices of 1,000 stocks; the effect of the outcome of tossing each of the 1,000 pennies was unique to a single stock.

executive. Widely diversified companies and companies with a balanced management team will tend to demonstrate less residual variability than others. A high level of fixed costs or a highly levered capital structure will, of course, amplify specific risk in the same way that it amplifies market risk.

Exhibit 1A demonstrates the meaning of the risk parameters for individual stocks in graphical terms. The horizontal axis measures the change in a market index (Fisher's Combination Investment Performance Index).[5] The vertical axis measures

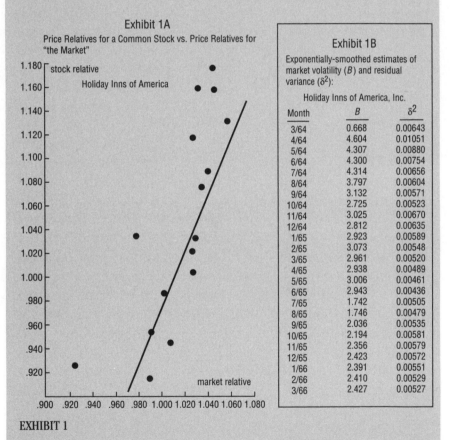

Exhibit 1A

Price Relatives for a Common Stock vs. Price Relatives for "the Market"

Exhibit 1B

Exponentially-smoothed estimates of market volatility (B) and residual variance (δ^2):

Holiday Inns of America, Inc.

Month	B	δ^2
3/64	0.668	0.00643
4/64	4.604	0.01051
5/64	4.307	0.00880
6/64	4.300	0.00754
7/64	4.314	0.00656
8/64	3.797	0.00604
9/64	3.132	0.00571
10/64	2.725	0.00523
11/64	3.025	0.00670
12/64	2.812	0.00635
1/65	2.923	0.00589
2/65	3.073	0.00548
3/65	2.961	0.00520
4/65	2.938	0.00489
5/65	3.006	0.00461
6/65	2.943	0.00436
7/65	1.742	0.00505
8/65	1.746	0.00479
9/65	2.036	0.00535
10/65	2.194	0.00581
11/65	2.356	0.00579
12/65	2.423	0.00572
1/66	2.391	0.00551
2/66	2.410	0.00529
3/66	2.427	0.00527

EXHIBIT 1

[5] Described in "Some New Stock Market Indexes," *Journal of Business*, loc. cit., pp. 191–225.

the change in the value of the security in question. Both are measured as the ratio of value at the end of a month (including intervening dividends) to value at the beginning. A straight line has been fitted to the data points in Exhibit 1A. The slope of the line is a measure of the sensitivity of the value of the security to fluctuations in the market index. The spread of data points around the line of best fit is a measure of residual variability.

The important distinction between market variability and residual variability in the individual security is that they affect portfolio returns in different ways. Sensitivity of a portfolio to variations in the market index is the average of the sensitivities of the individual securities held, weighted by the amounts. Residual variability in individual securities, on the other hand, tends to combine in such a way that it looms relatively less important in a portfolio (in comparison with market variability) than in the securities which comprise it. The spread is measured in terms of a number statisticians call the residual variance, which in terms of the present application is an average of the squares of the (residual) fluctuations over the time period covered by the sample. Under the assumptions of the Sharpe model there is a very simple rule for determining how specific risk in individual securities combines to determine specific risk in the portfolio: The residual variance for the portfolio can be expressed in terms of residual variance σ_i^2 for the individual stocks. Letting x^i equal the number of shares of the ith stock held in the portfolio and assuming that the relevant measures are expressed on a per-share basis, we have

$$(1) \quad \textit{Residual variance} = \Sigma x \sigma t^2$$

In like fashion we can define market variance as the average over time of (squared) fluctuations in portfolio value due to market fluctuations. Letting regression-slope coefficients B_i measure sensitivity of prices of individual stocks to fluctuations in the general market, and a variance $\sigma_m{}^2$ describe the variability of the general market, we have

$$(2) \quad \textit{Market variance} = [\Sigma x_i B_i]^2 \; \sigma_m^2$$

Finally, expressions (1) and (2) can be combined to estimate total portfolio variance $\sigma_m{}^2$. We have

$$(3) \quad \sigma^2 - [\Sigma x_i B_i]^2 \sigma_m^2 + \Sigma x t^2 \; \sigma_i^2$$

Equation (3) will hold only approximately since the residual variances for individual stocks are not strictly independent. As previously noted, a number of writers have challenged the Sharpe model on the assumptions underlying the way specific risks in individual securities combine in a portfolio. Nevertheless Equation (3) is probably the simplest model which has any reasonable hope of predicting the risk character of a diversified portfolio.

The values for the regression coefficients and residual variances are obtained by regressing price change histories for individual common stocks against a suitable market average. From these values and composition data, a model of the risk character of the portfolio is constructed. Predictions of a change in the value of the portfolio (given the change in market level) are compared with the actual change in order to test this model.

Our basic idea (in which we were anticipated by the work of Fanning and Steglitz, and also by that of Marshall Blume) is that if we knew the risk parameters for individual common stocks then we could estimate the risk character of a portfolio instantaneously—even though the composition was continuously changing. In order to test this idea we have studied all the common stocks held in an actual mutual-fund portfolio during a period of more than two years. The price history of each common stock was traced back as far as conveniently possible—in some cases, up to 40 years. From the price and dividend histories for the common stocks, we made running estimates of the risk parameters for each common stock held. Then, once a month for each month during the test period, we made an instantaneous estimate of the risk character of the mutual fund portfolio, based on its composition at the end of that month. Our estimate of market risk for the portfolio enabled us to predict how rapidly the value of the fund would change as the market level fluctuated. Our estimate of residual risk for the fund gives an estimate of the amount by which the true market value of the fund will differ from our predictions. For each month of the test period we estimated both risk parameters for the fund and observed the actual change in market level and the actual change in the value of the fund. How well we succeeded in predicting the observed changes in the value of the fund, given the actual changes in market level, is discussed at the end of this paper.

Although the risk character of a fund may change quickly if the composition of the fund changes, our scheme assumes that risk parameters for individual common stocks change relatively slowly. In most cases the assumption seems valid to us, since they change through the gradual evolution of products, manufacturing processes, and markets. The risk character of a company's common stock may change quickly, however, if the company enters into a wide ranging diversification program or undergoes a profound change in capital structure. The essence of the measurement problem is that they are measured subject to random fluctuations in the data and that reliable estimates can be obtained only with samples large enough to "average out" these random fluctuations to some degree. Unfortunately, over time, the underlying parameters which we are attempting to measure are themselves changing. Thus, we are confronted with an inescapable dilemma: If we confine our samples to very recent data, possible error due to random fluctuations in sample data may be excessively large. If, on the other hand, we include in our sample a longer time span we may be including data which are no longer relevant because of changes over time in the risk character of the common stock in question. In principle, there are ways of weighting more and less recent data which are optimal in the sense of minimizing the combined effects of both problems. We are currently experimenting with techniques which select optimum weights automatically. For this study, however, we used exponential smoothing techniques with arbitrary weights (see Appendix).

Using exponential smoothing we obtained running (that is, continually changing) estimates of the risk character of a large group of common stocks covering as much as 40 years. Exhibit 1B shows how estimates of the risk parameters for a single common stock have behaved over time.

Perhaps the most striking thing about our estimates of risk parameters for individual common stocks is the range of values encountered in our modest sample. Exhibit 2 shows current estimates for market risk of stocks in the sample. A regression-slope coefficient B_i equal to 1 implies that the stock in question has an average degree of market risk, and that if the market rises or falls 10% other things equal the stock in question will rise or fall respectively 10%. Values B_i in Exhibit 2 range from less than 0.5 to more than 2.5. In other words some stocks in Exhibit 2 have more than 5 times as much market risk as some others. Clearly the degree of market risk in a portfolio is determined, not only by the proportions devoted to common stock and fixed income securities respectively, but also by the kind of common stocks held.

RANKED BY B_i				
			17. Texas Instru.	1.575
			18. TWA	1.524
1.	Holiday Inns	2.427	19. Pan Am World Airways	1.517
2.	Warner & Swasey	2.088	20. Financial Federation	1.506
3.	Admiral	2.025	21. Ampex	1.505
4.	Collins Radio	1.954	22. First Charter Financial	1.504
5.	General Instru.	1.898	23. Control Data	1.500
6.	Vornado	1.817	24. Crowell Collier	1.498
7.	Piper Aircraft	1.798	25. Foxboro	1.496
8.	Beckman Instru.	1.763	26. Universal Oil Prod.	1.479
9.	Fairchild Camera	1.717	27. EJ Korvette	1.472
10.	Northwest Airlines	1.687	28. William H. Rorer	1.446
11.	Commonwealth Oil	1.679	29. Magnavox	1.438
12.	Max Factor	1.624	30. Polaroid	1.425
13.	Phila & Reading	1.609	31. Eastern Airlines	1.404
14.	Raytheon	1.595	32. Cerro	1.398
15.	Bell & Howell	1.595	33. Reynolds Metal	1.394
16.	Avon	1.589	34. National Airlines	1.378

35.	Perkin Elmer	1.378	85.	Chesebrough Ponds	1.022
36.	Zenith Radio	1.358	86.	Southern Co.	1.019
37.	Cons. Electronics Inds.	1.375	87.	Aluminum Co Amer.	1.011
38.	Rayonier	1.449	88.	W. Virginia Pulp & Paper	1.000
39.	Celanese	1.357	89.	Caterpillar Tractor	0.985
40.	Xerox	1.352	90.	Beaunit	0.982
41.	Revere Copper & Brass	1.350	91.	Crown Cork & Seal	0.978
42.	Motorola	1.344	92.	Tidewater	0.978
43.	Litton Inds.	1.337	93.	Chrysler	0.966
44.	Penn RR	1.332	94.	Montgomery Ward	0.953
45.	Ginn & Co.	1.320	95.	Texas Gulf Sulphur	0.945
46.	Douglas Aircraft	1.308	96.	Cons. Cigar	0.936
47.	Indian Head Mills	1.307	97.	Ex-Cell-O	0.936
48.	Mallory	1.306	98.	Westinghouse Electric	0.932
49.	Sunstrand	1.303	99.	Upjohn	0.920
50.	Delta Airlines	1.302	100.	Holt Rinehart & Winston	0.914
51.	I T & T	1.296	101.	Wesco Financial	0.911
52.	Carter Products	1.291	102.	Grumman	0.904
53.	General Precision	1.290	103.	Halliburton	0.893
54.	Sperry-Rand	1.290	104.	Florida Pwr & Light	0.888
55.	Western Airlines	1.277	105.	Cone Mills	0.887
56.	Hewlett Packard	1.262	106.	Colgate Palmolive	0.851
57.	ACF Inds.	1.242	107.	Union Oil Cal.	0.850
58.	Great Northern Paper	1.233	108.	Merck	0.850
59.	Owens Corning	1.207	109.	Columbia Brdestg.	0.837
60.	Kayser Roth	1.205	110.	Bobbie Brooks	0.825
61.	Grace	1.194	111.	Gillette	0.819
62.	Kaiser Alum	1.191	112.	Lockheed	0.805
63.	Frito Lay	1.171	113.	United Fruit	0.782
64.	Air Prd & Chem	1.157	114.	Coastal States Gas Prod.	0.774
65.	Allis Chalmers	1.157	115.	United Carr	0.764
66.	Whirlpool	1.156	116.	IBM	0.757
67.	Pfizer Chas.	1.133	117.	Marathon	0.752
68.	Corning Glass Works	1.123	118.	Allied Chemical	0.738
69.	General Dynamics	1.120	119.	Gulf Oil	0.727
70.	Bigelow Sanford	1.115	120.	McDonnell Aircraft	0.721
71.	Texas Oil & Gas	1.114	121.	Socony Mobil Oil	0.665
72.	Wetson & Co.	1.105	122.	Texaco	0.661
73.	Pennzoil	1.098	123.	Monsanto	0.649
74.	National Can	1.093	124.	Sunbeam	0.639
75.	Schering	1.092	125.	S. Carolina Elec. & Gas	0.610
76.	Union Bag Camp Paper	1.078	126.	Central Southwest	0.607
77.	Burroughs	1.072	127.	Abbott Labs	0.593
78.	Mueller Brass	1.059	128.	Standard Oil Cal.	0.587
79.	Allied Supermarkets	1.054	129.	Petrolane Gas Service	0.576
80.	MGM	1.048	130.	Beneficial Finance	0.565
81.	Bethlehem Steel	1.045	131.	Gulf States Utilities	0.549
82.	Fibreboard Paper Prds.	1.039	132.	Southwestern Public Sve.	0.451
83.	Olin Mathieson	1.035	133.	A T & T	0.403
84.	Harbison Walker	1.030			

EXHIBIT 2

Exhibit 3 shows current estimates of σ_i^2, the spread in residual risk for the common stocks studied. Here too the range is impressive. As one might expect there is some tendency for stocks that rank high in Exhibit 2 to rank high in Exhibit 3.

RANKED BY RESIDUAL VARIANCE

1.	Control Data Corp.	0.02116	43.	Pan Am Wld Airways	0.00666
2.	Fairchild Camera & Instru.	0.02071	44.	Phil. & Reading Corp.	0.00660
3.	Texas Gulf Sulphur	0.01576	45.	National Airlines	0.00659
4.	Texas Instru.	0.01453	46.	Allied Supermarkets	0.00648
5.	Admiral Corp.	0.01431	47.	Delta Air Lines Inc.	0.00645
6.	EJ Korvette	0.01344	48.	General Precision	0.00636
7.	Collins Radio	0.01326	49.	Ginn & Co.	0.00628
8.	Wesco Financial Corp.	0.01244	50.	Kaiser Alum & Chem	0.00622
9.	Xerox Corp.	0.01217	51.	Pennzoil Co.	0.00619
10.	Financial Federation	0.01200	52.	Beaunit Corp.	0.00613
11.	General Instru. Corp.	0.01145	53.	Kayser Roth Corp.	0.00603
12.	First Charter Finan. Corp	0.01045	54.	Lockheed Aircraft	0.00603
13.	Ampex Corp.	0.01011	55.	Litton Inds.	0.00590
14.	Cons. Electronics Inds.	0.00946	56.	Grumman Aircraft	0.00582
15.	Beckman Instru.	0.00939	57.	Western Airlines	0.00578
16.	Commonwealth Oil Refining	0.00900	58.	Bobbie Brooks	0.00576
			59.	Sunstrand Corp.	0.00573
			60.	Motorola Inc.	0.00571
17.	Raytheon Co.	0.00893	61.	United Fruit	0.00565
18.	Vornado Inc.	0.00892	62.	Great Northern Paper Co.	0.00564
19.	Max Factor & Co.	0.00878	63.	Schering Corp.	0.00558
20.	Polaroid Corp.	0.00874	64.	Sperry-Rand Corp.	0.00540
21.	Magnavox Co.	0.00861	65.	Wetson & Co.	0.00540
22.	Crowell-Collier	0.00820	66.	Cerro Corp.	0.00539
23.	William H. Rorer	0.00812	67.	Southern Co.	0.00537
24.	Douglas Aircraft Co.	0.00780	68.	Chrysler Corp.	0.00532
25.	Zenith Radio Corp.	0.00765	69.	Cons. Cigar Corp.	0.00529
26.	Texas Oil & Gas	0.00762	70.	Holiday Inns of Amer.	0.00527
27.	General Dynamics	0.00752	71.	Tidewater Oil Co.	0.00515
28.	McDonnell Aircraft Corp.	0.00730	72.	Bigelow-Sanford Inc.	0.00504
29.	TW A Inc.	0.00725	73.	Air Prod. & Chem	0.00501
30.	Bell & Howell Co.	0.00717	74.	Indian Head Mills	0.00498
31.	Hewlett Packard Co.	0.00711	75.	Burroughs Corp.	0.00493
32.	Crown Cork & Seal	0.00705	76.	Warner & Swasey Co.	0.00489
33.	Piper Aircraft Corp.	0.00697	77.	Holt Rinehart & Winston	0.00488
34.	Universal Oil Prds.	0.00694	78.	Revere Copper & Brass	0.00482
35.	Northwest Airlines	0.00692	79.	MGM	0.00480
36.	Perkin Elmer Corp.	0.00691	80.	Whirlpool Corp.	0.00476
37.	Carter Prod. Inc.	0.00688	81.	Celanese Corp Amer.	0.00475
38.	Mueller Brass Co.	0.00686	82.	Owens Corning Fiberglass	0.00465
39.	Eastern Airlines	0.00685	83.	Corning Glass Works	0.00449
40.	Reynolds Metals	0.00679	84.	Sunbeam Corp.	0.00447
41.	National Can Corp.	0.00668	85.	Rayonier Inc.	0.00439
42.	Foxboro Co.	0.00666	86.	Alum. Co Amer.	0.00433

87.	Petrolane Gas Srv. Inc.	0.00429	112.	Marathon Oil Co.	0.00323
88.	Intern. T & T	0.00428	113.	Union Bag Camp Paper	0.00318
89.	Gillette Co.	0.00406	114.	Montgomery Ward	0.00309
90.	ACF Inds.	0.00404	115.	Pfizer Chas	0.00294
91.	Penn RR	0.00404	116.	Harbison Walker	0.00291
92.	Columbia Brdestg	0.00402		Refractories	
93.	W. Virginia Pulp & Paper	0.00402	117.	Olin Mathicson Chem	0.00274
94.	Avon Prod.	0.00401	118.	Gulf Oil	0.00267
95.	Frito Lay	0.00396	119.	Westinghouse Electric	0.00267
96.	Fibreboard Paper Prds	0.00394	120.	Grace WR & Co.	0.00255
97.	Merck & Co.	0.00387	121.	Union Oil of Cal.	0.00245
98.	Mallory Pr & Co	0.00373	122.	IBM	0.00242
99.	Caterpillar Tractor	0.00363	123.	Florida Pwr & Light	0.00234
100.	United Carr Inc.	0.00359	124.	Beneficial Finance	0.00232
101.	Bethlehem Steel	0.00356	125.	Socony Mobil Oil	0.00225
102.	Abbott Lab	0.00354	126.	Texaco	0.00217
103.	Upjohn Co.	0.00353	127.	Gulf States Utilities	0.00216
104.	Coastal States Gas Prd Co.	0.00352	128.	S. Carolina Electric	0.00203
105.	Chesebrough Ponds Inc.	0.00341		& Gas	
106.	Ex-Cell-O	0.00340	129.	Central S. West	0.00200
107.	Cone Mills	0.00336	130.	Allied Chem Corp.	0.00185
108.	Colgate Palmolive	0.00330	131.	Southwestern Public	0.00181
109.	Halliburton Co.	0.00331		Svc.	
110.	Monsanto Co.	0.00329	132.	Standard Oil of Cal.	0.00174
111.	Allis Chalmers Mfg.	0.00327	133.	Amer Tel & Tel	0.00091

EXHIBIT 3

Ultimately our interest in the risk character of common stocks derives entirely from their possible impact on the risk character of a portfolio. The risk character of the mutual fund portfolio considered in this study is displayed in Exhibit 4.[6] The rate of return for an appropriate market index (the same Fisher Index referred to above) is measured along the horizontal axis and a rate of return for the fund is measured on the vertical axis. (The scatter diagram in Exhibit 4 covers 27 consecutive months of investment results for the fund.) The slope of the regression line fitted to these points (the Characteristic Line) is a measure of the average level of market risk in the fund over this period. If the actual level of market risk in the fund had

---

[6] The "fund" studied was the portion of Diversified Growth Stock Fund that was invested in common stocks listed on the New York Stock Exchange. These stocks comprised over 90 per cent of the net assets of the fund throughout the period studied (December 31, 1964 to March 31, 1966).

been maintained constant over the period, then the dispersion of month-to-month results around the line of best fit would be a measure of the degree of specific risk in the fund. If on the other hand, the actual degree of market risk in the fund was changing from month to month, then the dispersion of the data around the line of best fit over-states the degree of specific risk in the fund. It is obviously necessary to accumulate data over a substantial period of time in order to measure market risk in a fund using the Characteristic Line technique.

Fund Return vs. Market Return

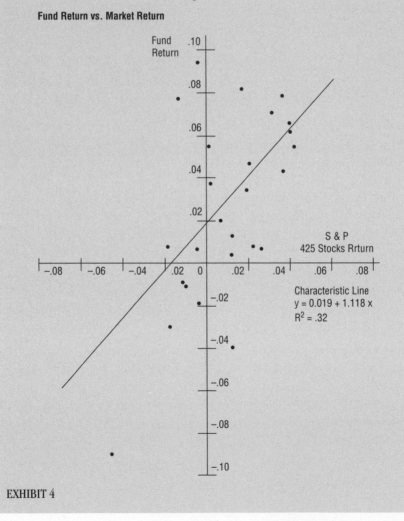

EXHIBIT 4

Exhibit 5 compares actual month-to-month results for the fund with results predicted, using the technique described in this paper. A comparison of Exhibits 4 and 5 shows that our forecast of investment results for the fund is improved by using risk estimates for the individual common stocks held. In fact, roughly half the variance left unexplained by the Characteristic Line is accounted for by allowing for changes in the composition of the fund (hence changes in the risk character of the fund) over the sample period. We conclude that our risk-measuring technique is producing numbers which are both meaningful and useful—not only for estimating portfolio risk after the fact but also for estimating the impact on fund risk of making contemplated changes in the composition of the fund. The numbers have other uses which will be described in a sequel.

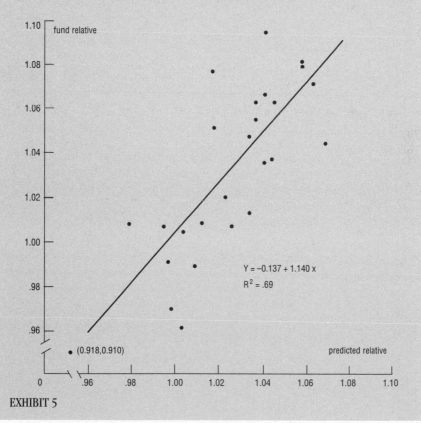

Fund Return vs. Predictions based on risk character of stocks listed

$Y = -0.137 + 1.140\,x$

$R^2 = .69$

(0.918,0.910)

EXHIBIT 5

The Canary in the Coal Mine: Subprime Mortgages, Mortgage-Backed Securities, and the US Housing Bust

By John Reddan, Managing Director, and William W. Priest, CEO. Published by Epoch Investment Partners, April 23, 2007. Available online at: www.eipny.com/index.php/epoch_insights/papers/mortgages_us-housing-bust.

Introduction

Recent events in the residential mortgage industry have verified what many of us expected all along: that the bursting of the housing bubble is already exerting dramatic and wide-ranging pressure on the US economy. As the housing market continues to decline, consumer spending will contract and financial institutions will suffer as housing-related financing instruments take the plunge.

Based on much of the analysis available today, it is tempting to blame the housing market's duress on the recent implosion of the subprime lending industry. However, we believe the decline of subprime mortgages is merely the weakest link in a long and tangled financial chain. In this paper, we hope to explore the causes and effects of the housing boom and bust, identify the impact on the market at large, clarify the nature and magnitude of the troubles on the horizon, and, in so doing, show why the subprime mortgage collapse is merely the most visible canary in the dangerous coal mine of the US housing finance market.

The U.S. Housing Boom—A Fragile Bubble

The recent housing boom—the unprecedented increase in US home prices and homeownership—was primarily caused by a combination of the Federal Reserve's aggressively easy monetary policy, the widespread abandonment of sensible lending practices, and an exponential increase in mortgage securitization, which was largely unregulated. As a result of these factors, US home prices, whether measured in real terms or in relation to incomes, rose to multiple standard deviations above the norm: up 98% from 1998 to 2006 on average. Similarly, home ownership increased from 64% to 69% of households (Figures 1 through 3). Intuitively, this should not have happened. As housing became more expensive, home ownership should have gone down, not up. In reality, therefore, this housing "boom" was actually a bubble of unreliable construction and unsustainable proportions.

This bubble was perpetuated by the widespread issuance of cheap, low-standard debt, which caused many homebuyers to engage in reckless overleveraging. And today, the dangers of this imprudence are becoming clear. Despite the continuation of benign US economic conditions (long term interest rates and unemployment near 50 year lows), mortgage delinquencies and defaults are currently rising at alarming rates. Home prices are falling across the country. According to the *High-Tech Strategist*, unsold new

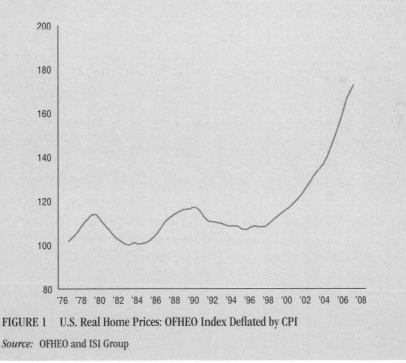

FIGURE 1   U.S. Real Home Prices: OFHEO Index Deflated by CPI

Source: OFHEO and ISI Group

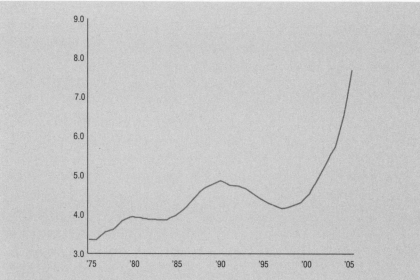

FIGURE 2   House-Price-to-Income Ratio in "Bubble Zone"

Source: HSBC and ISI Group

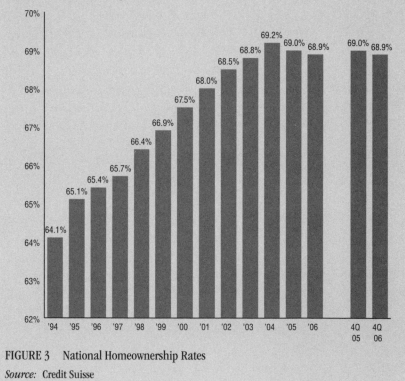

FIGURE 3   National Homeownership Rates

Source: Credit Suisse

home inventories are at 16-year highs (an estimated 8 months' supply), while sales of new homes are the slowest in nearly eight years. A near-record level of 3.75 million existing homes are on the market, more than 25% higher than a year ago. Building permits are down 30% year over year and are near recession levels.

Subprime and Alt-A Mortgages

There are a variety of ways to approach a discussion of the housing bubble and its decline. For our purposes, it will be helpful to start by focusing on residential mortgage debt. As mentioned previously, one of the bubble's primary causes was the increase in mortgage debt outstanding, which in turn was facilitated by wanton disregard of credit standards and a massive increase in securitization. In recent years, the growth in residential mortgage debt has been truly impressive: according to UBS, it increased at an 11% CAGR between 1997 and 2006, including rates of growth of 14% in 2004 and 15% in 2005. Residential mortgage debt outstanding of $10.2 trillion is now more than twice the US Treasury debt outstanding. During the growth of the housing bubble, subprime and Alt-A1 mortgages—extremely high-risk forms of mortgage debt—comprised an increasing percentage of total mortgage originations. Credit Suisse estimates that between 2002 and 2006, subprime mortgages increased from 6% to 20% of purchase dollar mortgage originations, while Alt-A mortgages increased from 5% to 20%. See Figure 4.

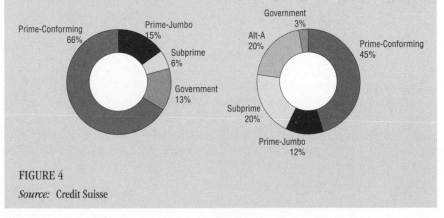

FIGURE 4
Source: Credit Suisse

In other words, 40% of purchase mortgage originations in 2006 were the result of dubious lending practices. At the end of 2006, subprime mortgages made up 12%-14% of outstanding residential mortgages, while it is estimated Alt-A mortgages[1] accounted for between 11% and 27% of mortgages outstanding.[2]

Before we continue, a brief word on Alt-A versus subprime loans. In reality, there is very little difference between the two. Both categories share virtually the same risky features: no or low documentation, piggyback borrowing, option ARM, interest only, etc. as shown in Figure 5.

	Subprime	Alt-A
ARM share	92%	63%
Interest-only share	22%	27%
Neg am share (option ARMs)	0%	32%
Average debt-to-income	42%	38%
Piggyback loan share	55%	54%
No or low documentation share	50%	81%
Prepayment penalty share	70%	48%
Non-owner occupied share	10%	22%
Average FICO score	627	710

Source: ISI Group, Loan Performance, Lehman, Fannie Mae, UBS, Fitch.

FIGURE 5   Alt-A Loans Share Subprime's Risky Features

Source: ISI

---

[1] A classification of mortgages where the risk profile falls between prime and subprime

[2] This wide range of estimated percentages is a result of the specific characteristic of Alt-A loans. Unlike subprime loans, Alt-A loans are not required to be reported by lenders. That is why there is such a large discrepancy in estimates of outstanding Alt-A loans. In reality, there is no hard and fast cut-off point for subprime loans either, with lenders using differing FICO scores in the low-600 range. There is a possibility that both categories are understated.

While Alt-A loans have higher FICO scores than subprime loans, more than 80% of Alt-A's are low or no documentation loans, which almost renders the FICO score meaningless. As lenders and securities holders are finding out, a FICO score is a credit history, not a credit analysis. Alt-A loans, therefore, arc far more risky than ratings agencies would have investors believe.

To further illustrate how subprime and Alt-A loans fall far short of traditional lending standards, we can contrast the requirements for these loans—which are minimal to nonexistent—with the requirements for a typical borrower in the mid-'90s. Before the housing bubble, the criteria for a residential loan approval included a down payment of at least 20%, three years of W-2s, one year of bank and brokerage statements (to ensure that the down payment was not wired in by a friend or relative), verification of employment and an appraisal of the property. In the subprime and Alt-A universe, these standards are vastly less stringent, resulting in a dramatic increase in default risk.

Therefore, in today's bubble-deflating marketplace, it is no surprise that the decline of the subprime lending industry (and, by inference, the Alt-A lending industry) is among the first harbingers of a widespread housing market collapse. But, as previously asserted, we believe this is merely the tip of a large and perilous iceberg. The mostly unseen yet extremely hazardous majority of this iceberg consists of the rampant securitization of these high-risk subprime and Alt-A loans.

The Rise of RMBS

Concurrent with the increase in residential subprime and Alt-A mortgage debt, the *securitization* of this debt into residential mortgage-backed securities (RMBS) also experienced phenomenal growth. Between 1997 and 2006, total RMBS increased at an 11% CAGR to $5.7 trillion, driven by 20% compound growth in non-agency RMBS, the majority of which are comprised of subprime and Alt-A loans.

RMBS are bonds that have been created by highly questionable structured finance techniques. These bonds are divided into tranches that are rated by the ratings agencies from AAA thru BBB– depending upon the amount of collateral of each tranche and the sequencing of the cash flows for the mortgages in that collateral. There is an unrated "equity" tranche below the BBB-tranche.

What is troubling about this arrangement is that, through the black art of structured finance, RMBS have turned low-quality, high-risk subprime and Alt-A loans into AAA rated securities through the sequencing of their cash flows in a highly leveraged structure. *Grant's Interest Rate Observer* uses the analogy of waterfalls and termites to describe the cash flow sequencing that can "alchemize" low quality loans into AAA rated securities: the first dollar of income goes to the AAA rated tranche, then income cascades down to the lower rated tranches, while the first dollar of losses is borne by the unrated "equity" tranches then migrates up the capital structure.

In addition to repackaging subprime and Alt-A loans into high-rated securities, the securitization process also reinforced the very process by which subprime and Alt-A loans came into being. Securitization of subprime and Alt-A loans into RMBS caused a further abandonment of lending standards because it freed lenders from holding a loan to maturity. Since, after an initial period, the lender of a securitized loan was only on the hook for a small residual value of the loan, there was no incentive for a lender to maintain rational lending standards. Historical due diligence processes virtually ceased. Therefore, as housing prices ratcheted higher, lenders began to progressively abandon standards with the goal of boosting loan volumes, fees and earnings; standards were also relaxed in order to bridge the widening affordability gap for the marginal homebuyer. As volume demands increased, there was no time or rationale for doing a traditional appraisal and credit analysis, as the marginal buyer would likely not qualify and the lender would not be on the hook if or when trouble hit. Therefore, it is easy to see how the relationship between securitization and subprime/Alt-A lending has created a dangerous feedback loop within the residential mortgage industry.

The Rise of CDOs

Collateralized debt obligations (CDOs) are the next increasingly hazardous rung in the rickety ladder of housing loan securitization. CDOs "re-securitize" RMBS in a highly leveraged structure, thereby further repackaging and obscuring the risks inherent in subprime and Alt-A loans.

The ultra-low interest rates in the early part of this decade, and today's persistently low long-term rates, have created enormous demand for CDOs from yield-starved investors. As a result, these securities have grown exponentially. CDO issuance increased almost sevenfold between 2001 and 2006 to approximately $500 billion. According to the Securities Industry and Financial Markets Association, structured finance (which includes RMBS, CMBS, CDOs, and other ABS) accounted for 60% of the collateral pools backing 2006 CDO issuance. Yet, as pointed out by Joseph R. Mason and Joshua Rosner in their paper "How Resilient Are Mortgage Backed Securities to Collateralized Debt Obligation Market Disruptions?" these securities are complex, non-standardized, nontransparent and highly leveraged They are traded "over-the-counter" and are "marked-to-model" not "marked-to-market." Because of their complexity, they are highly dependent on rating agency ratings: something Mason and Rosner feel is beyond the agencies' scope.[3]

There are two forms of CDOs: cash and synthetic. Cash CDOs are bonds divided into tranches that are backed primarily by the

---

[3] This paper is a must-read and can be found at: papers.ssrn.com/sol3/papers.cfm?abstract_id=1027472.

lower rated tranches of RMBS. Using the same "waterfall/termite" cash flow sequencing as RMBS (with income cascading down and losses migrating up), the ratings agencies "alchemize" bonds backed primarily by low rated RMBS into tranches with a range of ratings from AAA through BBB-. CDOs also have an unrated equity tier. According to Mason and Rosner, 77% of the funding structure of a typical CDO is rated AAA in order to ensure the lowest funding costs, while the unrated equity portion only makes up 8% of the structure.

Synthetic CDOs are bonds backed by the cash flows from the sale of credit default swaps. They sell default insurance on mortgage securities. However, as *Grant's Interest Rate Observer* points out, synthetic CDOs, unlike traditional insurance companies, are not required to hold reserves against the insurance they have written. They also are mostly unfunded as senior lenders are not required to put up the majority of their capital until losses force a capital call. Synthetic CDOs increased the supply of credit default swaps (CDS), which lowered the price of insuring mortgage securities thereby helping to increase demand for those securities. Synthetic CDOs tranches have ratings similar to those of cash CDOs and RMBS.

While CDOs—both cash and synthetic—have grown exponentially and are crucial to mortgage securitization, they are as opaque, illiquid and lightly regulated as their constituent parts. CDOs have been described as debt acquisition vehicles whose primary purpose is to provide a bid for the lower rated tranches of RMBS. Without the CDO bid, the RMBS market would be a lot smaller. But, while RMBS are static pools whose composition does not change, CDOs are managed pools whose assets can change dramatically during their term, with some CDOs closing before the asset pool is complete. CDOs are heterogeneous: some hold as little as twenty assets while others can hold several hundred. What's more, investors' ability to do due diligence on these asset pools is restricted, leading to an overreliance on the rating agencies. CDO secondary market trading is also limited, leading to "mark to model" valuation, which can lead to sudden write-downs by holders. Most importantly, Rosner and Mason point out that only "qualified investors" have access to CDO documents and performance reports. Currently none of the bank regulatory authorities in the US, including the Federal Reserve, the FDIC and the Office of the Comptroller of the Currency, are considered "qualified investors." (Astounding, is it not?)

CDOs and RMBS—Risks That Lie Beyond the Subprime Decline

What, then, are the big-picture ramifications of this CDO/RMBS house of cards? To return to the idea originally postulated by this paper, the collapse of CDOs and RMBS is the larger disaster presaged by the implosion of the subprime (and Alt-A) lending industry.

Before we discuss the specific dangers of the CDO/RMBS situation, it is important to remember that mortgages, as a group, have many obvious risks. Mason and Rosner describe three specific risks that make mortgages exceedingly difficult to value: credit risk, interest rate risk and prepayment risk. A mortgage investor could lose, therefore, if the borrower defaults (credit risk), if interest rates rise (interest rate risk) or if interest rates fall (prepayment risk). Given the extremely lax credit policies of the past several years, credit risk is surely greater now than it has ever been, making extrapolations of historical default rates unreliable. Furthermore, Mason and Rosner describe the relationship between interest rate risk and prepayment risk as a "double-edge sword" that creates a nonlinear estimation environment. Yet despite these risks and complexities, mortgages have been packed into opaque, highly leveraged CDOs and RMBS.

The crux of the matter is this: we believe these mortgage securities could magnify the deflation of the housing bubble as easily as they magnified its inflation. Given their highly leveraged structures, CDOs and RMBS are extremely sensitive to home prices, as illustrated in the following table from Paul Singer of Elliott Associates as portrayed in *Grant's Interest Rate Observer* (Figure 6).

This table shows the estimated losses to the different tranches of a hypothetical CDO backed by the BBB-rated tranches of subprime mortgage-backed securities (MBS). If house prices are flat-to-down 4% over two years, the BBB+ tranche of the MBS will get written off, while losses will reach all the way up to the AAA tranche of the CDO, which will suffer a partial write down. If house prices depreciate 4-7% over the same two year period, losses reach all the way up to the A tranche of the MBS, which would be written off, while the CDO would be wiped out. Given the historic run-up in house prices, still stretched affordability levels, and the coming credit contraction, a 4-7% two-year decline in house prices does not seem extreme. In fact, it seems like a reasonable base case. It is why Mason and Rosner

Home Price** Appreciation	Mortgage Pool Cumulative Loss	Most Senior MBS Class Written Off	Loss to CDO	Most Senior CDO Class Written Off
+7% to +10%	2%	—	0%	—
+4% to +7%	4%	BB	3%	—
0% to +4%	6%	BBB–	39%	AA
0% to –4%	10%	BBB+	84%	AAA (partial
–4% to –7%	12%	A	100%	AAA
–7% to –10%	16%	AA–	100%	AAA

FIGURE 6   Mortgage Schematic,* House Prices, Mortgage Defaults, and CDO Loss Transmission Mechanism

*Assumes CDO constructed from BBB-rated tranches of subprime mortgage-backed securities; rough approximation of estimated collateral losses and trance write-downs.

**Cumulative appreciation over two years.

Source: Paul Singer

conclude that even the investment grade rated tranches of CDOs will experience significant losses if house prices depreciate.

Before we examine the potentiality of an upcoming CDO-related injury to the housing market, it's helpful to look at the history of this financial instrument. CDOs backed by other collateral have run into problems in the past. Mason and Rosner point out that CDO issuance dropped off dramatically between 1998 and 2002—from just under $150 billion to about $90 billion—as the economy weakened and problems arose in the collateral that backed the CDOs of that era. That "problem collateral" included corporate loans and bonds, manufactured housing and franchise business loans as well as aircraft leases. Deutsche Bank estimates that between 1999 and 2004, $123 billion of AAA ABS were downgraded by at least one rating agency due to collateral performance problems. Given the current accelerating level of mortgage delinquencies and defaults, the same thing could happen to CDOs backed by RMBS. Many holders of senior CDO securities are limited to holding investment grade securities, thus they could be forced to liquidate in a falling market, if the securities are downgraded.

Today, as in the past, CDOs and RMBS are vulnerable because of the weakness of their underlying securities: subprime and Alt-A mortgages, which have fallen prey to a recent spike in delinquencies. According to First American Loan performance, 14.3% of securitized subprime loans were at least 60 days delinquent in January up from 13.4% in December and 8.4% a year ago. For securitized Alt-A loans, 60-day delinquencies rose to 2.6% in January compared to 2.3% in December and 1.3% a year ago. Recently both M&T Bank Corp and American Home Mortgage Investment Corp were forced to lower their earnings forecasts due to problems selling Alt-A loans into securitization as well as credit deterioration in their Alt-A portfolios.

Resets of adjustable rates are the likely cause of these growing delinquencies. In recent years, large quantities of poorly
underwritten adjustable rate debt have been taken out at low
teaser rates that are currently resetting in a flat-to-falling home
price environment. According to both Goldman Sachs and Bank
of America, this phenomenon is at the heart of the increase in
defaults. Bank of America shows that Alt-A ARM delinquencies
in 2006 ran at four times historical averages (Figure 7), while
Goldman estimates that subprime ARM delinquencies are over
400 bps higher than subprime fixed rate mortgages, and are
accelerating at seven times the rate.

Flat-to-falling home prices in 2006 are unmasking the
incredibly lax lending policies of the last few years. Prior to this
year, rising home prices allowed troubled borrowers to sell to
avoid delinquency. However, approximately $1.0 to $1.5 trillion
of mortgages will reset this year and next, according to the

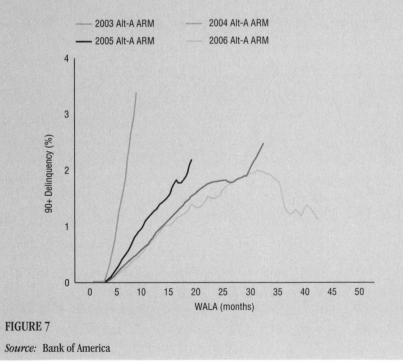

FIGURE 7

Source: Bank of America

Mortgage Bankers Association. This will increase the average monthly payment by 25% or more. With income per household flat or up only slightly, this incremental claim will stretch homeowner's budgets even further. As a result, it is reasonable to expect continued defaults to subprime and Alt-A loans, with a resulting negative impact on mortgage-backed securities such as RMBS and CDOs.

The Future of the Subprime Residential Mortgage Industry

As previously discussed, the collapse of the residential subprime/Alt-A market will cascade into the RMBS and CDO industries, tripping the wire of a large-scale credit contraction. In our view, this credit contraction is only just beginning. As a result of the recent sharp spike in delinquencies, 59 subprime lenders have closed or been acquired in distress sales, including the third, fifth and seventh largest players in the industry. Subprime mortgage issuance is expected to fall 50% this year from over $600B in 2006. Having been burned, lenders are raising teaser rates and requiring down payments and greater documentation for loans. Credit Suisse estimates that 21% of 2006 mortgage originations with the riskiest features—high cumulative loan to value, low credit scores and low or no documentation—will no longer be made (Figure 8).

Product	Share of Purchase Market	Elimination Due to Standards	Impact on Total Market
Subprime	20%	50%	10%
Alt-A	20%	25%	5%
Prime and Government	60%>	10%	6%
Total	**100%**		**21%**

FIGURE 8

Source: Credit Suisse

This 21% estimate could be low as it is only slightly more than half of the riskiest loans made last year. In the first quarter of this year, a Federal Reserve survey found that more banks are tightening mortgage standards today than at any point in the past 15 years (Figure 9).

It is not only the banks that have recently embraced a more rigorous approach to lending standards. Congress has also acknowledged the urgency of this matter and has intensified its focus on regulatory legislation. Congress has demanded that regulators specifically extend their recently released Intra-agency Guidelines on Non-traditional Mortgages to include the "2-28" loan, the most popular subprime loan that features a low teaser rate for 2 years. The guidelines require the lender to qualify the borrower on the fully amortizing rate and not on the teaser

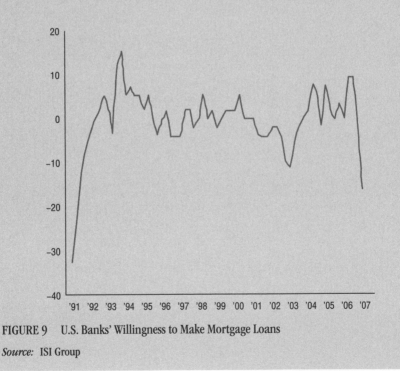

FIGURE 9   U.S. Banks' Willingness to Make Mortgage Loans

Source: ISI Group

rate. Countrywide Financial and Washington Mutual, two of the largest mortgage lenders, testified at recent Congressional hearings that the new guidelines would cut their subprime issuance by 50%. Indeed, since the issuance of the new guidelines last September, nontraditional loan volume has fallen dramatically (Figure 10).

In addition to these new Congressional guidelines, legislators are now enacting or promising to enact harsh retribution for predatory loans (FKA affordability loans). During the housing boom, as home prices soared relative to incomes and housing affordability fell, lenders loosened standards dramatically. Ostensibly, these relaxed standards were put in place to qualify otherwise unqualified borrowers for the "American Dream" of home ownership; but they also served to feed the demands of the securitization machine and to fatten bottom lines of the lending institutions. National and local legislators are now denouncing these "payment stretching" loans as predatory lending and are holding hearings and beginning to undertake serious enforcement actions against lenders. Ohio, for example, has recently passed legislation that will empower a task force to investigate predatory lending with penalties ranging from criminal and civil prosecutions through monetary damages and stays and injunctive relief. The Ohio attorney general is quoted in *Grant's Interest Rate Observer* as having said, "We're looking

2006	Option ARMs	Interest Only	Total Mortgage Originations
1Q	+43%	+49%	6%
2Q	+32%	+50%	1%
3Q	−12%	−17%	−14%
4Q	−14%	−21%	−9%

FIGURE 10   Nontraditional Loan Origins Fall Sharply in 3Q as New Rules Took Effect. Year-over-Year Change in Origination Volume

Source: Inside Mortgage Finance and ISI Group

at jail time for some of these folks." As evidence of this legislation in action, Ohio has recently placed an injunction on all foreclosures in the state by New Century Financial, the now defunct subprime lender, until it can determine whether the loan violated existing law. If a violation is found, the stay will be extended until there is a satisfactory adjustment in the borrowers' favor.

The Future of CDOs and RMBS

Grant's quotes an analyst as saying that a mortgage without the ability to foreclose is an unsecured loan. So what is an RMBS backed by that same mortgage? And what is a CDO backed that RMBS? As the answers to these questions become increasingly obvious, the manner in which these mortgages are securitized is also coming into the legislative crosshairs. A series of Congressional Hearings is underway as part of the process of drafting an anti-predatory lending bill. It will likely impose an obligation on lenders to ensure a loan is suitable for a borrower, similar to the fiduciary duty imposed on stockbrokers. Recognizing the major role that securitization played in the current housing bust, legislators are also examining an "assignee liability" provision which would hold investors that purchase RMBS liable for predatory loans. Needless to say, such a provision would limit demand for RMBS and CDOs in particular and the availability of mortgage credit in general. Investment banks and rating agencies will have to explain their roles in creating AAA rated securities backed primarily by subprime mortgage loans (RMBS) as well as AAA securities backed by the lowest rated tranches of RMBS (CDOs).

Conclusion

The bursting of the housing bubble is already well underway. Lenders are collapsing or raising lending standards, while regulators are cracking down on the imprudent lending that financed the marginal US homebuyer. Many of these imprudent loans will re-set this year and next, raising questions about the ability of these borrowers to re-finance. With the marginal buyer no longer able to get financing and a large inventory of homes for sale, US housing prices are likely to decline, possibly quite sharply, over the next several years. With the marginal home-buyer all but unfinanceable, and with the current dearth of first-time homebuyers, a decline in home prices seems inevitable. And the effect on the US economy will be profound: according to *The New York Times*, more than 20% of global private debt securities are tied to the US housing market. That is equivalent to $7.5 trillion: a sum far larger than the US Treasury market. Even if house prices decline only modestly, a significant portion of these securities would still suffer substantial losses.

In light of the housing market's unstable present and perilous future, mortgage-backed securities have become a significant and largely underestimated danger. In our view, mortgage-backed CDOs and RMBS are analogous to termites in their ability to silently wreak fatal, widespread and immediate havoc. Because of the manner in which they are structured, these instruments are capable of infecting unsuspecting financial institutions that, due to a blind overreliance on the rating agencies' conclusions, have inadequately reserved for the liabilities associated with these products. Opaqueness and "mark to model" are no substitutes for proper due diligence and "mark to market" pricing. In 2007, many financial intermediaries with investments in mortgage-backed securities will learn this the hard way. The "subprime canary" has dropped—and that's very bad news for the rest of the coal mine.

The Financial Crisis: A "Whodunit" Perspective

Commentary Prepared for the Foreign Policy Association's World Leadership Forum, September 23, 2009. Available at: www.eipny.com/epoch_insights/papers/the_financial_crisis_a_whodunit_perspective.

The Argument

This paper will argue that the recent financial crisis occurred at the intersection of: (1) an asymmetric compensation system inside banks that benefited from balance sheet leverage; (2) a deregulated banking system; (3) a waning memory of crises past; (4) the promotion of self-regulation by the financial industry's government authorities; and (5) a near catastrophic Federal Reserve Policy under Greenspan.

A Perspective

After the events of 2008, there is little doubt that the future of Wall Street will be very different from its past. The public outcry and the blame game have ensured that a new era of regulation and responsibility is on the horizon. But, as we begin to shape our new economic reality, it is important to take a careful look at the many causes of the recent financial meltdown. When a football team loses the "big game," it is tempting to blame the quarterback, the team's most visible player. But the people behind the design of the game plan—the coach and the general manager—bear as much responsibility as the quarterback, if not more. In the same way, it is true that bankers may bear the primary responsibility for the situation in which we find ourselves, but they cannot be blamed for the prevailing climate of moral laxity that fostered the recession. To understand this nuance requires a broader context and a bit of history.

The Role of Investment Banking

Let us begin with a look at the evolution of the investment banking industry. In many respects, the passage of the Glass-Steagall

Act in 1933 laid the foundation for investment banks in postwar America. Following this legislation, commercial banks and investment banks came to occupy separate spheres. As a result, there was little regulation of investment banks. After all, they existed solely as handmaidens to industry: underwriting security offerings and initial public offerings, and advising on mergers and acquisitions.

How did this business model change so profoundly over the past seven decades? When Donaldson, Lufkin & Jenrette, formerly a private brokerage firm and investment bank, went public in the 1960s, the notion of OPM, or "other people's money," was unleashed. No longer did an investment firm's partners have to provide 100% of the capital and assume 100% of the business risk. Instead, a firm's permanent capital availability was determined by its access to public market capital with a by-product being a lower cost of capital for firms choosing this path. This lower cost of capital facilitated an acceleration of growth for public firms versus private ones. Soon, the choice to stay private became a growth-limiting choice. The burden of assumed risk also changed—for public companies, risk was now shared between management owners and public owners. Later, this concept would set the stage for the investment banker's management model of "heads we win, tails you lose."

The second big event that shaped the investment banking industry was the development of option theory. The invention of the option pricing model by Fischer Black, Myron Scholes, and Bob Merton inaugurated a multiyear explosion of new innovations in hedging balance sheet risk, arbitraging risk opportunities, shifting profits/risks among countries, asset classes, and so on. The derivative strategies that were deployed as a result of this model altered the risk profile of both investment banks and the financial markets, so much so that the Swedes saw fit to reward Scholes and Merton with the Noble Prize in Finance. Much like the moment in physics when the atom was split, the insights derived from the application of the option pricing model would prove capable of doing great good or great harm depending on how they were deployed. In recognition of this dangerous duality, and in a statement of remarkable prescience, Warren Buffet deemed these instruments "Financial Weapons of Mass Destruction." In 2007, Richard Bookstaber also made some insightful comments on the subject in his book, *A Demon of Our Own Design*, a must-read for any student of finance.

Following the arrival of OPM and the deployment of derivative strategies, we reached a point at which leverage entered the scene in a big way and changed the business of investment banking dramatically. Starting in the early 1980s, after Paul Volcker slayed the inflation dragon, we entered the greatest period for investing in 100 years. Over the next two decades, interest rates declined over 1000 basis points! Bond and stock market values soared. This period became known as the "Great Moderation." Macro economists and central bankers—including Alan Greenspan—basked in the notion that the business cycle had been tamed.

The caution bred in the two decades prior to 1980, when interest rates rose dramatically and economic growth was sub-par, had given way to a new and more cavalier attitude toward risk. This attitude was validated by the stock market's unprecedented performance. In the equity market, for example, one dollar invested in the S&P 500 in 1980 became $25 in 2000. Therefore, if one was not "fully invested" throughout the period, one underperformed any equity benchmark. Portfolio managers could quite literally lose their jobs if they allowed an aversion to risk to influence their investment decisions. Risk-taking was in, and the lessons learned in the 1960–1980 period were deemed irrelevant for the new era.

Think of the mind-set that must have existed for the people running investment banks in 1980. OPM had only just begun, interest rates had risen from 2.5 to 13.5 percent, and the Dow Jones Industrial Average was no higher in 1980 than it was in

1965. Most industry executives, even then, had never heard of Myron Scholes or Fischer Black.

They awoke quickly, however, to the advantage of leverage when a little known private equity company called Wesray Corporation bought Gibson Greeting Cards from RCA in 1982. The purchase price was $81 million. The management team received a 20% interest. Eighty million dollars were borrowed. To finance the rest of the purchase price, Gibson sold and leased back its manufacturing and distribution facilities. Eighteen months later, Wesray floated an IPO of Gibson at $27.50. For their one million dollars of equity, the cofounders of Wesray, Bill Simon and Ray Chambers, realized a payoff of $66 million. This launched not only the private equity boom (then called leveraged buyouts or LBOs) but also allowed investment banks to enter a new line of business. Leverage was "in," and it grew and grew until 2008 when, for some investment banks, asset to equity ratios reached 40 to 1.

With leverage came a "new, improved" investment banking model that looked like this. Roughly 50% of the revenues within the bank went for compensation. Think about it: the more leverage, the more revenues, and the more revenues, the more compensation for employees. Leverage was rising and why not? The viability of this model seemed all but guaranteed via "The Great Moderation" and the "Greenspan Put", through which the Fed would bail everyone out by lowering interest rates and creating an accommodative monetary policy should trouble arise. After all, we only know there is a bubble after it bursts said the Maestro—Greenspan.

After leverage took hold of the business model, one more piece of the puzzle was still missing. There was money still left on the table as a result of the investment bank's inability to function like commercial banks, which made the investment banks unable to compete with their tough, farsighted European equivalents who did not separate the commercial function from the investment banking function.

Enter Bob Rubin, the Secretary of the Treasury and sort of an unofficial lobbyist for the U.S. banking industry. He encouraged the repeal of Glass-Steagall, largely under the rationalization that U.S. banks were at a global disadvantage to their overseas counterparts. The evils that the enactment of Glass-Steagall was designed to address were not a worry in the new competitive marketplace. The industry, Rubin reasoned, would regulate itself via the "unseen hand" of competition. Self-interest assured a constructive outcome. The repeal of Glass-Steagall occurred in 1999, allowing commercial banks and investment banks to merge. About a week following its passage, Bob Rubin resigned as Secretary of the Treasury to join Citibank as Vice Chairman.

While the repeal of Glass-Steagall may have made sense in the leverage-crazed halcyon days of the new millennium, the new legislation failed to fully account for the fundamental differences between commercial banks and investment banks. Whereas most commercial banks were deposit-based institutions, investment banks were not. The latter relied on their ability to issue commercial paper with investment grade ratings to finance their asset base. As long as confidence existed in the institution, there was seldom a question of rolling over the commercial paper. However, should that confidence be questioned, the inability to rollover short term debt combined with the high leverage that existed within these firms and the questionable quality of assets contained on the balance sheet could create a catastrophic condition for many firms, as evidenced in the events of 2008. Indeed, the investment banking model, as we came to know it, died last year with Lehman's bankruptcy.

Lehman defaulted on some $165 billion in unsecured debt. Most important, however, the bank was the number one dealer in commercial paper. Lehman was the middleman between issuers of commercial paper and money market funds. When the bank collapsed unexpectedly, the commercial paper market froze. Lehman's collapse demonstrated that the A1, P1 ratings of commercial paper by Moody's and S&P did not signal safety. As a result, money market funds stopped buying commercial paper and issuers stopped issuing it.

Lehman was also a major player in credit default swaps. Banks all over the world were now at risk if Lehman defaulted on the swaps. If the bank was the insured party, they worried about the extent of their protection against Lehman's default; and if they were the insuring party, they worried about the extent of their liability.

Similarly, Lehman played a critical role in the market for letters of credit. Letters of credit are bank guarantees that a negotiated transaction will go through according to its terms. Such instruments are very standard in international trade. Lehman's collapse exacerbated problems in international trade, which was already declining due to the emerging freeze of global credit.

The Lehman bankruptcy signaled that any financial firm could go broke. The failure to save Lehman shook confidence in the government's management of the crisis. Arguably, it was the worst decision made by the Bush team.

Waning Memory of Financial History

From my point of view, the 100,000-foot perspective can be expressed in two simple quotations: one from George Santayana and one from Confucius. The former states "Those who fail to remember the past are condemned to repeat it;" and the second, "I hear and I forget, I see and I remember, I do and I understand." Some of the current problems in our economy today reflect a loss of memory, an erosion of knowledge gained, and an explosion of ignorance as a result.

Allow me to digress for a moment with a personal story. My father was born in 1906 and lived through the turmoil of the 1920s and 1930s. Although he never lost his job at the steel company where he worked, plenty of his friends did. He saw the devastation, the broken families, and even suicides. All of those stories were told to his children with the message being: avoid debt at all costs, save something from every paycheck for the inevitable rainy day, and never think the government can save you. When he died in 1986, those lessons had already become part of our family's heritage.

My father never had any debt, not even a mortgage. (Granted, houses were a lot cheaper in Ohio in 1939. When he had finally saved enough to buy one, it cost just under $10,000.) This profound aversion to debt was not, however, something that fully carried through to my generation. For us, mortgages were necessary and credit cards had just appeared on the scene. Saving was still a virtue but debt in certain forms was necessary and culturally acceptable.

Skip another generation. Save? What for? You only go around once, and one can always get a job. After all, unemployment was seldom over 5% and, if you had a college education, it was even less. Remember, if you do not fly first class, your children will! The present replaced the future as a cultural goal. Deferred consumption was old-fashioned. One can argue that, by 2008, the U.S. culture and value system was at the apex of this frenzy for immediate gratification. Now, in the last months of 2009, it is a very different world, with the highest unemployment rates in nearly 30 years and the largest government stimulus in place since the 1930s.

Capitalism: Did It Fail Us?

Capitalism will survive simply because all other alternatives have been thoroughly discredited. However, the form it took from 1980 through 2008 has ended in my view. So-called "laissez-faire" capitalism, with minimum government influence and maximum self-regulation, simply did not work.

The Role of Government

Was government responsible for this crisis as some conservatives believe? If true, there is little need for re-regulation. I agree with Richard Posner—distinguished jurist, writer and author of the insightful book, *A Failure of Capitalism*—when he says "this depression (Great Recession, in my words) is the result of normal business activity in a laissez-faire economic regime. Bankers and consumers alike...have been acting in conformity with their rational self-interest throughout the period that saw the increase in risky banking practices, the swelling and bursting of the housing bubble, and a reduction in the rate of personal savings combined with an increase in the riskiness of those savings." (Just imagine what would have happened if we had privatized Social Security!)

Laissez-faire capitalism *did* fail us, but the policies of both parties created the preconditions of the Great Recession. What's more, our government's responses were late, slow, indecisive and almost impossible to understand. Perhaps the worst outcome so far is the rise of "moral hazard." When risky behavior is insured against the consequences of its failure, that is considered moral hazard. If performed on a broad enough scale, it can be catastrophic for a nation.

Many of the policies that have been enacted in response to the catastrophes of 2008 may have been necessary at the moment, but have almost certainly given rise to the moral hazard argument. These include the elimination of limits of FDIC insurance on bank deposits, extending that insurance to money market funds, and bailing out firms thought to be "too big to fail." The latter encourages the pursuit of corporate gigantism and financial irresponsibility. By substantially increasing the federal deficit—again, a necessary step in the short term—the government has sown the seeds of future inflation. While all of these policies were necessary in the immediate sense, they will have certain long-term consequences, few of which will be positive.

The critical role of government, as pointed out by Posner, was one of permission rather than encouragement. By largely deregulating banking over a period of decades, and by loosening the requirements for credit in general, the government inadvertently allowed the rational, self-interested decisions of private actors—bankers, mortgage brokers, real estate salesmen, homeowners, and others—to bring on a financial crisis that the government was unable to prevent from morphing into the situation in which we now find ourselves. The market's failure was abetted by the government's inaction. That inaction was partly the result of political pressures (to keep interest rates down, to maintain the illusion of prosperity, and to conciliate powerful political interests that are, not incidentally, large financial contributors to political campaigns.) All in all, government policies set the stage for this calamity, but did not create it. That responsibility lies with the incentive systems embodied in the laissez-faire banking model.

The government failed to take timely and coherent measures to check the downturn. As stated earlier, the seeds of failure were sown in the movement to reduce the regulation of banking and credit, which began in the 1970s. These seeds then germinated during the Clinton administration, when the housing bubble began and the deregulation of banking culminated with the repeal of the Glass-Steagall Act. Further encouraging the market's eventual boom and crash was the decision not to bring a profusion of new financial instruments, in particular credit-default swaps, under the regulatory oversight that would have given the public information about the scope, risks, and value of these instruments. The key architects of the nation's economic policy in the Clinton era (Greenspan, Rubin, and Summers) allowed the build-up of forces that would eventually blow the housing and banking industries sky-high. These forces were then multiplied by the reckless fiscal policy of the Bush Administration that enlarged the size of the national debt and set the stage for an economic train wreck.

The Role of the Federal Reserve

Today, we are in an economic crisis that is the result of a financial crisis that reflects two ill-considered government policies.

First, the Federal Reserve was guilty of an overreliance on their ability to control short-term interest rates. In the eyes of the Fed, every problem could be solved by interest rate manipulation; and there was, in fact, some history to support this point. (After all, if the only tool in the tool kit is a hammer, then every problem looks like a nail!) But the ensuing decade of low interest rates had a clear downside: it made borrowing cheap and safe saving unattractive. Hence, under this policy, personal debt soared and personal savings rates fell. Low rates combined with a government policy of an "owner in every house" (a modern version of Herbert Hoover's "a chicken in every pot") caused a bubble in housing prices. Similarly, low rates created high valuations on stocks, as P/E ratios and interest rates are inversely correlated.

The second policy that led to the recent recession began almost thirty years ago with the end of Regulation Q, which put a limit on the interest rates banks could pay on savings deposits. When Reg Q was phased out in the early 1980s, it reflected a decision to stop controlling the price of credit by controlling savings rates on deposits, thus ushering in a long term policy of deregulation within the banking system. Unregulated financial entities were soon able to operate just like banks, with the important distinction of being unregulated, hence the term "shadow banking system." The banking industry, therefore, became more competitive with lower profit margins. As a result, banks had to incorporate either scale or leverage into their business models in order to maintain return on capital targets.[1] The most aggressive players ramped up the riskiness of their loans or other investments, thus boosting their returns, at least in the short run. The more timid competitors were then forced to match the strategies of the industry's more aggressive players or else drop out of the competition altogether. Ultimately, this proved

---

[1] Return on capital is determined by the product of three factors: profits per dollar of revenues (profit margins), revenues per dollar of assets (scale), and assets per dollar of capital (leverage).

to be a race to the bottom, which was reached in 2008. In the infamous words of Chuck Prince, then-CEO of Citicorp, "If the music keeps playing, we have to keep dancing."

Summary

The most important lesson here is that what is tolerable risk for a company may well be intolerable for a nation. This is particularly true in banking. There is no real economy if the financial economy fails. As elaborated by Posner, "The risk to the nation is not the bankruptcy of a single major bank but the collapse of the banking industry, precipitating a financial crisis that can bring on a depression." The likelihood of this occurring is increased if one of the consequences of easy credit is a high level of personal debt. When credit markets seize, as a result of a crisis in the banking industry, economic output falls because the normal course of business, which depends heavily on credit, is disrupted. When output drops, layoffs begin. People with heavy debt, who lose or fear losing their jobs, reduce their spending, which causes a further drop in output.

What now? Without proper perspective, any attempt to make appropriate adjustments to the system whether by rules, legislation, or penalties can make matters worse rather than better. Before we do anything of substance, I would suggest we form a blue ribbon panel similar to the Pecora Committee of the 1930s or the 9/11 Commission to examine the management, or mismanagement, of the economy over the past several years. Examine the role of government policy including that of the Federal Reserve. Examine the incentives inside capitalism that encourage individual risk taking but may create "moral hazard" at the firm, industry, or national level. Only with that understanding will we be able to create the standards and safeguards to prevent a future disaster.

The Power of Zero + The Power of the Word

By William W. Priest, Co-CIO and Portfolio Manager; David N. Pearl, Executive Vice President, Co-CIO and Portfolio Manager; and Kenneth H. Hightower, Director, Quantitative Research and Risk Management; May 29, 2014

The stock market's appreciation from 2011 is nothing short of spectacular. From December 31, 2011 through December of 2013, the S&P 500 Index gained 54% and the MSCI World Index 47%. If we go back to the bottom of the market following the global financial crisis, these two indices have risen 200% and 165%, respectively. Few, if any, market participants saw this coming.

What are the elements that explain this spectacular surge in equity asset prices? We believe there were two powerful contributors—the first is the "power of zero" and the second is attributable to the voice of central bankers, the "power of the word."

The Power of Zero

The stock market is often characterized as a "present value machine." Its level reflects the perceived stream of cash flows from publicly traded companies worldwide, discounted by a rate that reflects the real rate of interest plus other measures of future uncertainties. When central banks lower that real rate of interest to zero or near zero, the present value of the numerator, corporate cash flows, rises sharply.

The numerator of that equation, corporate earnings, is driven primarily by the level and the growth rate of global GDP. In Figure 1, we observe the growth of real U.S. GDP and real reported earnings over the past century. The correlation between these two components is very high through time.

Real GDP is driven by only two variables—growth in the work force and growth in productivity. These two variables over the past several decades have averaged 1.0% and 2.0%, respectively. Add inflation to that number and you have nominal GDP. Thus, a realistic expectation for nominal GDP growth is 4 to 6% over the long term, and a forecast for earnings growth of a similar rate is a reasonable one.

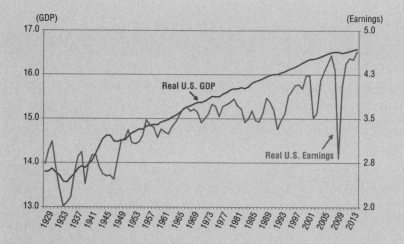

FIGURE 1   Earnings Are Correlated with GDP

Source: Bureau of Economic Analysis; Robert Shiller; Epoch Investment Partners, Inc.; 2013.

When the discount is lowered for that long-term stream of expected earnings or cash flows, it has a powerful effect on the present value of that stream. In Figure 2, we show both short- and long-term interest rates before and after the global financial

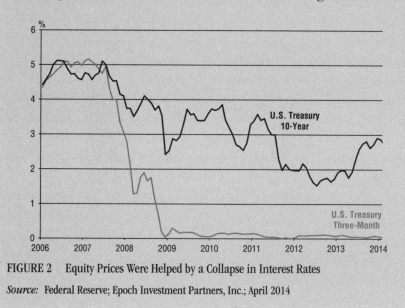

FIGURE 2   Equity Prices Were Helped by a Collapse in Interest Rates

Source: Federal Reserve; Epoch Investment Partners, Inc.; April 2014

crisis. In our view, the introduction of quantitative easing (QE) has been the single most important factor contributing to the rise in equity prices over this period.

The Power of the Word

The second important element, however, is what we call the "power of the word." On July 26, 2012, Mario Draghi made the following statement: "Within our mandate, the ECB is ready to do whatever it takes to preserve the euro. And believe me, it will be enough."

Although he was speaking for the ECB, his comments eventually came to represent the mantra for all central bankers at the time. He said in effect that central bankers will not allow the monetary system built over the past many decades to fail. Central bank policies will effectively ensure that the left-hand tail of the typical return/risk curve will not happen.

In Figure 3, we show the combined effects on stock market levels of the "power of zero" and the "power of the word." Whereas P/E ratios declined in 2011, they soared in 2012 and

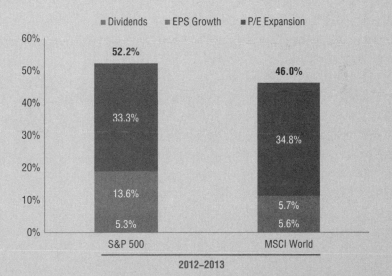

FIGURE 3   Recent Returns Predominantly the Result of Expanding P/E Multiples

Source: Standard & Poor's; MSCI; Epoch Investment Partners, Inc.; December 31, 2013.

2013. Nearly two-thirds of the stock market gains in the U.S. and three-quarters of the gains globally were attributable to P/E multiple expansion, with the balance coming from dividends and earnings. Even the earnings line needs some qualification, as much of those gains were impacted by share buybacks (more than half in 2013 alone for the S&P 500!).

Speculation in financial assets was encouraged by these two elements. Government bonds performed well but high-yield bonds performed even better as yields fell and credit spreads tightened. Blue chip stocks rose, but speculative stocks rose even more. The "earnings line" was replaced with the "dream line" particularly evident in the prices of many biotech and social media companies.

Consider one example of the dream line: Tesla Motors. One has to be impressed with the intellect and success of the company's visionary leader. But with a market capitalization of $26 billion for an automaker that can barely produce 35,000 cars per year, what about Tesla's valuation? The market for $80,000 electric cars with no dealership network to service them is unknown and is largely dependent on government subsidies for buyers and tax credits for the company.

Nevertheless, some analysts on the sell-side have justified Tesla's valuation. We recently observed a televised analyst say "when Tesla is earning $25 a share. ..." That estimate, presumably at some point in the future, is used as an anchor for a target price as the stock shifts into a "concept holding." The analyst accomplishes this transition by changing what the company does (making cars) into something entirely different: making high-tech consumer products.

The argument goes something like this: "one cannot value Tesla as an ordinary auto maker where the $25-per-share earnings might be valued at a multiple of 10 times earnings. It is really a high-tech consumer products company, which deserves a multiple of 20 to 30 times earnings, so the target share price could be in the $500-$750 range." The question of how many technology companies sell for 20 to 30 times earnings is another matter. Many large tech firms sell at multiples closer to auto stocks.

We do not mean to single out Tesla, as there are dozens of stocks that have recently been wrapped in "concepts" that provide flexibility in estimating valuation multiples. (That is, if there are earnings to provide multiples! The majority of companies in the IPO market over the past twelve months had no earnings.) What is driving these concept stories and their valuations?

The answer appeared to us in a sign outside a bar recently. "Alcohol served here: because no good story ever started with a salad!" The "alcohol" fueling today's market is QE. By artificially impacting the discount rate for future (or imaginary?) earning streams, we are witnessing the power of zero. Concept stocks are effectively options, whether they appear in biotech, fuel cells, social media, or Tesla. They are enormously and positively affected by the power of zero because the "dream line" is essentially a long-duration "wish line" that is affected more by the power of zero than any other type of investment.

QE has made life more difficult for traditional equity asset managers. We need real businesses with real cash flows along with managements who are good capital allocators. Those firms will avoid history's dustbin of failed businesses, but their stock prices may well lag in markets fueled by QE, where "dreamin'" pays. At Epoch we seek to identify companies that generate free cash flow each and every year and possess managements with a record of wise capital allocation decisions between capital returned to shareholders in the form of dividends (cash, buybacks or debt pay downs) and capital reinvested for growth via cap ex or acquisitions.

While this methodology has proven to be highly successful over many decades, it can falter when market returns are dominated by P/E expansion rather than earnings and dividends. In Figure 4, we show over eighty years of rolling ten-year returns for the S&P 500. From point to point, P/Es added little to long-term returns, as shown in Table 1. But within that long time

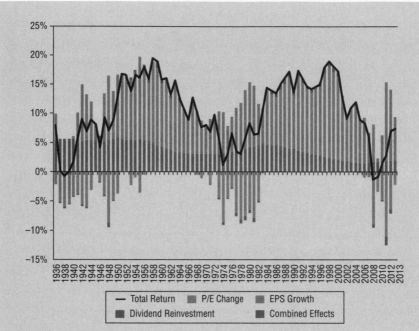

FIGURE 4   Components of Compound Annual Equity Returns for Trailing
10-Year Periods

Source: Epoch Investment Partners, Inc.; Standard & Poor's; April 2014.

frame, certain periods were dominated by P/E multiple expansion. And unless one can forecast the drivers of P/E multiples, namely inflation and interest rates, the fundamental investor's performance may lag during these periods.

TABLE 1.1   Long-Term History

	1927–2013
Earnings	5.3%
Dividends	4.0%
P/E	0.6%
Annualized Returns[1]	9.9%

[1]S&P 500 total return (USD)

Source: Epoch Investment Partners, Inc.; Standard & Poor's; April 2014

Today, we find ourselves in a world with sluggish real growth and interest rates at all-time lows, reflecting extremely low inflation and a huge surplus of excess savings. Inflation may remain very low in these circumstances, causing P/E ratios to remain relatively high on a historical basis.

Might P/Es rise even further from here? Not likely, in our view. QE is being withdrawn in the U.S. and reduced in the U.K. However, it remains the most likely monetary policy choice for the eurozone, even if the mechanisms for its implementation are not at all clear. Japan, too, appears to have little choice except to expand its current version of QE, as inflation remains well below government targets.

All in all, P/Es are more likely to contract than expand, reflecting either continued sluggish growth as a result of the huge global overhang of debt (Figure 5) or the outcome of the end of QE in the U.S. and the U.K.

The gradual end of QE will signal that the artificial depressant imposed on the real interest rate, and therefore supporting stock market levels, is ending. Hence, the discount rate for financial

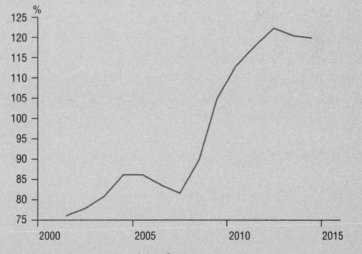

FIGURE 5   G7 Gross Government Debt % of GDP

Source: International Monetary Fund; World Economic Outlook Database; April 2014.

assets will begin to rise. The "dream line" will become more of a nightmare for speculators as this rise in the real rate of interest occurs, but the "earnings line," free cash flow to us, will become ever more important. Put another way, we believe the multiple expansion phase of this market is over and free cash flow analysis will again be required for superior equity returns.

As our colleague David Pearl says, "If you own a company that generates free cash flow each and every year, that possesses little or no debt, it will never go broke. Purchased at a reasonable price, such companies should become the long-term winners history recognizes and clients desire."

Financial Asset Valuation

In this appendix we review principles of valuation for financial assets, to illustrate how securities prices change with variations in interest rates. We first consider the case of hypothetical simple bonds, to establish two basic principles: (1) for a given financial asset, prices tend to rise as interest rates fall, and fall as interest rates rise, and (2) for a given change in interest rates, bonds with longer maturities show greater variations in price than those with short maturities.

Then we apply the methods of bond valuation to equity securities, through a technique known as the dividend discount model. We also consider duration measures for equities.

Bonds—A Basic Case

Bonds provide simple illustrations of the principles of valuation of financial assets. They typically have a finite life, and involve many fixed terms—their beginning, ending, payments in between, and many other factors—so their prices can be precisely calculated. The one dynamic in most cases is the market rate of interest at a given time, but with the knowledge or assumption of that data point, prices can be readily estimated. We rely on two simple examples of a bond—with annual coupon payments based on fixed interest rates, and respective maturities of five and 10 years.

1. Prices of Bonds at Issuance

Two hypothetical bonds are issued for $1,000 each at the start of Year 1. One matures in five years, and pays interest at a rate of 6% (the market rate for a bond of that maturity), while the other matures in 10 years and pays interest at 8% (also the market rate for its maturity).

The value an investor realizes from a bond is the stream of its cash flows, so that the prices of each bond at any point in time are the sums of the present values of each of the future interest and principal payments. The present value of a cash flow is a function of (1) the amount of cash to be received, (2) the timing of the payment, and (3) the interest rate (or discount rate) used to calculate the present value. For a given payment t, its present value (PV) is defined as:

$$PV_t = \frac{cash\ flow\ in\ period\ t}{(1 + discount\ rate)^t}$$

The examples show each year's cash flows for interest and principal, and the discount factors applied to each (Table B.1). Note that the present value of the each year's interest payment declines the further ahead in time it is to be received, due to the compounding of the discount factor. Also note that the largest component in the price of each bond is the present value of its principal payment. Because it is paid at the end of the bond's life, the principal is subject to the greatest discounting.

In these examples the coupon rate of interest is equal to the market rate at issuance, so the bonds are priced at "par," or $1,000.

TABLE B.1   Bonds at Issuance

	Years				
	1	2	3	4	5
5-Year Bond					
Cash Flows:					
Interest	$60	$60	$60	$60	$60
Principal					$1,000
Discount Factors:	$(1 + 6\%)^1$	$(1 + 6\%)^2$	$(1 + 6\%)^3$	$(1 + 6\%)^4$	$(1 + 6\%)^5$
Present Values at Start of Year 1:					
Interest	$56.60	$53.40	$50.38	$47.53	$44.84
Principal					$747.26
Sum of Present Values at Start of Year 1:	**$1,000.00**				

(*Continued*)

275

TABLE B.1 (*Continued*)

				Years						
	1	2	3	4	5	6	7	8	9	10
10-Year Bond										
Cash Flows:										
Interest	$80	$80	$80	$80	$80	$80	$80	$80	$80	$80
Principal										$1,000
Discount Factors:	$(1 + 8\%)^1$	$(1 + 8\%)^2$	$(1 + 8\%)^3$	$(1 + 8\%)^4$	$(1 + 8\%)^5$	$(1 + 8\%)^6$	$(1 + 8\%)^7$	$(1 + 8\%)^8$	$(1 + 8\%)^9$	$(1 + 8\%)^{10}$
Present Values at Start of Year 1:										
Interest	$74.07	$68.59	$63.51	$58.80	$54.45	$50.41	$46.68	$43.22	$40.02	$37.06
Principal										$463.19
Sum of Present Values at Start of Year 1:	$1,000.00									

2. Bond Prices with Changing Interest Rates

Time moves ahead to the start of Year 2. The first interest payment on each bond has been paid to the bond holders. If market interest rates happen to be the same as they were at issuance—that is, equal to the coupon rate—the price of each bond would again be $1,000. Although there are fewer payments to be received, the present values of the interest and principal payments have increased, due to lower discount factors applied to each (Table B.2 shows the example of the five-year bond as of the start of Year 2). For example, the present value of the principal payment has increased from $747 to $792.

However, if interest rates have changed, the discount factors and prices of the bonds change with them. Higher interest rates bring a higher discount factor, and each interest and principal payment is divided by a greater number, lowering the present values. (The opposite holds if interest rates have fallen.)

TABLE B.2   Five-Year Bond at Year 2

	Years			
	2	**3**	**4**	**5**
Cash Flows:				
Interest	$60	$60	$60	$60
Principal				
Discount Factors:	$(1 + 6\%)^1$	$(1 + 6\%)^2$	$(1 + 6\%)^3$	$(1 + 6\%)^4$
Present Values at Start of Year 2:				
Interest	$56.60	$53.40	$50.38	$47.53
Principal				$792.09
Sum of Present Values at Start of Year 2:	**$1,000.00**			

Table B.3 shows the effect of a 1 percentage point rise in rates for the five-year bond (to a yield of 7% from 6%). Due to compounding at a higher discount rate, each payment would be divided by a greater discount factor and have a lower present value, and in this case the bond price would have fallen from $1,000 at issuance to $966 (a decline of 3.4%). Details of the 10-year bond example are not shown, but on a one percentage point rise in rates, to a yield of 9%, its value too would have dropped—to $940, for a fall of 6.0%.

If interest rates had instead fallen from the date of issuance to the start of Year 2, the prices of both bonds would have risen, because in each case the cash flows would be divided by a smaller discount factor.

3. Bond Duration

In general, the longer the maturity of a bond, the greater the sensitivity in its price to changes in interest rates. This is due in great part to the back-loading of the present value of a bond's

TABLE B.3   Higher Interest Rates: 7 Percent

	Years			
	2	**3**	**4**	**5**
Five-Year Bond				
Cash Flows:				
Interest	$60	$60	$60	$60
Principal				$1,000
Discount Factors:	$(1 + 7\%)^1$	$(1 + 7\%)^2$	$(1 + 7\%)^3$	$(1 + 7\%)^4$
Present Values at Start of Year 2:				
Interest	$56.07	$52.41	$48.98	$45.77
Principal				$762.90
Sum of Present Values at Start of Year 2:	**$966.13**			

price in its principal payment. In the case of the five-year bond, the rise in market rates from 6 percent to 7 percent caused the present value in Year 2 of the principal to fall from $792 to $763, accounting for most of the $34 decrease in the bond's price (Table B.2 versus Table B.3).

Bond math allows for a calculation of a bond's "modified duration"—a weighted average of its term to maturity (weighted by the present value of the cash flow to be received in each year), which expresses the approximate sensitivity of a bond's price to a 1 percentage point (or 100 basis point) change in market interest rates. The modified duration of the five-year bond at the start of Year 2 is 4.2 (which multiplied by the one percentage point rise in rates is approximately equal to the drop in price). Modified duration for the 10-year bond is far higher, however, at 6.6, reflecting the increased effects of discounting on its longer stream of cash flows over a greater time span.

Stock Valuation through Cash Flows

1. Dividend Discount Models

These present value principles of bond valuation can be applied to the estimating the fair value of equities as well. In 1938, investment manager John Burr Williams authored *The Theory of Investment Value*, which sought to apply a mathematical framework to investing in stocks. His goal was not to show how to build wealth, but rather to provide investors an understanding, as he put it, of the physiology of the markets:

> The wide changes in stock prices in the last eight years, when prices fell as much as 80 or 90 per cent from the 1929 peaks only to recover much of their decline later, are a serious indictment of past practice in Investment Analysis. Had there been any general agreement among analysts themselves concerning the proper criteria of value, such enormous fluctuations should not have

occurred, because the long-run prospects for dividends have not in fact changed as much as the prices have. Prices have been based too much on current earning power, too little on long-run dividend paying power.[1]

Williams defined the investment value of a stock as the present value of all the dividends to be paid, in the same way that a bond's value is the present value of its interest and principal payments:

Most people will object at once to the foregoing formula for stocks by saying that it should use the present worth of future *earnings*, not future *dividends*. . . . Earnings are only a means to an end. . . . Therefore we must say that a stock derives its value from its dividends, not its earnings. In short, *a stock is worth only what you can get out of it*.[2]

He developed several models, applicable to companies in various financial situations—declining, stable and growing dividends. The mechanics of some are quite complicated (which he acknowledged): the "sudden expansion" variety entailed 11 known or assumed variables, and seven additional unknowns. He also conceded that the hardest part of valuing stocks on future cash flows would be estimating the dividends for each year over a long future.

In 1956 Myron Gordon, a professor at the University of Toronto, introduced a simpler dividend discount model that relieved analysts of forecasting earnings and dividends far into the future, and instead allowed them to substitute assumptions on the future growth rates of earnings and dividends. The Gordon growth model is best suited to situations with expected stable growth, and earnings and dividends not much affected by the business cycle, such as utilities and consumer staples companies. Here is its basic form:

$$Estimate\ of\ share\ value = \frac{D_{t+1}}{k - g}$$

D represents the dividend per share, *k* the company's cost of equity capital, and *g* the rate of growth in dividends.

The Gordon growth model is appealing for its simplicity, but with so few inputs is highly sensitive to the analyst's assumptions, particularly the reasonableness of expected growth in dividends (as the model assumes that such growth will last forever).

Other forms of dividend discount models have been devised to account for different stages of a company's growth—typically with one segment showing more rapid growth early on, and a second for slowing growth as a company's business matures. Dividend discount models can also be adjusted for firms not currently paying dividends, through estimates of dividends to be paid in the future.

One shortcoming of dividend discount models is their focus on dividends, particularly in a world where companies are making larger distributions to owners in the form of share repurchases (considered in Chapter 10). However, models can be modified by combining dividends and share repurchases, and looking at the firm's returns to owners in the aggregate rather than on a per share basis.

2. Duration

The prices of equities are sensitive to interest rates shifts just as bonds are, but while measuring the variations of bond prices from changes in interest rates is scientific and well established, the evolution of duration measures for equity has been ad hoc.[3] As with dividend discount models, a proper evaluation would call for developing long-term, detailed forecasts of future cash distributions, which lack the certainty of expected cash flows from bonds' interest and principal payments.

The same principles apply to equities, however: as with bonds, the sooner cash is paid out, the lower the duration. Thus shares of a mature company that pays high dividends have a shorter duration than those of a growth company that pays little or no dividends. In turn, the prices of stocks that pay higher current returns to shareholders should generally be less vulnerable to rising interest rates, all else being equal.[4]

Professors Patricia Dechow, Richard Sloan, and Mark Soliman developed a two-stage duration model for equities in 2001, and found it to perform well in empirical tests. Overall they concluded that "[D]uration tends to be low for firms with high ROE, low growth and low market valuations and high for firms with low ROE, high growth and high market valuations."[5]

A rough-and-ready duration measure, not calling for detailed cash flow forecasts, was described in 1985 by investment practitioner James Farrell.[6] His formulation is similar to the Gordon growth model, and based on dividend growth and required return:

$$Duration = \frac{1}{k - g}$$

Where k is the stock's required return, and g is the growth rate in dividends. Rearranging the terms makes the duration measure even simpler:

$$Duration = \frac{1}{dividend\ yield}$$

Farrell comments that stocks with low yields carry longer durations, and are relatively more sensitive to discount rate changes, and that "High-growth stocks, which are generally characterized by relatively low dividend yields, would be more subject to this risk than low-growth stocks." Overall he concludes that because stocks have a perpetual life and growing dividends, "[They] should thus be more responsive than bonds to changes in real interest rates, and carry a correspondingly higher premium (via the discount rate)."[7]

Notes

1. John Burr Williams, *The Theory of Investment Value* (Flint Hill, VA: Fraser Publishing Company, 1997), 191.
2. Ibid.
3. Patricia M. Dechow, Richard Sloan, and Mark Soliman, "Implied Equity Duration: A New Measure of Equity Security Risk" (June 2001). Available at: dx.doi.org/10.2139/ssrn.551644.
4. Eric Sappenfield, John Tobin, William W. Priest, Kera Van Valen, Michael A. Welhoelter. "Shareholder Yield: The Case for the Next Decade," Epoch Investment Partners White Paper, July 2015.
5. Dechow, Sloan, and Soliman.
6. James Farrell Jr., "The Dividend Discount Model: A Primer," *Financial Analysts Journal* (November/December 1985), 16–25.
7. Ibid.

Appendix C

Feathered Feast: A Case

At the time this article was published, its author, Jack L. Treynor was President of Treynor Capital Management, Inc. in Palos Verdes Estates, California, and a member of the editorial board of the *Financial Analysts Journal*, in which this piece originally appeared.

Feathered Feast: A Case

Jack L. Treynor, *Financial Analysts Journal*, November/December 1993.

Feathered Feast is a case about disclosure—about the relation between the reporting accountant and the outside user and about the framework within which these professionals perform mutually complementary roles. Like all cases, it confers little or no insight on those who merely read it. Rather, one has to live the case—to feel the frustration and anguish of the protagonist, Shepard Saunders.

Feathered Feast Inc. (III)

In May 1993, Shepard Saunders, manager of the Amalgamated Iceman's Pension Fund, was reviewing certain purchases that, in retrospect, had not worked out as successfully as he had originally hoped. Among these was Feathered Feast, Inc., purchased for the fund in December 1991.

Feathered Feast, Inc. (FF) was at that time one of a number of rapidly growing fast-food chains specializing in fried chicken. FF was distinguished by the fact that, instead of selling franchises, it retained complete control of all FF retail outlets, owning them outright. Management argued that outright ownership gave them better control over the quality of the final product. But outright ownership, together with management's effort to keep pace with its rapidly growing competition, had also led to a heavy demand for funds.

Despite FF's rapid growth, its management had controlled costs very successfully, maintaining profit margins virtually constant until 1992. In order to conserve funds, management had subcontracted the warehousing, distribution and food-preparation functions. New funds were mainly used for the construction of new outlets, which were built on leased land.

Each outlet was basically a standardized, sheet-metal structure fabricated in the shape of a giant chicken, with integral refrigeration, deep-fry vats and warming ovens. Standing nearly 30-feet high, these structures served to excite the eating public's interest in FF's principal product, the Featherburger. They were, in fact, rapidly becoming a familiar sight along heavily traveled suburban arteries when fast-food retailing margins collapsed in 1992.

The shock and disappointment of FF shareholders was heightened by the fact that, until that time, FF's profit performance had been spectacular (see Table 1). It was, in fact, the profit performance that had induced Shepard Saunders to "swing a little bit," as the institutional salesman from the First Hoboken Corporation had put it, cashing in Treasury bills amounting to roughly 5% of the fund's portfolio and devoting the proceeds to FF shares.

TABLE 1:   Foresight Depreciation and Profit Analysis for Feathered Feast

	1987	1988	1989	1990	1991 (est)
Net Income (After Taxes)	$58	$64	$71	$78	$85
Net Income Plus Depreciation	$100	$110	$121	$133	$146
Dividends	$50	$55	$60	$67	$73
Capital Investment	$0	$50	$55	$60	$67
Gross Plant	$500	$550	$605	$665	$732
Dividends/Net Income	0.86	0.86	0.86	0.86	0.86

The salesman from First Hoboken had explained why Feathered Feast, selling at 40 times earnings, was a bargain: Since the company, with its aggressive merchandising and innovative product concept, had burst onto the fast-food service scene in 1987, earnings had grown steadily at 10% per year (see Table 2). The performance was all the more impressive because, as the First Hoboken research report had made clear, the quality of

TABLE 2   Salesman's Estimate of the Investment Value of Feathered Feast (Year-End 1991)

Basic Assumptions

5-Year Growth Rate	10%
Discount Rate	12%

Dividend Payout Detail

Depreciation (12 years, straight-line)	5/12 of gross
Earnings after Depreciation	7/12 of gross
Cash Investment	6/12 of gross
Cash Available for Dividends	6/12 of gross
Dividends/Earnings	6/7 of net

earnings was high. The growth was entirely genuine, internal, organic growth, unadulterated by "dirty pooling" acquisitions. There were no franchise contracts to be taken into sales at inflated figures. Depreciation was conservative: The retail structures were fully depreciated in 12 years on a straight-line basis, despite the fact that, with proper maintenance, they would easily last 40 or 50 years.

In view of this rapid yet steady growth, coupled with the demonstrably high quality of earnings, a discount rate (total return) of 12% was surely conservative. Feathered Feast had consistently succeeded in paying out over 85% of its earnings in dividends, and it had achieved this high dividend payout without borrowing to finance its rapid expansion. Using the famous Gordon-Shapiro formula to translate these assumptions about growth rate, discount rate and dividend payout rate into an estimate of the investment value of Feathered Feast (see Table 2), the salesman had argued that Feathered Feast was worth at least a price/earnings ratio of 43, in contrast to the ratio of 40, at which it was selling in December of 1991.[1] Although Saunders had never entirely bought the salesman's argument that these achievements made Feathered Feast the "bluest of the blue chips," he had been prepared to believe that it was a far sounder investment than many of the "story stocks" that lacked its tangible assets and record of solid earnings growth.

Shepard Saunders's first inkling that all was not well with FF came when he read in *The Wall Street Journal* that FF was defaulting on some of the lease contracts for retail sites (these contracts had 12 years' duration, with subsequent options to renew). Declining unit volume and cutthroat price cutting quickly transformed formerly profitable outlets into money losers. The prob-

---

[1] Professors Gordon and Shapiro are the authors of a widely used formula according to which the appropriate price/earnings ratio for a common stock is equal to the proportion of earnings paid out in dividends divided by the appropriate discount rate (or total return) minus the expected growth rate.

lem, which appeared first in California and then spread across the country, was—at least in hindsight—clearly excess capacity. At the end of 1992, most of FF's retail outlets were barely covering out-of-pocket costs of operation. Unable to cover corporate overhead costs, FF auctioned off its assets for scrap value.

Although most of FF's competition had encountered the same problem at about the same time, it was hard to understand how a company that sold at 40 times earnings one year could be broke the next. In his attempt to understand why Feathered Feast had been such a disappointment, Saunders developed the figures shown in Table 3. He noted that, by 1992, Feathered Feast's existing outlets, being scarcely able to cover out-of-pocket operating costs, were essentially worthless. That meant, he reasoned, that the outlets that came into operation at the beginning of 1987 had, at least in hindsight, a five-year economic life. In similar fashion, he reasoned that the outlets that went into operation in 1988 had a four-year economic life, and so forth. Using these new assumptions about the economic lives of units coming into operation in each of the years from 1987 through 1991, Saunders recalculated earnings after depreciation (see Table 3).

TABLE 3   Hindsight Depreciation and Profit Analysis for Feathered Feast

	1987	1988	1989	1990	1991 (est)
Gross Plant	$500	$550	$605	$665	$732
New Investment	$0	$50	$55	$60	$67
Restated Depreciation	$100	$112	$131	$161	$228
Net Plant	$400	$338	$262	$161	$0
Net Income (after taxes plus depreciation)	$100	$110	$121	$133	$146
Depreciation	$100	$112	$131	$161	$228
Net Income	$0	(2)	(10)	(28)	(82)

When depreciation was adjusted with the benefit of hindsight, Feathered Feast still displayed a rapid earnings growth rate—but the earnings and the growth were negative. If Table 3 rather than Table 1 represented the true earnings history for Feathered Feast, Saunders reasoned, then it had not been worth 43 times 1991 earnings (estimated) in December 1991. But it had not been until 1992 when fast-food margins collapsed, that it became clear that Table 3 was a better representation of the earnings history than Table 1.

Perhaps Saunders was misusing historical earnings data. Perhaps he didn't understand what the data meant. He decided to go to a well-recognized accountant, someone who had given a lot of thought to the objectives of financial statements and the conceptual framework for accounting. The obvious choice was the noted accounting theorist, Stamford Ridges. Saunders was delighted when Ridges granted him an interview. A transcript of Saunders's questions and Ridges's answers follows.

Saunders: Was I wrong to rely on the earnings history of Feathered Feast in estimating the value of its common stock?

Ridges: Earnings for an enterprise for a period measured by accrual accounting are generally considered to be the most relevant indicator of relative success or failure of the earnings process of an enterprise in bringing in needed cash. Measures of periodic earnings are widely used by investors, creditors, security analysts and others.[2]

Saunders: Is it appropriate to extrapolate historical earnings trends into the future?

Ridges: The most important single factor determining a stock's value is now held to be the indicated future earning

---

[2] All of Ridges's answers are excerpted, out of context and with malice aforethought, from two documents—*Tentative Conclusions on Objectives of Financial Statements of Business Enterprises* and (the discussion memorandum) *Conceptual Framework for Financial Accounting and Reporting*, published December 2, 1976, by the Financial Accounting Standards Board.

power—that is, the estimated average earnings for a future span of years. Intrinsic value would then be found by first forecasting this earning power and then multiplying that prediction by an appropriate "capitalization factor." "Earning power" means the long-term average ability of an enterprise to produce earnings and is estimated by normalizing or averaging reported earnings and projecting the resulting trend into the future.

Saunders: My experience with Feathered Feast suggests that earnings, earnings trend and estimates of investment value based on these numbers can be very sensitive to the life of fixed assets.

Ridges: Assets are not inherently tangible or physical. An asset is an economic quantum. It may be attached to or represented by some physical object, or it may not. One of the common mistakes we all tend to make is that of attributing too much significance to the molecular concept of property. A brick wall is nothing but mud on edge if its capacity to render economic service has disappeared; the molecules are still there, and the wall may be as solid as ever, but the value has gone.

Saunders: So it's the economic, rather than the physical, life that matters. How is the outside user to know whether reported earnings are true earnings and reported earnings trend true trend unless he knows the economic life of major assets?

Ridges: The success or failure of a business enterprise's efforts to earn more cash than it spends on resources can be known with certainty only when the enterprise is liquidated.

Saunders: How, then, does the accountant arrive at the figures he reports?

Ridges: In the purest, or ideal, form of accrual accounting, sometimes called direct valuation, each noncash asset represents expected future cash receipts and each liability represents expected future cash outlays.

Saunders: Wouldn't I be better off if I focused on financial data that were untainted by the subjectivity of an accountant's expectations?

Ridges: The standard of verifiability is a necessary attribute of accounting information, allowing persons who have neither access to the underlying records nor the competence to audit them to rely on those records.

Saunders: If I wanted to base my analysis on numbers relatively free from the influence of an accountant's expectations regarding the future, what numbers might I use?

Ridges: The fundamental concern of investors and creditors with an enterprise's cash flows might suggest that financial statements that report cash receipts and cash disbursements of an enterprise during a period would provide the most useful information for investor and creditor analyses. That information is readily available, can be reported on a timely basis at minimum cost, and is essentially factual because it involves a minimum of judgment and assumption.

Saunders: Would you mind telling me again why outside users like myself are supposed to pay so much attention to earnings?

Ridges: The relation between cash flows to an enterprise and the market price of its securities, especially that of common stock, is complex, and there are significant gaps in the knowledge of how the market determines the prices of individual securities. Moreover, the prices of individual securities are affected by numerous other factors that affect market prices in general. Nevertheless, the expected cash inflows to the enterprise are the ultimate source of value for its securities, and major changes in expectations about these cash inflows immediately affect market prices significantly.

Intrinsic value is the value that the security ought to have and will have when other investors have the same insight and knowledge as the analyst. Because the intrinsic value of a stock usually cannot be measured directly, given the uncertainty of its future cash dividends and market prices, investors and security analysts commonly attempt to estimate it indirectly or to estimate some surrogate for intrinsic value, such as what a stock's price ought to be in a price/earnings ratio. The procedure involves estimating average earnings for a future span of years—the indicated future average earning power—and multiplying that prediction by an appropriate "capitalization" to obtain intrinsic value. For example, estimated average earnings per share may be multiplied by a price/earnings ratio to obtain a price that reflects intrinsic value. If that price is higher than the market price, the analysis advises the investor to buy; if it is less than the market price, the analysis advises the investor to sell.

Saunders: So that's why you accountants place heavy emphasis on reported earnings.

Ridges: Decisions about what information should be included in financial statements and what information should be excluded or summarized should depend primarily on what is relevant to investors' and creditors' decisions.

Sensing that he had gone about as far as he could go with Ridges, Saunders thanked him and brought the interview to a close. Although he found Ridges's answers enigmatic and mildly confusing, he had the feeling that they held the key to his problems with Feathered Feast. In a few days, Saunders would be meeting with the trustees of the Amalgamated Iceman's Pension Fund to explain its investment performance since 1991. They had selected him to manage the portfolio largely because of his reputation for emphasizing tangible earning assets, rather than "stories." He was sure the trustees would ask him to defend the Feathered Feast decision and to explain the subsequent investment disappointment. Should he show them Tables 1 and 2? Or should he show them Table 3? Saunders was uncertain exactly what to say.

ACKNOWLEDGEMENTS

When the New York Yankees beat the Kansas City Athletics to clinch the 1958 American League pennant, Yankees manager Casey Stengel famously remarked that "I realize I couldn't have done it without the players." This book, too, was a long and considerable effort, and would not have been possible without the important contributions of many people other than the authors.

For their views on the investment management industry, we thank James MacLachlan, Laurence Siegel, Ted Aronson, and Barton Waring. Behind the scenes at Epoch Investment Partners, Lilian Quah brought our attention to crucial academic research and wrote up the Epoch Core Model, David Pratter crunched invaluable numbers, while Huma Bari deftly juggled schedules, paperwork, and personalities. At our publisher, John Wiley & Sons, Christina Verigan and Susan Cooper brought the manuscript together, while Vincent Nordhaus and Bill Falloon kept us on track toward production.

And most important, we give a special shout-out to the employees of Epoch Investment Partners--who collectively define our culture, carry out our investment philosophy, and are the heart of innovating and evolving the firm to the next level.

Thanks to all of you.

William W. Priest is Chief Executive Officer and Co-Chief Investment Officer of Epoch Investment Partners. Prior to co-founding Epoch in 2004 with David Pearl, Tim Taussig, and Phil Clark, Bill was a Co-Managing Partner and portfolio manager at Steinberg Priest & Sloane Capital Management, LLC for three years. Before joining Steinberg Priest, he was Chairman and Chief Executive Officer of Credit Suisse Asset Management-Americas and CEO and portfolio manager of its predecessor firm BEA Associates, which he co-founded in 1972. During his 30-year tenure at BEA and CSAM, he developed the firm into a well-recognized investment manager with over $100 billion under management. Bill is the author of several published articles and papers on investing and finance, as well as two books: *The Financial Reality of Pension Funding Under ERISA* and more recently, *Free Cash Flow and Shareholder Yield: New Priorities for the Global Investor,* published by John Wiley & Sons. Bill holds the Chartered Financial Analyst designation, is a former CPA, and a graduate of Duke University and the University of Pennsylvania Wharton Graduate School of Business. He is a member of the Council on Foreign Relations and the *Barron's* Roundtable.

Steven D. Bleiberg is a Managing Director of Epoch Investment Partners. Steven is responsible for the design and development of investment strategies at Epoch, and also serves as a portfolio manager for the firm's Capital Reinvestment strategy. Prior to joining Epoch, Steven served as a portfolio manager for $7.5 billion in asset allocation funds at Legg Mason. Earlier, he was the head of investment strategy at Citigroup Asset Management, and a portfolio manager at Credit Suisse Asset Management and its predecessor firm, BEA Associates. Steven is a graduate of Harvard College, where he served as an editor of the *Harvard Lampoon*, and the Sloan School of Management at MIT. He has contributed articles to the *Financial Analysts Journal, The Journal of Portfolio Management*, and the *New York Times*, and wrote a chapter on behavioral finance in *Multi-Manager Funds: Long-Only Strategies for Managers and Investors* (2006).

Michael A. Welhoelter is Epoch Investment Partners' Chief Risk Officer. He heads the firm's Quantitative Research and Risk Management team, and is responsible for integrating risk management into the investment process. Prior to joining Epoch in 2005, he was a Director and portfolio manager in the Quantitative Strategies Group at Columbia Management Group, Inc. Previously, Mike was a portfolio manager in the Structured Equity group at Credit Suisse Asset Management Group and a portfolio manager and quantitative research analyst at Chancellor/LGT Asset Management. Mike holds a BA degree in Computer and Information Science from Colgate University. He is a member of the New York Society of Security Analysts, the Society of Quantitative Analysts, and holds the Chartered Financial Analyst designation.

John Keefe is a New York-based freelance writer, having covered investment and retirement topics for such publications as *Institutional Investor, Financial Times*, and *PlanSponsor*. His training is in finance, and he spent ten years as an analyst on the sell side of Wall Street following the financial services industry. John is a former CPA, and a graduate of Villanova University and the University of Pennsylvania Wharton Graduate School of Business.

INDEX